Lóegaire Humphrey (Ed.)

Daniel D. McCracken

Lóegaire Humphrey (Ed.)

Daniel D. McCracken

Computer science, City College of New York, Computer programming, Fortran

Claud Press

Imprint

Publisher:
Claud Press is a trademark of
International Book Market Service Ltd., 17 Rue Meldrum, Beau Bassin, 1713-01 Mauritius
Email: info@bookmarketservice.com
Website: www.bookmarketservice.com

Published in 2011

Printed in: U.S.A., U.K., Germany. This book was not produced in Mauritius.

ISBN: 978-613-7-46688-9

Contents

Articles

Daniel D. McCracken 1
Computer science 3
City College of New York 14
Computer programming 32
Fortran 38
Central Washington University 56
General Electric 61
United States Atomic Energy Commission 73
New York University 77
Courant Institute of Mathematical Sciences 98
Master of Divinity 109
Union Theological Seminary in the City of New York 110
Association for Computing Machinery 116
Fellow 123
Computer Professionals for Social Responsibility 126
Golden Key International Honour Society 128

References

Article Sources and Contributors 132
Image Sources, Licenses and Contributors 136

Daniel D. McCracken

Daniel D. McCracken	
Born	July 23, 1930Hughesville, Judith Basin County, Montana
Died	July 30, 2011 (aged 81)New York City
Nationality	USA
Occupation	professor, author, and computer scientist
Known for	Computer pioneer, computer programmer, computer scientist, and author of computer programming books

Daniel D. McCracken (July 23, 1930 – July 30, 2011) was a computer scientist in the United States. He was a Professor of Computer Sciences at the City College of New York, and the author of over two dozen textbooks on computer programming. His *A Guide to Fortran Programming* (Wiley, 1961) and its successors were the standard textbooks on that language for over two decades. His books have been translated into fourteen languages.

Career

McCracken was born in 1930 in Hughesville, Judith Basin County, Montana, a mining town, and graduated in 1951 from Central Washington University with degrees in mathematics and chemistry. He worked seven years with the General Electric Company in computer applications and programmer training. After that, he worked at the New York University Atomic Energy Commission Computer Center, and was a graduate student at the Courant Institute of Mathematical Sciences. In 1959 he became a consultant and continued writing on computer subjects. In 1970 he earned a Master of Divinity degree from the Union Theological Seminary in New York.[1]

From 1976-78, he was vice president of the Association for Computing Machinery (ACM), from 1978-80 he was president of the the ACM, and in 1994 he was inducted as a Fellow of ACM. He joined the City College of New York Computer Sciences Department in 1981. In 1989 he received the Norbert Weiner Award for Social and Professional Responsibility from Computer Professionals for Social Responsibility and is an honorary member of the Golden Key International Honour Society.[2]

Death

McCracken died of cancer a week after his 81st birthday on July 30, 2011 in New York City.[3] [1]

Books

- McCracken, Daniel D. (1957). *Digital Computer Programming* (1 ed.). Wiley.
- McCracken, Daniel D.; Harold Weiss, Tsai H. Lee (1959). *Programming Business Computers* (1 ed.). Wiley. ISBN B000MFMTLG.
- McCracken, Daniel D. (1961). *A Guide to Fortran Programming* (1 ed.). Wiley. ISBN B0000EGLDD.
- McCracken, Daniel D. (1962). *A Guide to Algol Programming* (1 ed.). Wiley.
- McCracken, Daniel D. (1962). *A Guide to IBM 1401 Programming* (1 ed.). Wiley.
- McCracken, Daniel D. (1963). *A Guide to Cobol Programming* (1 ed.). Wiley.
- McCracken, Daniel D.; Fred J. Gruenberger (1963). *Introduction to Electronic Computing* (1 ed.). Wiley.
- McCracken, Daniel D.; William S. Dorn (1964). *Numerical Methods and Fortran Programming* (1 ed.). Wiley.
- McCracken, Daniel D. (1965). *A Programmer's Introduction to the IBM System/360 Architecture, Instructions, and Assembler Language* (1 ed.). IBM.
- McCracken, Daniel D. (1966). *A Guide to Fortran IV Programming* (1 ed.). Wiley. ISBN B000GSBIIE.

- McCracken, Daniel D. (1967). *Fortran with Engineering Applications* (1 ed.). Wiley.
- McCracken, Daniel D.; Umberto Garbassi (1970). *A Guide to Cobol Programming* (2 ed.). Wiley. ISBN 978-0471582441.
- McCracken, Daniel D. (1972). *To Love or to Perish: The Technological Crisis and the Churches*. J. Edward Carothers, Margaret Mead, Roger L. Shinn (eds.) (1 ed.). Friendship Press.
- McCracken, Daniel D.; William S. Dorn (1972). *Numerical Methods with Fortran IV Case Studies* (1 ed.). Wiley.
- McCracken, Daniel D. (1974). *A Simplified Guide to Fortran Programming* (1 ed.). Wiley.
- McCracken, Daniel D. (1976). *A Simplified Guide to Structured Cobol Programming* (1 ed.). Wiley.
- McCracken, Daniel D.; William S. Dorn (1976). *Introductory Finite Mathematics with Computing* (1 ed.). Wiley.
- McCracken, Daniel D. (1978). *A Guide to PL/M for Microcomputer Applications* (1 ed.). Addison-Wesley.
- McCracken, Daniel D. (1981). *A Guide to Nomad for Applications Development* (1 ed.). Addison-Wesley.
- McCracken, Daniel D. (1984). *Computing for Engineers and Scientists with Fortran 77* (1 ed.). Wiley.
- McCracken, Daniel D. (1986). *A Second Course in Computer Science with Pascal* (1 ed.). Wiley. ISBN B001NBX18S.
- McCracken, Daniel D.; William I. Salmon (1987). *A Second Course in Computer Science with Modula-2 [data structures]* (1 ed.). Wiley.
- McCracken, Daniel D.; William I. Salmon (1988). *Computing for Engineers and Scientists with Fortran 77* (2 ed.). Wiley. ISBN 978-0471625520.
- McCracken, Daniel D.; Donald G. Golden (1990). *Simplified Structured Cobol with Microsoft/MicroFocus Cobol* (1 ed.). Wiley. ISBN 978-0471514077.
- McCracken, Daniel D. (1992). *Learning GEL By Example* (1 ed.). Gain Technology.
- McCracken, Daniel D.; Rosalee J. Wolfe (2003). *User-Centered Website Development: A Human-Computer Interaction Approach* (1 ed.). Prentice Hall. ISBN 978-0130411617.

References

[1] Lohr, Steve, "Daniel D. McCracken, Expert on Computers, Dies at 81" (http://www.nytimes.com/2011/08/13/technology/daniel-d-mccracken-dies-at-81-wrote-best-sellers-on-using-computers.html), *The New York Times*, August 12, 2011

[2] Daniel D. McCracken Biography (http://www.cwu.edu/~glasbys/DDM_BIO.HTM) - Central Washington University

[3] Swalec, Andrea, "Washington Heights Computer Science Expert Dies" (http://www.dnainfo.com/20110801/washington-heights-inwood/washington-heights-computer-science-expert-dies), *DNAinfo*, August 1, 2011

External links

- "Daniel McCracken, Interview by Arthur L. Norberg, January 7-9, 2008" (http://portal.acm.org/ft_gateway.cfm?id=1452135&type=pdf), Association for Computing Machinery historical interview.
- Dan McCracken's webpage at City College of New York (http://www1.ccny.cuny.edu/facultystaff/directory/profile-record.cfm?customel_datapageid_1237265=1240063)
- Daniel D. McCracken Papers, 1958-1983 (http://purl.umn.edu/41426). Charles Babbage Institute, University of Minnesota, Minneapolis.
- "Obituary: Daniel D. McCracken" (http://www.legacy.com/obituaries/nytimes/obituary.aspx?n=daniel-d-mccracken&pid=152831055), *The New York Times*, August 1, 2011

Computer science

Computer science or **computing science** (abbreviated **CS**) is the study of the theoretical foundations of information and computation and of practical techniques for their implementation and application in computer systems.[1] [2] Computer scientists invent algorithmic processes that create, describe, and transform information and formulate suitable abstractions to model complex systems.

Computer science has many sub-fields; some, such as computational complexity theory, study the fundamental properties of computational problems, while others, such as computer graphics, emphasize the computation of specific results. Still others focus on the challenges in implementing computations. For example, programming language theory studies approaches to describe computations, while computer programming applies specific programming languages to solve specific computational problems, and human-computer interaction focuses on the challenges in making computers and computations useful, usable, and universally accessible to humans.

The general public sometimes confuses computer scientists with other computer professionals having careers in information technology, or think that computer science relates to their own experience with computers, which typically involves activities such as gaming, web-browsing, and word-processing. However, the focus of computer science is more on understanding the properties of the programs used to implement software such as games and web-browsers, and using that understanding to create new programs or improve existing ones.[3]

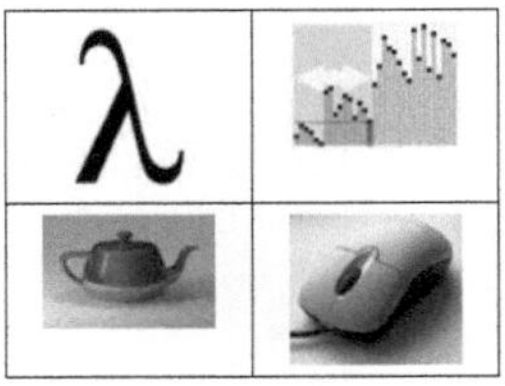

Computer science deals with the theoretical foundations of information, computation, and with practical techniques for their implementation and application.

History

The early foundations of what would become computer science predate the invention of the modern digital computer. Machines for calculating fixed numerical tasks, such as the abacus, have existed since antiquity. Wilhelm Schickard designed the first mechanical calculator in 1623, but did not complete its construction.[4] Blaise Pascal designed and constructed the first working mechanical calculator, the Pascaline, in 1642. Charles Babbage designed a difference engine and then a general-purpose Analytical Engine in Victorian times,[5] for which Ada Lovelace wrote a manual. Because of this work she is regarded today as the world's first programmer.[6] Around 1900, punched card machines were introduced.

During the 1940s, as newer and more powerful computing machines were developed, the term *computer* came to refer to the machines rather than their human predecessors.[7] As it became clear that computers could be used for more than just mathematical calculations, the field of computer science broadened to study computation in general. Computer science began to be established as a distinct academic discipline in the 1950s and early 1960s.[8] [9] The world's first computer science degree program, the Cambridge Diploma in Computer Science, began at the University of Cambridge Computer Laboratory in 1953. The first computer science degree program in the United States was formed at Purdue University in 1962.[10] Since practical computers became available, many applications of computing have become distinct areas of study in their own right.

Although many initially believed it was impossible that computers themselves could actually be a scientific field of study, in the late fifties it gradually became accepted among the greater academic population.[11] It is the now well-known IBM brand that formed part of the computer science revolution during this time. IBM (short for International Business Machines) released the IBM 704 and later the IBM 709 computers, which were widely used during the exploration period of such devices. "Still, working with the IBM [computer] was frustrating...if you had misplaced as much as one letter in one instruction, the program would crash, and you would have to start the whole process over again".[11] During the late 1950s, the computer science discipline was very much in its developmental stages, and such issues were commonplace.

Time has seen significant improvements in the usability and effectiveness of computer science technology. Modern society has seen a significant shift from computers being used solely by experts or professionals to a more widespread user base. Initially, computers were quite costly, and for their most-effective use, some degree of human aid was needed, in part by professional computer operators. However, as computers became widespread and far more affordable, less human assistance was needed, although residues of the original assistance still remained.

Major achievements

Despite its short history as a formal academic discipline, computer science has made a number of fundamental contributions to science and society. These include:

The German military used the Enigma machine (shown here) during World War II for communication they thought to be secret. The large-scale decryption of Enigma traffic at Bletchley Park was an important factor that contributed to Allied victory in WWII.[12]

- The start of the "digital revolution," which includes the current Information Age and the Internet.[13]
- A formal definition of computation and computability, and proof that there are computationally unsolvable and intractable problems.[14]
- The concept of a programming language, a tool for the precise expression of methodological information at various levels of abstraction.[15]
- In cryptography, breaking the Enigma machine was an important factor contributing to the Allied victory in World War II.[12]
- Scientific computing enabled practical evaluation of processes and situations of great complexity, as well as experimentation entirely by software. It also enabled advanced study of the mind, and mapping of the human genome became possible with the Human Genome Project.[13] Distributed computing projects such as Folding@home explore protein folding.
- Algorithmic trading has increased the efficiency and liquidity of financial markets by using artificial intelligence, machine learning, and other statistical and numerical techniques on a large scale.[16]
- Image synthesis, including video by computing individual video frames.
- Human language processing, including practical speech-to-text conversion and automated translation of languages
- Simulation of various processes, including computational fluid dynamics, physical, electrical, and electronic systems and circuits, as well as societies and social situations (notably war games) along with their habitats, among many others. Modern computers enable optimization of such designs as complete aircraft. Notable in electrical and electronic circuit design are SPICE as well as software for physical realization of new (or modified) designs. The latter includes essential design software for integrated circuits.

Philosophy

Following Peter Wegner, Amnon H. Eden proposes that there are three paradigms at work in various areas of computer science:[17]

- a "rationalist paradigm", which treats computer science as branch of mathematics, which is prevalent in theoretical computer science, and mainly employs deductive reasoning,
- a "technocratic paradigm", readily identifiable with engineering approaches, most prominent in software engineering, and
- a "scientific paradigm", which approaches computer-related artifacts from the empirical perspective of natural sciences, and identifiable in some branches of artificial intelligence (the study of artificial life for instance).

Areas of computer science

As a discipline, computer science spans a range of topics from theoretical studies of algorithms and the limits of computation to the practical issues of implementing computing systems in hardware and software.[18] [19] CSAB, formerly called *Computing Sciences Accreditation Board* – which is made up of representatives of the Association for Computing Machinery (ACM), and the IEEE Computer Society (IEEE-CS)[20] – identifies four areas that it considers crucial to the discipline of computer science: *theory of computation*, *algorithms and data structures*, *programming methodology and languages*, and *computer elements and architecture*. In addition to these four areas, CSAB also identifies fields such as software engineering, artificial intelligence, computer networking and communication, database systems, parallel computation, distributed computation, computer-human interaction, computer graphics, operating systems, and numerical and symbolic computation as being important areas of computer science.[18]

Theoretical computer science

The broader field of theoretical computer science encompasses both the classical theory of computation and a wide range of other topics that focus on the more abstract, logical, and mathematical aspects of computing.

Theory of computation

According to Peter J. Denning, the fundamental question underlying computer science is, *"What can be (efficiently) automated?"*[8] The study of the theory of computation is focused on answering fundamental questions about what can be computed and what amount of resources are required to perform those computations. In an effort to answer the first question, computability theory examines which computational problems are solvable on various theoretical models of computation. The second question is addressed by computational complexity theory, which studies the time and space costs associated with different approaches to solving a multitude of computational problems.

The famous "P=NP?" problem, one of the Millennium Prize Problems,[21] is an open problem in the theory of computation.

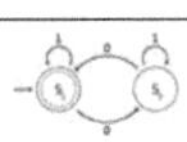		**P = NP** ?	**GNITIRW-TERCES**	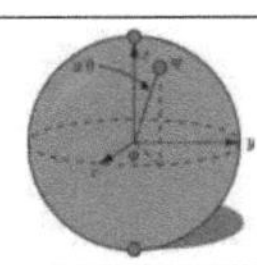
Automata theory	Computability theory	Computational complexity theory	Cryptography	Quantum computing theory

Information and coding theory

Information theory is related to the quantification of information.This was developed by Claude E. Shannon to find fundamental limits on signal processing operations such as compressing data and on reliably storing and communicating data. Coding theory is the study of the properties of codes and their fitness for a specific application. Codes are used for data compression, cryptography, error-correction and more recently also for network coding. Codes are studied for the purpose of designing efficient and reliable data transmission methods.

Algorithms and data structures

	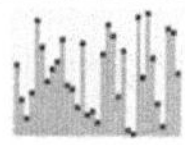	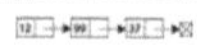	
Analysis of algorithms	Algorithms	Data structures	Computational geometry

Programming language theory

Programming language theory is a branch of computer science that deals with the design, implementation, analysis, characterization, and classification of programming languages and their individual features. It falls within the discipline of computer science, both depending on and affecting mathematics, software engineering and linguistics. It is a well-recognized branch of computer science, and an active research area, with results published in numerous journals dedicated to PLT, as well as in general computer science and engineering publications.

	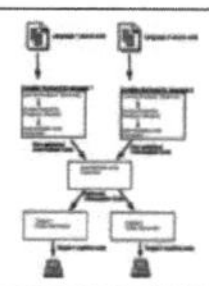	
Type theory	Compiler design	Programming languages

Formal methods

Formal methods are a particular kind of mathematically-based techniques for the specification, development and verification of software and hardware systems. The use of formal methods for software and hardware design is motivated by the expectation that, as in other engineering disciplines, performing appropriate mathematical analysis can contribute to the reliability and robustness of a design. However, the high cost of using formal methods means that they are usually only used in the development of high-integrity systems, where safety or security is of utmost importance. Formal methods are best described as the application of a fairly broad variety of theoretical computer science fundamentals, in particular logic calculi, formal languages, automata theory, and program semantics, but also type systems and algebraic data types to problems in software and hardware specification and verification.

Concurrent, parallel and distributed systems

Concurrency is a property of systems in which several computations are executing simultaneously, and potentially interacting with each other. A number of mathematical models have been developed for general concurrent computation including Petri nets, process calculi and the Parallel Random Access Machine model. A distributed system extends the idea of concurrency onto multiple computers connected through a network. Computers within the same distributed system have their own private memory, and information is often exchanged amongst themselves to achieve a common goal.

Databases and information retrieval

A database is intended to organize, store, and retrieve large amounts of data easily. Digital databases are managed using database management systems to store, create, maintain, and search data, through database models and query languages.

Applied computer science

Despite its name, a significant amount of computer science does not involve the study of computers themselves. Because of this, several alternative names have been proposed. Certain departments of major universities prefer the term *computing science*, to emphasize precisely that difference. Danish scientist Peter Naur suggested the term *datalogy*, to reflect the fact that the scientific discipline revolves around data and data treatment, while not necessarily involving computers. The first scientific institution to use the term was the Department of Datalogy at the University of Copenhagen, founded in 1969, with Peter Naur being the first professor in datalogy. The term is used mainly in the Scandinavian countries. Also, in the early days of computing, a number of terms for the practitioners of the field of computing were suggested in the *Communications of the ACM* – *turingineer*, *turologist*, *flow-charts-man*, *applied meta-mathematician*, and *applied epistemologist*.[22] Three months later in the same journal, *comptologist* was suggested, followed next year by *hypologist*.[23] The term *computics* has also been suggested.[24] In continental Europe, terms derived from "information" and "automatic" are often used, e.g. *informatique* (French), *Informatik* (German), Informatica (Spain, Italy) or *informatika* (Slavic languages) are also used.

Renowned computer scientist Edsger Dijkstra once stated: "Computer science is no more about computers than astronomy is about telescopes."[25] The design and deployment of computers and computer systems is generally considered the province of disciplines other than computer science. For example, the study of computer hardware is usually considered part of computer engineering, while the study of commercial computer systems and their deployment is often called information technology or information systems. However, there has been much cross-fertilization of ideas between the various computer-related disciplines. Computer science research also often intersects other disciplines, such as philosophy, cognitive science, linguistics, mathematics, physics, statistics, and logic.

Computer science is considered by some to have a much closer relationship with mathematics than many scientific disciplines, with some observers saying that computing is a mathematical science.[8] Early computer science was strongly influenced by the work of mathematicians such as Kurt Gödel and Alan Turing, and there continues to be a useful interchange of ideas between the two fields in areas such as mathematical logic, category theory, domain theory, and algebra.

The relationship between computer science and software engineering is a contentious issue, which is further muddied by disputes over what the term "software engineering" means, and how computer science is defined. David Parnas, taking a cue from the relationship between other engineering and science disciplines, has claimed that the principal focus of computer science is studying the properties of computation in general, while the principal focus of software engineering is the design of specific computations to achieve practical goals, making the two separate but complementary disciplines.[26]

The academic, political, and funding aspects of computer science tend to depend on whether a department formed with a mathematical emphasis or with an engineering emphasis. Computer science departments with a mathematics emphasis and with a numerical orientation consider alignment with computational science. Both types of departments tend to make efforts to bridge the field educationally if not across all research.

Artificial intelligence

This branch of computer science aims to synthesise goal-orientated processes such as problem-solving, decision-making, environmental adaptation, learning and communication which are found in humans and animals. From its origins in cybernetics and in the Dartmouth Conference (1956), artificial intelligence (AI) research has been necessarily cross-disciplinary, drawing on areas of expertise such as applied mathematics, symbolic logic, semiotics, electrical engineering, philosophy of mind, neurophysiology, and social intelligence. AI is associated in the popular mind with robotic development, but the main field of practical application has been as an embedded component in areas of software development which require computational understanding and modeling such as finance and economics, data mining and the physical sciences. The starting-point in the late 1940s was Alan Turing's question "Can computers think?", and the question remains effectively unanswered although the "Turing Test" is still used to assess computer output on the scale of human intelligence. But the automation of evaluative and predictive tasks has been increasingly successful as a substitute for human monitoring and intervention in domains of computer application involving complex real-world data.

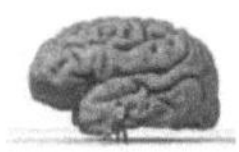	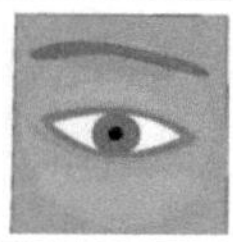	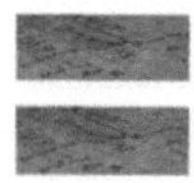	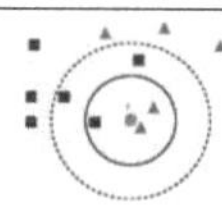
Machine Learning	Computer vision	Image Processing	Pattern Recognition
	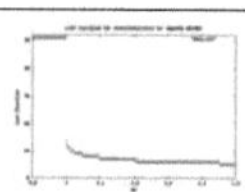	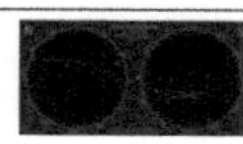	
Cognitive Science	Data Mining	Evolutionary Computation	Information Retrieval
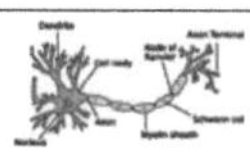	abcdefghijk lmnopqrstuvwxyz ABCDEFGHIJKLMN OPQRSTUVWXYZ		
Knowledge Representation	Natural Language Processing	Robotics	

Computer architecture and engineering

Computer architecture, or digital computer organization, is the conceptual design and fundamental operational structure of a computer system. It focuses largely on the way by which the central processing unit performs internally and accesses addresses in memory. The field often involves disciplines of computer engineering and electrical engineering, selecting and interconnection hardware components to create computers that meet functional, performance, and cost goals.

		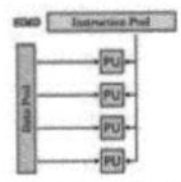	
Digital logic	Microarchitecture	Multiprocessing	
	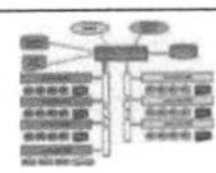		
Operating systems	Computer networks	Databases	Computer security
	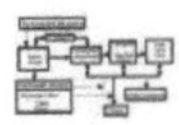	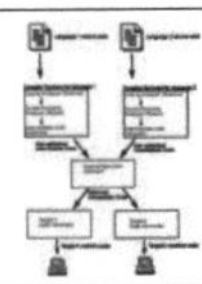	
Ubiquitous computing	Systems architecture	Compiler design	Programming languages

Computer graphics and visualization

Computer graphics is the study of digital visual contents, and involves syntheses and manipulations of image data. The study is connected to many other fields in computer science, including computer vision, image processing, and computational geometry, and are heavily applied in the fields of special effects and video games.

Computer security and cryptography

Computer security is a branch of computer technology, whose objective includes protection of information from unauthorized access, disruption, or modification while maintaining the accessibility and usability of the system for its intended users. Cryptography is the practice and study of hiding (encryption) and therefore deciphering (decryption) information. Modern cryptography is largely related to computer science, for many encryption and decryption algorithms are based on their computational complexity.

Computational science

Computational science (or scientific computing) is the field of study concerned with constructing mathematical models and quantitative analysis techniques and using computers to analyze and solve scientific problems. In practical use, it is typically the application of computer simulation and other forms of computation to problems in various scientific disciplines.

	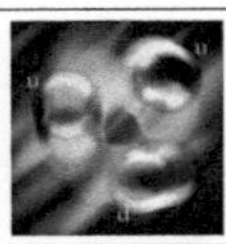	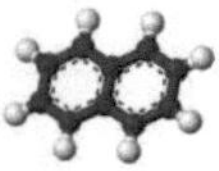	
Numerical analysis	Computational physics	Computational chemistry	Bioinformatics

Information science

	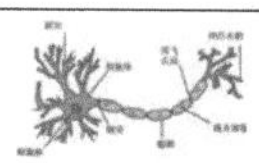	abcdefghijk lmnopqrstuvwxyz ABCDEFGHIJKLMN OPQRSTUVWXYZ	
Information Retrieval	Knowledge Representation	Natural Language Processing	Human–computer interaction

Software engineering

Software engineering is the study of designing, implementing, and modifying software in order to ensure it is of high quality, affordable, maintainable, and fast to build. It is a systematic approach to software design, involving the application of engineering practices to software. Software engineering deals with the organizing and analyzing software to get the best out of them. it does not just deal with the creation or manufacture of new software but the internal maintenance and arrangement.

Academia

Conferences

Further information: List of computer science conferences

Journals

Further information: Category:Computer science journals

Education

Some universities teach computer science as a theoretical study of computation and algorithmic reasoning. These programs often feature the theory of computation, analysis of algorithms, formal methods, concurrency theory, databases, computer graphics, and systems analysis, among others. They typically also teach computer programming, but treat it as a vessel for the support of other fields of computer science rather than a central focus of high-level study.

Other colleges and universities, as well as secondary schools and vocational programs that teach computer science, emphasize the practice of advanced programming rather than the theory of algorithms and computation in their computer science curricula. Such curricula tend to focus on those skills that are important to workers entering the software industry. The process aspects of computer programming are often referred to as software engineering.

Yet while computer science professions increasingly drive the U.S. economy, computer science education is absent in most American K-12 curricula. A report entitled "Running on Empty: The Failure to Teach K-12 Computer Science in the Digital Age" [27] was released in October 2010 by Association for Computing Machinery (ACM) [28] and Computer Science Teachers Association (CSTA) [29], and revealed that only 14 states have adopted significant education standards for high school computer science. The report also found that only nine states count high school computer science courses as a core academic subject in their graduation requirements. In tandem with "Running on Empty," a new, non-partisan advocacy coalition--Computing in the Core (CinC) [30]--was founded to influence federal and state policy, such as the Computer Science Education Act [31], which calls for grants to states to develop plans for improving computer science education and supporting computer science teachers.

See also

- Academic genealogy of computer scientists
- Computer scientist
- Computing
- History of computer science
- Informatics
- List of academic computer science departments
- List of computer science conferences
- List of computer scientists
- List of open problems in computer science
- List of publications in computer science
- List of pioneers in computer science
- List of software engineering topics
- Philosophy of computer science
- Women in computing

References

[1] Denning, P. J.; Comer, D. E.; Gries, D.; Mulder, M. C.; Tucker, A.; Turner, A. J.; Young, P. R. (Jan 1989). "Computing as a discipline". *Communications of the ACM* **32**: 9–23. doi:10.1145/63238.63239. volume = 64 "Computer science and engineering is the systematic study of algorithmic processes-their theory, analysis, design, efficiency, implementation, and application-that describe and transform information."

[2] Wegner, P. (October 13–15, 1976). "Research paradigms in computer science". *Proceedings of the 2nd international Conference on Software Engineering*. San Francisco, California, United States: IEEE Computer Society Press, Los Alamitos, CA. "Computer science is the study of information structures"

[3] "*Common myths and preconceptions about Cambridge Computer Science*" Computer Science Department (http://web.archive.org/web/20110718081431/http://www.cl.cam.ac.uk/admissions/undergraduate/myths/), University of Cambridge

[4] Nigel Tout (2006). "Calculator Timeline" (http://www.vintagecalculators.com/html/calculator_time-line.html). *Vintage Calculator Web Museum*. . Retrieved 2006-09-18.

[5] "Science Museum - Introduction to Babbage" (http://web.archive.org/web/20060908054017/http://www.sciencemuseum.org.uk/on-line/babbage/index.asp). Archived from the original (http://www.sciencemuseum.org.uk/on-line/babbage/index.asp) on 2006-09-08. . Retrieved 2006-09-24.

[6] "A Selection and Adaptation From Ada's Notes found in "Ada, The Enchantress of Numbers," by Betty Alexandra Toole Ed.D. Strawberry Press, Mill Valley, CA" (http://www.scottlan.edu/Lriddle/women/ada-love.htm). . Retrieved 2006-05-04.

[7] The Association for Computing Machinery (ACM) was founded in 1947.

[8] Denning, P.J. (2000). "Computer Science: The Discipline" (http://web.archive.org/web/20060525195404/http://www.idi.ntnu.no/emner/dif8916/denning.pdf) (PDF). *Encyclopedia of Computer Science*. Archived from the original (http://www.idi.ntnu.no/emner/dif8916/denning.pdf) on 2006-05-25. .

[9] CAM.ac.uk (http://www.cl.cam.ac.uk/conference/EDSAC99/statistics.html)

[10] Computer science pioneer Samuel D. Conte dies at 85 (http://www.cs.purdue.edu/feature/conte.html) July 1, 2002

[11] Levy, Steven (1984). *Hackers: Heroes of the Computer Revolution*. Doubleday. ISBN 0-385-19195-2.

[12] David Kahn, The Codebreakers, 1967, ISBN 0-684-83130-9.

[13] Cornell.edu (http://www.cis.cornell.edu/Dean/Presentations/Slides/bgu.pdf)

[14] Constable, R.L. (March 2000) (PDF). *Computer Science: Achievements and Challenges circa 2000* (http://www.cs.cornell.edu/cis-dean/bgu.pdf). .

[15] Abelson, H.; G.J. Sussman with J. Sussman (1996). *Structure and Interpretation of Computer Programs* (2nd ed.). MIT Press. ISBN 0-262-01153-0. "The computer revolution is a revolution in the way we think and in the way we express what we think. The essence of this change is the emergence of what might best be called *procedural epistemology* — the study of the structure of knowledge from an imperative point of view, as opposed to the more declarative point of view taken by classical mathematical subjects."

[16] Black box traders are on the march (http://www.telegraph.co.uk/money/main.jhtml?xml=/money/2006/08/27/ccsoft27.xml) The Telegraph, August 26, 2006

[17] Eden, A. H. (2007). "Three Paradigms of Computer Science" (http://www.eden-study.org/articles/2007/three_paradigms_of_computer_science.pdf). *Minds and Machines* **17** (2): 135–167. doi:10.1007/s11023-007-9060-8. .

[18] Computing Sciences Accreditation Board (28 May 1997). "Computer Science as a Profession" (http://web.archive.org/web/20080617030847/http://www.csab.org/comp_sci_profession.html). Archived from the original (http://www.csab.org/comp_sci_profession.html) on 2008-06-17. . Retrieved 2010-05-23.

[19] Committee on the Fundamentals of Computer Science: Challenges and Opportunities, National Research Council (2004). *Computer Science: Reflections on the Field, Reflections from the Field* (http://www.nap.edu/catalog.php?record_id=11106#toc). National Academies Press. ISBN 978-0-309-09301-9. .
[20] CSAB, Inc. (http://www.csab.org/)
[21] Clay Mathematics Institute (http://www.claymath.org/millennium/P_vs_NP/) P=NP
[22] Communications of the ACM 1(4):p.6
[23] Communications of the ACM 2(1):p.4
[24] IEEE Computer 28(12):p.136
[25] Research Methods for Science By Michael P. Marder page 14. Published by Cambridge University Press
[26] Parnas, D. L. (1998). *Annals of Software Engineering* **6**: 19–37. doi:10.1023/A:1018949113292., p. 19: "Rather than treat software engineering as a subfield of computer science, I treat it as an element of the set, Civil Engineering, Mechanical Engineering, Chemical Engineering, Electrical Engineering, [...]"
[27] http://www.acm.org/runningonempty/
[28] http://www.acm.org/
[29] http://csta.acm.org/
[30] http://www.computinginthecore.org/
[31] http://www.govtrack.us/congress/bill.xpd?bill=h111-5929&tab=summary

Further reading

Overview

- Tucker, Allen B. (2004). *Computer Science Handbook* (2nd ed.). Chapman and Hall/CRC. ISBN 158488360X.
    - "Within more than 70 chapters, every one new or significantly revised, one can find any kind of information and references about computer science one can imagine. [...] all in all, there is absolute nothing about Computer Science that can not be found in the 2.5 kilogram-encyclopaedia with its 110 survey articles [...]." (Christoph Meinel, *Zentralblatt MATH*)
- van Leeuwen, Jan (1994). *Handbook of Theoretical Computer Science*. The MIT Press. ISBN 0262720205.
    - "[...] this set is the most unique and possibly the most useful to the [theoretical computer science] community, in support both of teaching and research [...]. The books can be used by anyone wanting simply to gain an understanding of one of these areas, or by someone desiring to be in research in a topic, or by instructors wishing to find timely information on a subject they are teaching outside their major areas of expertise." (Rocky Ross, *SIGACT News*)
- Ralston, Anthony; Reilly, Edwin D.; Hemmendinger, David (2000). *Encyclopedia of Computer Science* (http://portal.acm.org/ralston.cfm) (4th ed.). Grove's Dictionaries. ISBN 156159248X.
    - "Since 1976, this has been the definitive reference work on computer, computing, and computer science. [...] Alphabetically arranged and classified into broad subject areas, the entries cover hardware, computer systems, information and data, software, the mathematics of computing, theory of computation, methodologies, applications, and computing milieu. The editors have done a commendable job of blending historical perspective and practical reference information. The encyclopedia remains essential for most public and academic library reference collections." (Joe Accardin, Northeastern Illinois Univ., Chicago)

Selected papers

- Knuth, Donald E. (1996). *Selected Papers on Computer Science*. CSLI Publications, Cambridge University Press.
    - "Covering a period from 1966 to 1993, its interest lies not only in the content of each of these papers — still timely today — but also in their being put together so that ideas expressed at different times complement each other nicely." (N. Bernard, *Zentralblatt MATH*)

Articles

- Peter J. Denning. *Is computer science science?* (http://portal.acm.org/citation.cfm?id=1053309&coll=&dl=ACM&CFID=15151515&CFTOKEN=6184618), Communications of the ACM, April 2005.

- Peter J. Denning, *Great principles in computing curricula* (http://portal.acm.org/citation.cfm?id=971303&dl=ACM&coll=&CFID=15151515&CFTOKEN=6184618), Technical Symposium on Computer Science Education, 2004.
- Research evaluation for computer science, Informatics Europe report (http://www.informatics-europe.org/docs/research_evaluation.pdf). Shorter journal version: Bertrand Meyer, Christine Choppy, Jan van Leeuwen and Jorgen Staunstrup, *Research evaluation for computer science*, in Communications of the ACM, vol. 52, no. 4, pp. 31–34, April 2009.

Curriculum and classification

- Association for Computing Machinery. 1998 ACM Computing Classification System (http://www.acm.org/class/1998/overview.html). 1998.
- Joint Task Force of Association for Computing Machinery (ACM), Association for Information Systems (AIS) and IEEE Computer Society (IEEE-CS). Computing Curricula 2005: The Overview Report (http://www.acm.org/education/curric_vols/CC2005-March06Final.pdf). September 30, 2005.
- Norman Gibbs, Allen Tucker. "A model curriculum for a liberal arts degree in computer science". *Communications of the ACM*, Volume 29 Issue 3, March 1986.

External links

- Computer science (http://www.dmoz.org/Computers/Computer_Science//) at the Open Directory Project
- Scholarly Societies in Computer Science (http://www.lib.uwaterloo.ca/society/compsci_soc.html)
- Best Papers Awards in Computer Science since 1996 (http://jeffhuang.com/best_paper_awards.html)
- Photographs of computer scientists (http://se.ethz.ch/~meyer/gallery/) by Bertrand Meyer
- EECS.berkeley.edu (http://www.eecs.berkeley.edu/department/history.shtml)

Bibliography and academic search engines

- CiteSeer^{x} (http://citeseerx.ist.psu.edu/) (article): search engine, digital library and repository for scientific and academic papers with a focus on computer and information science.
- DBLP Computer Science Bibliography (http://dblp.uni-trier.de/) (article): computer science bibliography website hosted at Universität Trier, in Germany.
- The Collection of Computer Science Bibliographies (http://liinwww.ira.uka.de/bibliography/) (article)

Webcasts

- Directory of free university lectures in Computer Science (http://www.lecturefox.com/computerscience/)
- Collection of computer science lectures (http://videolectures.net/Top/Computer_Science/)
- UCLA Computer Science 1 Freshman Computer Science Seminar Section 1 (http://www.oid.ucla.edu/webcasts/courses/2006-2007/2006fall/cs1)

ltg:Datorzineiba rue:Інформатіка

City College of New York

City College of New York	

Motto	Respice, Adspice, Prospice (*Look back, look at, and look ahead*)
Established	1847
Type	Public
Endowment	$131 million [1]
President	Dr. Lisa Staiano-Coico, (2010-)
Provost	Dr. Martin Moskovits
Academic staff	508 (full time)
Admin. staff	401
Students	15,889
Undergraduates	12,541
Postgraduates	3,282
Location	New York City, NY, USA
Campus	Urban
Athletics	16 sports teams
Colors	Lavender and Black
Mascot	Beaver
Affiliations	City University of New York
Website	www1.ccny.cuny.edu [2]

The **City College of the City University of New York** (known more commonly as the **City College of New York** or simply **City College**, **CCNY**, or colloquially as **City**) is a senior college of the City University of New York (CUNY), in New York City. It is also the oldest of the City University's twenty-three institutions of higher learning.[3] City College's thirty-five acre Manhattan campus along Convent Avenue from 130th Street to 141st Street[4] is on a hill overlooking Harlem; its neo-Gothic campus was mostly designed by George Browne Post, and many of its buildings are landmarks.

CCNY was the first free public institution of higher education in the United States[5] and also for many years has been considered the flagship campus of the CUNY public university system.[6]

History

Early history - 19th century

The City College of New York was originally founded as the Free Academy of the City of New York in 1847 by wealthy businessman and president of the Board of Education Townsend Harris.[7] A combination prep school and college, it would provide children of immigrants and the poor access to free higher education based on academic merit alone.

Shepard Hall, rear entrance, viewed the west from Convent Avenue, City College of New York, 2010.

The Free Academy was the first of what would become a system of municipally-supported colleges. Hunter College, the second, was founded as a women's institution in 1870. Brooklyn College, the third, was established as a coeducational institution in 1930.

In 1847, New York State Governor John Young had given permission to the Board of Education to found the Free Academy, which was ratified in a statewide referendum. Founder Townsend Harris proclaimed, "Open the doors to all... Let the children of the rich and the poor take their seats together and know of no distinction save that of industry, good conduct and intellect."

City College of New York in 2010, North Campus, looking West. Wingate Hall on the left, Townsend Harris Hall in the background.

Dr. Horace Webster, a West Point graduate, was the first president of the Free Academy. On the occasion of The Free Academy's formal opening, January 21, 1849, Webster said:

> The experiment is to be tried, whether the children of the people, the children of the whole people, can be educated; and whether an institution of the highest grade, can be successfully controlled by the popular will, not by the privileged few.[8]

A view of the original entrance to Shepard Hall, the main building of City College of New York, in the early 1900's, on its new campus in Hamilton Heights, from St. Nicholas Avenue looking up westward to St. Nicholas Terrace.

In 1847, a curriculum was adopted which had nine main fields: mathematics, history, language, literature, drawing, natural philosophy, experimental philosophy, law, and political economy. The Academy's first graduation took place in 1853 in Niblo's Garden Theatre,[9] a large theater and opera house on Broadway, near Houston Street at the corner of Broadway and Prince Street.

Even in its early years, the Free Academy showed tolerance for diversity, especially in comparison to its urban neighbor, Columbia College, which then wasn't much more than a finishing school for wealthy young gentlemen. The Free Academy had a framework of tolerance that extended beyond the admission of students from every social stratum. In 1854, Columbia's trustees denied Oliver Wolcott Gibbs, a distinguished chemist and scientist, a faculty position because of Gibbs's religious beliefs. He was a Unitarian. Gibbs was a professor and held an appointment at the Free Academy since 1848.[10] (In 1863, Gibbs went on to an appointment at Harvard University, the Rumsford Professorship in Chemistry, where he had a distinguished career. In 1873, he was awarded an honorary degree from Columbia with a unanimous vote by its Trustees with the strong urging of President Barnard.[11] [12]) Later in the history of CCNY, in the early 1900s, President John H. Finley gave the College a more secular orientation by abolishing mandatory chapel attendance.[13] This change occurred at a time when more Jewish students were enrolling in the College.

In 1866, the Free Academy, a men's institution, was renamed the College of the City of New York. In 1929, the College of the City of New York became the City College of New York.[6] [14] [15] Finally, the institution became known as the City College of the City University of New York when CUNY was formally established as the umbrella institution for New York City's municipal-college system in 1961. The names City College of New York and City College, however, remain in general use.

With the name change in 1866, lavender was chosen as the College's color. In 1867, the academic senate, the first student government in the nation, was formed. Having struggled over the issue for ten years, in 1895 the New York State legislature voted to let the College build a new campus. A four-square block site was chosen, located in Manhattanville, within the area which was enclosed by the North Campus Arches; the College, however, quickly expanded north of the Arches (see below).

Statue of Alexander S. Webb, second president of CCNY

Like President Webster, the second president of City College was a West Point graduate. The second president, General Alexander S. Webb, assumed office in 1869. One of the Union's heroes at Gettysburg, General Webb was the commander of the Philadelphia Brigade. When the Union Army repulsed the Confederates at Cemetery Hill, General Webb played a central role in the battle. Coddington[16] wrote about Webb's conduct during Pickett's Charge: "Refusing to give up, [Webb] set an example of bravery and undaunted leadership for his men to follow...." In 1891, while still president of City College, he was awarded the Congressional Medal of Honor for heroism at Gettysburg. A full-length statue of Webb, in full military uniform, stands in his honor at the heart of the campus.[17]

The College's curriculum under Webster and Webb combined classical training in Latin and Greek with more practical subjects like chemistry, physics, and engineering. One of the outstanding Nineteenth Century graduates of City College was the Brooklyn-born George Washington Goethals, who put himself through the College in three years before going on to West Point. He later became the chief engineer on the Panama Canal. General Webb was succeeded by John Huston Finley in 1903. Finley relaxed some of the West Point-like discipline that characterized the College, including compulsory chapel attendance.[13] Delta Sigma Phi [18] was founded at CCNY in 1899 as a Jewish and Christian Fraternity, however the chapter did not last long due to Delta Sigma Phi becoming only Christian in 1914.

20th century

Education courses were first offered in 1897 in response to a city law that prohibited the hiring of teachers who lacked a proper academic background. The School of Education was established in 1921. The college newspaper, *The Campus*, published its first issue in 1907, and the first degree-granting evening session in the United States was started. Separate Schools of Business and Civic Administration and of Technology (Engineering) were established in 1919. Students were also required to sign a loyalty oath. In 1947, the College celebrated its centennial year, awarding honorary degrees to Bernard Baruch (class of 1889) and Robert F. Wagner (class of 1898). A 100 year time capsule was buried in North Campus.

Until 1929, City College had been an all-male institution. During that time, specifically in 1909, the first chapter of Sigma Alpha Mu fraternity was founded. [19]. In 1930, CCNY admitted women for the first time, but only to graduate programs. In 1951, the entire institution became coeducational.

In the years when top-flight private schools were restricted to the children of the Protestant Establishment, thousands of brilliant individuals (including Jewish students) attended City College because they had no other option. CCNY's academic excellence and status as a working-class school earned it the titles "Harvard of the Proletariat", the "poor man's Harvard", and "Harvard-on-the-Hudson".[20]

Even today, after three decades of controversy over its academic standards, no other public college has produced as many Nobel laureates who have studied and graduated with a degree from a particular public college.[21] CCNY's official quote on this is "Nine Nobel laureates claim CCNY as their Alma Mater, the most from any public college in the United States."[22] [23] This should not be confused with Nobel laureates who teach at a public university; UC Berkeley boasts 19.

In its heyday of the 1930s through the 1950s, CCNY became known for its political radicalism. It was said that the old CCNY cafeteria in the basement of Shepard Hall, particularly in alcove 1, was the only place in the world where a fair debate between Trotskyists and Stalinists could take place.[24] [25] Being part of a political debate that began in the morning in alcove 1, Irving Howe reported that after some time had passed he would leave his place among the arguing students in order to attend class. When he returned to the cafeteria late in the day, he would find that the same debate had continued but with an entirely different cast of students.[24] Alumni who were at City College in the mid-20th century said that City College in those days made UC Berkeley in the 1960s look like a school of conformity.

The municipality of New York was considerably more conformist than CCNY students and faculty. The Philosophy Department, at the end of the 1939-1940 academic year, invited the British mathematician and philosopher Bertrand Russell to become a professor at CCNY. Members of the Catholic Church protested Russell's appointment. A woman named Jean Kay filed suit against the Board of Higher Education to block Russell's appointment on the grounds that his views on marriage and sex would adversely affect her daughter's virtue, although her daughter was not a CCNY student. Russell wrote "a typical American witch-hunt was instituted against me."[26] Kay won the suit, but the Board declined to appeal after considering the political pressure exerted.[27] Also see the Bertrand Russell Case.

Russell took revenge in the preface of the first edition of his book *An Inquiry into Meaning and Truth*, which was published by the Unwin Brothers in the UK (the preface was not included in the U.S. editions). In a long précis that detailed Russell's accomplishments including medals awarded by Columbia University and the Royal Society and faculty appointments at Oxford, Cambridge, UCLA, Harvard, the Sorbonne, Peking (the name used in that era), the LSE, Chicago, and so forth, Russell added, "Judicially pronounced unworthy to be Professor of Philosophy at the College of the City of New York."

Many City College alumni served in the U.S. Armed Forces during the Second World War. A total of 310 CCNY alumni were killed in the War. Prior to World War II, a large number of City College alumni—relative to alumni of other U.S. colleges—volunteered to serve on the Republican side in the Spanish Civil War. Thirteen CCNY alumni were killed in Spain.[28]

In 1945, Professor William E. Knickerbocker, Chairman of the Romance Languages Department, was accused of anti-semitism by four faculty members. They claimed that "for at least seven years they have been subjected to continual harassment and what looks very much like discrimination ...." by Knickerbocker.[29] Four years later Knickerbocker was again accused of anti-semitism, this time for denying honors to high-achieving Jewish students.[30] [31] About the same time, Professor William C. Davis of the Economics Department was accused by students of maintaining a racially segregated dormitory at Army Hall.[30] [32] Professor Davis was the dormitory's administrator. CCNY students, many of whom were World War II veterans, launched a massive strike in protest against Knickerbocker and Davis.[30] [33] The *New York Times* called the event "the first general strike at a municipal institution of higher learning."[33] Also see the Knickerbocker Case.

CCNY is the only team in men's college basketball history to win both the National Invitation Tournament and the NCAA Tournament in the same year, 1950. However, this accomplishment was overshadowed by a point shaving scandal in which seven CCNY basketball players were arrested, in 1951, for taking money from gamblers to affect the outcome of games.[34] The scandal led to the decline of CCNY from a national powerhouse in Division I basketball to a member of Division III and damaged the national profile of college basketball in general. The College currently fields nine men's and seven women's varsity athletic teams.[35]

In 1955, a City College student named Alan A. Brown founded the economics honor society, Omicron Chi Epsilon. The purpose of the society was to confer honors on outstanding economics students, organize academic meetings, and publish a journal. In 1963, Omicron Chi Epsilon merged with Omicron Delta Gamma, the other economics honor society, to form Omicron Delta Epsilon, the current academic honor society in economics.[36]

During a 1969 takeover of South campus,[37] under threat of a riot, African American and Puerto Rican activists and their white allies demanded, among other policy changes, that City College implement an aggressive affirmative action program.[7] At some point, campus protesters began referring to CCNY as "Harlem University." The administration of the City University at first balked at the demands, but instead, came up with an open admissions or open-access program under which any graduate of a New York City high school would be able to matriculate either at City College or another college in the CUNY system. Beginning in 1970, the program opened doors to college to many who would not otherwise have been able to attend college. The program, however, came at the cost of City College's and the University's academic standing as well as New York City's fiscal health.[7]

City College began charging tuition in 1976. By the 1990s, CCNY stopped admitting and offering remedial classes to students who did not meet its academic entrance requirements. CUNY then enrolled less well prepared students in its community colleges.

As a result of the 1989 student protests and building takeovers concerning tuition increases, a community action center was opened on the campus called The Guillermo Morales/Assata Shakur Community and Student Center located in the NAC building. The center was named after 1960s CCNY student activists Assata Shakur and Guillermo Morales.[38] [39] [40]

CCNY's new Frederick Douglass Debate Society defeated Harvard and Yale at the "Super Bowl" of the American Parliamentary Debate Association in 1996. In 2003, the College's Model UN Team was awarded as an Outstanding Delegation at the National Model United Nations (NMUN) Conference, an honor that it would repeat for four years in a row.

The U.S. Postal Service issued a postcard commemorating CCNY's 150th Anniversary, featuring Shepard Hall, on Charter Day, May 7, 1997.

21st century

Engineering School

The City University of New York began recruiting students for the University Scholars program in the fall 2000, and admitted the first cohort of undergraduate scholars in the fall 2001. CCNY was one of five CUNY campuses, on which the program was initiated. The newly admitted scholars became undergraduates in the college's newly formed Honors Program. Students attending the CCNY Honors College are awarded free tuition, a cultural passport that admits them to New York City cultural institutions for free or at sharply reduced prices, a notebook computer, and an academic expense account that they can apply to such academic-related activities as study abroad. These undergraduates are also required to attend a number of specially developed honors courses. In 2001 CUNY initiated the CUNY Honors College, renamed Macaulay Honors College in 2007.[41] Both the CCNY Honors Program and the CCNY chapter of the Macaulay Honors College are run out of the CCNY Honors Center.

In October 2005, Dr. Andrew Grove, a 1960 graduate of the Engineering School in Chemical Engineering, and co-founder of Intel Corporation, donated $26 million to the Engineering School, which has since been renamed the Grove School of Engineering.[42] It is the largest donation ever given to the City College of New York.

In 2009, the School of Architecture moved into the former 'Y' Building.[43] The 'Y' building had been gutted and completely remodeled under the design direction of architect Rafael Viñoly. Also in 2009, school was renamed the Bernard and Anne Spitzer School of Architecture in honor of the $25 million gift the Spitzers gave to the school.[44]

Campus history

Downtown

The Free Academy at Lexington Avenue and 23rd Street in New York City in the 1800s.

City College was originally situated in downtown Manhattan, in the Free Academy Building, which was CCNY's home from 1849 to 1907. The building was designed by James Renwick, Jr. and was located at Lexington Avenue and 23rd Street. According to some sources, it was the first Gothic Revival college building on the East Coast.[45] Renwick's building was demolished in 1928, and replaced in 1930 with a 16-story structure that is part of the present-day Baruch College campus.

North Campus

The main City College building, Shepard Hall, looking West from St. Nicholas Avenue to Shepard Hall's main entrance on St. Nicholas Terrace (1907)

CCNY then moved to its current location in the upper Manhattan village of Manhattanville in 1906, when the Collegiate Gothic campus was erected.[46] [47] [48] [49]

This new campus was designed by George Browne Post.

According to CCNY's published history, "The Landmark neo-Gothic buildings of the North Campus Quadrangle were designed by the noted architect George Browne Post. They are superb examples of English Perpendicular Gothic style and are among the first buildings, as an entire campus, to be built in the U.S. in this style. Groundbreaking for the Gothic Quadrangle buildings took place in 1903".

The original neo-Gothic buildings on the new upper Manhattan campus were:

- Shepard Hall, standing on its own, across the street from the campus quadrangle on Convent Avenue
- Baskerville Hall
- Compton Hall
- Harris Hall
- Wingate Hall

Shepard Hall tower, seen from Harlem

Shepard Hall, the largest building and the centerpiece of the campus, was modeled after a Gothic cathedral plan with its main entrance on St. Nicholas Terrace.[50] It has a large chapel assembly hall called "The Great Hall" which has a mural painted by Edwin Blashfield called "The Graduate".[51] [52] [53]

Harris Hall, named in the original architectural plans as "the Sub-Freshman Building", housed City College's preparatory high school, Townsend Harris High School, from 1906 until it moved in 1930 downtown to the School of Business.[54]

Wingate Hall was named for George Wood Wingate (Class of 1858), an attorney and promoter of physical fitness. It served as the College's main gymnasium between 1907 and 1972.[55] [56] [57]

Baskerville Hall for many years housed the Chemistry Department, was also known as the Chemical Building, and had one of the largest original lecture halls on the campus, Doremus lecture hall.[58] It currently houses HSMSE, The High School for Mathematics, Science, and Engineering.

Compton Hall was originally designed as the Mechanical Arts Building.[59]

Five of these new Gothic campus buildings opened in 1906. The sixth, Goethals Hall,[60] was completed in 1930. The new building was named for George Washington Goethals, the CCNY civil engineering alumnus who, as mentioned above in the section on the history of the College, went on to become the chief engineer of the Panama Canal. Goethals Hall housed the School of Technology (engineering) and adjoins the Mechanical Arts Building, Compton Hall.

The six Gothic buildings are connected by a tunnel, which closed to public use in 1969.[61]

Six hundred grotesques on the original Gothic buildings represent the practical and the fine arts.[62] [63]

The North Campus Quadrangle contains four great arches on the main avenues entering and exiting the campus:

- the Hudson Gate on Amsterdam Avenue[64]
- the George Washington Gate at 138th Street and Convent Avenue
- the Alexander Hamilton Gate at the northern edge of Convent Avenue
- the Peter Stuyvesant Gate at St. Nicholas Terrace. (The Archway and north pedestrian arch over the north side of St. Nicholas Terrace was dismantled prior to March 25, 1927 when ground was broken for the soon to be completed Bowker Library fronting on St. Nicholas Terrace)

A stone grotesque on a CCNY building from 1906, holding a model of Shepard Hall.

Lewisohn Stadium (demolished)

In the early 1900s, after most of the Gothic campus had been built, CCNY President John H. Finley wanted the College to have a stadium because the existing facilities for the College's athletic teams were inadequate. New York City did not provide the money needed to build a stadium; however, the municipal government donated to the College two city blocks south of the campus which were open park land. Finley's wish for a stadium moved forward when in 1912 businessman and philanthropist Adolph Lewisohn expressed interest in financing construction of the stadium. Lewisohn donated $75,000 for the stadium's construction and Finley commissioned architect Arnold W. Brunner to design Lewisohn Stadium, which was influenced by Finley's memories of a small rock-hewn theatre in the Trastevere section of Rome.[65]

Lewisohn Stadium was built as a 6,000-seat stadium, with thousands more seats available on the infield during concerts, and was dedicated on May 29, 1915, two years after Dr. Finley had left his post at the College and Dr. Sidney Edward Mezes had become CCNY's fourth president. The stadium's dedication was enhanced by a performance of "The Trojan Women", produced by Granville Barker and Lillian McCarthy. College graduation services were held in Lewisohn for many years.

The former Adolph Lewisohn Stadium, now the site of the North Academic Center (1915)

Other demolished buildings

A separate library building originally planned in 1912 for the campus was never built but ground was broken on March 25, 1927 for a free-standing library to be built on St. Nicholas Terrace, between St. Nicholas & 141st St. Only 1/5 of the original library plan was constructed at a cost of $850,000, far above the $150,000 alumni had collected to establish a library at the original Amsterdam Avenue & 140th St. site. The Bowker/Alumni Library stood at the present site of the Steinman Engineering building until 1957.[66]

The Hebrew Orphan Asylum was erected in 1884 on Amsterdam Avenue between 136th and 138th Street, and was designed by William H. Hume.[67] It was already there when City College moved to upper Manhattan. When it closed in the 1940s, the building was used by City College to house members of the U.S. Armed Forces assigned to the Army Specialized Training Program (ASTP). From 1946 to 1955, it was used as a dormitory, library, and classroom space for the College. It was called "Army Hall" until it was demolished in 1955 and 1956.[68] <[69]

In 1946, CCNY purchased a former Episcopal orphanage on 135th Street and Convent Avenue (North campus), and renamed it Klapper Hall, after Paul Klapper (Class of 1904) Professor and the Dean of School of Education and who was later the first president of Queens College/CUNY (1937–1952). Klapper Hall was red brick in Georgian style and it served until 1983 as home of the School of Education.[70]

Postwar buildings

Steinman Hall, which houses the School of Engineering, was erected in 1962 on the north end of the campus, on the site of the Bowker Library and the Drill Hall to replace the facilities in Compton Hall and Goethals Hall, and was named for David Barnard Steinman (CCNY Class of 1906), a well known civil engineer and bridge designer.[71]

In 1963, the Administration Building was erected on the North Campus across from Wingate Hall. It houses the College's administration offices, including the President's, Provost's and the Registrar's offices. It was originally intended as a warehouse to store the huge number of records and transcripts of students since 1847.[72] [73] In early 2007, the Administration Building was formally named The Howard E. Wille Administration Building, in honor of Howard E. Wille, class of 1955, a distinguished alumnus and philanthropist.[74]

In 1971, the Marshak Science Building was completed on the site of the former Jasper Oval, an open space previously used as a football field.[75] [76] The building was named after Robert Marshak, renowned physicist and president of CCNY (1970–1979). The Marshak building houses all science labs and adjoins the Mahoney Gymnasium and its athletic facilities including a swimming pool and tennis courts.[77]

In the 1970s, construction of the massive North Academic Center (NAC) was initiated. It was completed in 1984, and replaced Lewisohn Stadium and Klapper Hall. The NAC building houses hundreds of classrooms, two cafeterias, the Cohen Library, student lounges and centers, administrative offices, and a number of computer installations. Designed by architect John Carl Warnecke, the building has received criticism for its lack of design and outsize scale in comparison to the surrounding neighborhood.

North Academic Center

Within the NAC, a student lounge space was created outside the campus bookstore, and murals celebrating the history of the campus were painted on the doors of the undergraduate Student Government.[78] Founded in 1869, it claims to be the oldest continuously operating student government organization in the country.

The first floor of the Administration Building was given a postmodern renovation in 2004. The first floor houses the admissions office and the registrar's office. The upper floors house the offices of the president and provost.

The New York Landmarks Preservation Commission made the North Campus Quadrangle buildings and the College Gates official landmarks in 1981. The buildings in the Quadrangle were put on the State and National Register of Historic Places in 1984. In the summer of 2006, the historic gates on Convent Avenue were restored.

South Campus

In 1953, CCNY bought the campus of the Manhattanville College of the Sacred Heart (which, on a 1913 map, was shown as The Convent of the Sacred Heart), which added a south section to the campus. This expanded the campus to include many of the buildings in the area between 140th Street to 130th Street, from St. Nicholas Terrace in the east to Amsterdam Avenue in the west.

1950's aerial view of the old South Campus of City College, bought in 1953 from Manhattanville College of the Sacred Heart. The photo is taken from the south looking northeast.

Former buildings of the Manhattanville College campus to be used by CCNY were re-named for City College's purposes: Stieglitz Hall, Downer Hall, Wagner Hall, the prominent Finley Student Center which contained the very active Buttenweiser Lounge, Eisner Hall, Park Gym, Mott Hall, and others.

As a result of this expansion, the South Campus of CCNY primarily contained the liberal arts classes and departments of the College. The North Campus, also as a result of this expansion, mostly housed classes and departments for the sciences and engineering, as well as Klapper Hall (School of Education), and the Administration Building.

In 1957, a new library building was erected in the middle of the campus, near 135th Street on the South Campus, and named Cohen Library, after Morris Raphael Cohen, an alumnus (Class of 1900) and celebrated professor of philosophy at the College from 1912 to 1938. When the Cohen Library moved to the North Academic Complex in the early 1980s, the structure was renamed the 'Y' building, and housed offices, supplies, the mail room, etc. The building was eventually gutted and renovated to become the home of the School of Architecture in 2009 (see below).

In the 1970s, many of the old buildings of the South Campus[79] were demolished, some which had been used by the Academy of The Sacred Heart. The buildings remaining on the South Campus at this time were the Cohen Library (later moved into the North Academic Center), Park Gym (now the Structural Biology Research Center[80]), Eisner Hall (built in 1941 by Manhattanville College of the Sacred Heart as a library, later remodeled and housed CCNY's Art Department and named for the Chairman of the Board of Higher Education in the 1930s),[81] the Schiff House (former President's residence, now a child care center), and Mott Hall (formerly the English Department, now a New York City Department of Education primary school[82]).

Some of the buildings which were demolished at that time were Finley Hall (housed The Finley Student Center, student activities center, originally built in 1888-1890 as Manhattanville Academy's main building, and purchased in 1953 by City College),[83] Wagner Hall (housed various social science and liberal arts departments and classes, originally built as a dormitory for Manhattanville Academy, and was named in honor of Robert F. Wagner Sr., member of the Class of 1898, who represented New York State for 23 years in the United States Senate),[84] Stieglitz Hall, and Downer Hall, amongst others.

Annotated 1950s aerial view of the main part of the old South Campus of City College, with many former CCNY buildings marked with their names. (Click on photo to enlarge)

New buildings were erected on the South Campus, including Aaron Davis Hall in 1981, and the Herman Goldman sports field in 1993. In August 2006, the College completed the construction of a 600-bed dormitory, called "The Towers" [85] [86] [87] There are plans to rename The Towers after a distinguished alumnus or donor.

The building that formerly housed Cohen Library, i.e., the 'Y' Building mentioned above, became the new home for the School of Architecture, with the renovation headed by architect Rafael Viñoly. Near the 133rd Street gate, a new science building is under construction in order to relieve pressure from Marshak Hall, which had a beam collapse in 2005. Part of this project is the elimination of the Herman Goldman sports field, a controversial move which will dramatically alter the South Campus.

In 2007, two new buildings had been proposed for the South Campus site by the Dormitory Authority of the State of New York (DASNY). One was a four story City College of New York Science Building, to serve as an adjunct to the Marshak Science Building on the North Campus, and the other was a six story City University of New York Advanced Science Research Center (ASRC).[88] [89] [90]

Campus location

The College is located between West 130th and West 141st Street in Manhattan, along Convent Avenue and St. Nicholas Terrace, between Amsterdam and St. Nicholas Avenues. The campus is served by:

- the 137th Street – City College subway station, served by the Broadway local 1 train
- the 125th and 145th stations, served by the A, B, C, and D trains
- numerous city buses and campus shuttle buses

College seal and medal logo

The design of the three-faced college seal took its roots in the 19th century when Professor Charles Anthon was inspired by views of Janus, the Roman god of beginnings, whose two faces connect the past and the future. He broadened this image of Janus in three faces to show the student, and consequently, knowledge, developing from childhood through youth into maturity.

It was redesigned again in 1947 by Professor Albert P. d'Andrea (CCNY class of 1918) for the college's Centennial Medal.[91] [92] Professor Albert P. d'Andrea came to the United States from Benevento, Italy in 1901. He was a faculty member of the City College of New York from 1918 to 1948 and Professor of Art and Chairman of the Art Department from 1948 to 1968.

In 2003, the college decided to create a logo distinct from its seal, with the stylized text "the City College of New York."[93]

Rankings

- City College was ranked [94] by Shanghai Jiao Tong University as 89-117 nationally and 203-304 internationally in 2007 and 115-139 nationally, 303-401 internationally in 2008 and 90-121 nationally, 340-451 internationally in 2009. It should be noted however that the study focuses heavily on institutions with strong hard science backgrounds, as the rating is based on a number of factors including articles published in scientific journals and Nobel laureates.
- The 2008 America's Best Colleges ranked by Forbes.com placed City College at #355.[95]
- U.S. News and World Report ranks City College 62 in the master's universities of the North category. [96]

Popular culture

Film

- *Marty* (1955) - the main character, Marty, says that he filled out an application and was accepted to City College, but had to turn it down after his father died.[97]
- *Love Story* (1970) - The Harvard graduation was in the Great Hall in CCNY's Shepard Hall.
- *Bananas* (1971) - the character Nancy, who is taking signatures for a petition in Fielding Mellish's apartment building, is a student at CCNY
- *Serpico* (1973) - Al Pacino's character has a meeting at Lewisohn Stadium, which also shows the Marshak building and North Campus at the time.
- *Fast Break* (1979) - Gabe Kaplan's character, David Greene, wears a City College sweatshirt during the movie.
- *Wall Street* (1987) - Michael Douglas's character, Gordon Gekko, tells Bud Fox (played by Charlie Sheen) that his accomplishments are "not bad for a City College boy. I bought my way in; now all these Ivy League schmucks are sucking my knee caps."
- *Crossing Delancey* (1988) - Sam is wearing a City College of New York sweater when playing handball
- *Cocktail* (1988) - the character Brian Flanagan was studying business at CCNY
- *Reversal of Fortune* (1989) - The CCNY campus was used to depict Harvard for this 1990 movie. Many of the scenes taking place in the law school, including the office of Professor Alan M. Dershowitz and several classroom scenes, were filmed in late 1989 at the CCNY School of Architecture, located in Shepard Hall.
- *The Substance of Fire* (1996) - Scenes in the publishing firm run by Isaac Geldhart (Ron Rifkin's character), a Holocaust survivor, were shot in Shepard Hall.
- Habit (film) (1997) - A horror film by Larry Fessenden. Scenes at the beginning of the film take place at City College as well as St. Nicholas Park behind CCNY.
- *The Royal Tenenbaums* (2001) - Shepard Hall's tower can be seen in the opening montage of this film as the young Richie Tenenbaum releases his eagle. Much of the film was shot at or near CCNY.
- *25th Hour* (2002) - Most scenes were shot in Shepard Hall, when Monty Brogan (Edward Norton's character) visits (and reminisces about the past) his old high school and friend Jacob Elinsky (Philip Seymour Hoffman's character) who teaches at a fancy private high school.
- *City Island* (2009) - Protagonist Vince Rizzo says, "Anyway I had 75 hundred bucks in my pocket that I had earned, you know, working at my father's boat here on City Island, I was gunna use it to go to City College, but I gave it to her instead."

Television shows

- *Mad Men* - Anna's niece, Stephanie, asks Don Draper where he went to college, he responds "I strung together several non-consecutive years in night school—City College."
- *Law & Order* - various scenes from *Law & Order* have been filmed on the City College campus.
- *The West Wing* - It is stated on occasion that Toby Ziegler attended City College.
- *Gossip Girl* - Some scenes from the *Gossip Girl* show have been filmed on the City College campus.
- *Weeds* - Shane Botwin obtains admission to CCNY during the seventh season by lying about his nation of origin.

Literature

- Allen Ginsberg - Allen Ginsberg referenced CCNY in multiple poems.
- Langston Hughes - Langston Hughes referenced CCNY in multiple poems, such as in "Theme for English B" as " ... to this college on the hill above Harlem." [98] [99]
- Thomas Pynchon - Thomas Pynchon referenced CCNY in his roman V. On p. 132, it speaks of Esther Harvitz who was an honors graduate of CCNY.[100]
- Woody Allen - Sidney Kugelmass, the protagonist of Allen's short story "The Kugelmass Episode," is stated to be a professor of humanities at CCNY.

Presidents

- 1. Horace Webster, 1847–1869
- 2. General Alexander S. Webb, 1869–1902
- 3. John Huston Finley, 1903–1913
- 4. Sidney Edward Mezes, 1914–1927
- 5. Frederick Robinson, 1927–1938
- 6. Harry N. Wright, 1941–1952
- 7. Buell G. Gallagher, 1953–1969
- 8. Robert Marshak, 1970–1979
- 9. Bernard W. Harleston, 1981–1992
- 10. Yolanda T. Moses, 1993–1999
  - Stanford A. Roman Jr., (interim) 1999-2000
- 11. Gregory H. Williams, 2001–2009
  - Robert "Buzz" Paaswell, (interim) 2009-2010 [101]
- 12. Lisa Staiano-Coico, 2010- [102] [103]

(source: *The Adolph Lewisohn Plaza of Honor* website - archived copy [104])

See also

- Mid-InfraRed Technologies for Health and the Environment (MIRTHE) (largely based at Princeton University)

Notes

[1] "Best Colleges 2010: CUNY--City College CUNY--City College" (http://colleges.usnews.rankingsandreviews.com/best-colleges/new-york-ny/city-college-2688), *U.S. News & World Report*
[2] http://www1.ccny.cuny.edu/
[3] CUNY's list of its 23 institutions (http://www1.cuny.edu/about/index.html)
[4] CCNY campus map (http://www1.ccny.cuny.edu/prospective/about/upload/CURRENTmap07.pdf) which shows the lower section extending to 130th St. where the new Towers dormitory is, and up north to 141st St. where Steinman Hall ends and CCNY Alumni House stands.
[5] "... the founding, in 1847, of the Free Academy, the very first free public institution of higher education in the nation.", Baruch College history website. (http://www.baruch.cuny.edu/about/glance.html)
[6] Rudy,Willis, *The College of the City of New York: A History 1847-1947*, City College Press 1949. Also issued as a thesis by Columbia University. Reprinted in 1977 by the Arno Press.
[7] Traub, James. *City on a Hill: Testing the American Dream at City College.* Addison-Wesley, 1984.
[8] Association of the Bar of the City of New York, Report of the Commission on the Future of CUNY: Part I Remediation and Access: To Educate the "Children of the Whole People", 1999. (http://www.abcny.org/Publications/reports/show_html.php?rid=47)
[9] "Niblo's Garden" (http://www.musicals101.com/bwaypast4.htm#Niblo's) - Demolished Theatres, *musicals101.com*
[10] Cf. Bender, pp. 271-273
[11] Cf. Bender, p. 273, footnotes.
[12] "The Wolcott Gibbs Affair at Columbia, 1854" (http://beatl.barnard.columbia.edu/stand_columbia/TimelineGibbsAffair.html). . Retrieved 2008-03-06.
[13] Cf. Bender, pp. 291-292
[14] Minutes, Trustees, Board of Higher Education, 1929, p. 194
[15] Subway College (http://www.time.com/time/magazine/article/0,9171,804043,00.html), in Time magazine, October 28, 1946.
[16] Coddington, Edwin B. *The Gettysburg campaign; a study in command*, Scribner's, 1984.
[17] The statue is on the east side of Convent Avenue near both Shepherd Hall and the Administration Building.
[18] http://www.deltasig.org
[19] http://www.sam.org/
[20] Robert Sobel (1994-11-21). "Review of *City on a Hill: Testing the American Dream at City College* by James Traub" (http://findarticles.com/p/articles/mi_m0EKF/is_n2041_v40/ai_16036295). Electronic News. . Retrieved 2007-12-12.
[21] see article Nobel Prize laureates by university affiliation

[22] "CCNY - An Experiment in Democracy Going Strong Over 160 Years Later" (http://www1.ccny.cuny.edu/advancement/pr/presskit/) - CCNY website press information
[23] "Nine graduates of City College have won the Nobel Prize" (http://www1.ccny.cuny.edu/advancement/pr/presskit/nobel/index.cfm), CCNY website press information
[24] "Arguing the World" (http://www.pbs.org/arguing/) - PBS documentary, 1997.
[25] "Finding My Way to the Alcoves" (http://www.pbs.org/arguing/about_essays_1.html) - Joseph Dorman, film director of "Arguing the World".
[26] Bertrand Russell, *The Autobiography of Bertrand Russell: The Middle Years: 1914-1944*. Bantam, 1969, p. 320.
[27] Thom Weidlich. *Appointment Denied: The Inquisition of Bertrand Russell*. Prometheus Books, 2000.
[28] Memorial plaques providing the numbers and honoring those who gave their lives can be found in the second floor rotunda of the NAC building on the CCNY campus.
[29] Morris Freedman, The Knickerbocker Case, *Commentary*, August 1945.
[30] Feinberg, Alexander (April 12, 1949). "City College Students Clash with Police in 'Bias' Strike" (http://select.nytimes.com/gst/abstract.html?res=F40C13FA3D5F177B93C0A8178FD85F4D8485F9). *New York Times*: pp. 1, 36. .
[31] This Wiki writer's personal communication with a 1949 student striker, 1989.
[32] "William C. Davis, Educator, Is Dead". *New York Times*: p. 33. August 16, 1948.
[33] Goodman, Walter E. (April 16, 1984). "C.C.N.Y. Alumni Recall 1949 Strike" (http://www.nytimes.com/1984/04/16/nyregion/ccny-alumni-recall-1949-strike.html). *New York Times*: p. B10. .
[34] Explosion: 1951 scandals threaten college hoops (http://espn.go.com/classic/s/basketball_scandals_explosion.html)
[35] CCNY Athletics page (http://www1.ccny.cuny.edu/athletics/)
[36] Omicron Delta Epsilon - The International Economics Honor Society (http://www.omicrondeltaepsilon.org/history.html)
[37] Reitano, Joanne R., "The Restless City: A Short History of New York from Colonial Times to the Present" (http://books.google.com/books?id=60bQLzwGVjsC&printsec=frontcover), CRC Press, 2006. ISBN 0415978491. Cf. page 176.
[38] "Shakur - Morales Student & Community Center Under Attack at City College of New York" (http://leftspot.com/blog/?q=node/220), *Left Spot*, December 12, 2006.
[39] "FOX Facts: Student Group Statement on Morales/Shakur Community Center" (http://www.foxnews.com/story/0,2933,236079,00.html), *FOX News*, Tuesday, December 12, 2006
[40] Wise, Daniel, "First Amendment Violation Claim Proceeds Against College Over Removed Plaque" (http://www.law.com/jsp/article.jsp?id=1202447703512&slreturn=1&hbxlogin=1), *New York Law Journal*, April 8, 2010
[41] "History: Macaulay Honors College" (http://macaulay.cuny.edu/about/history.php), CUNY website
[42] Grove School of Engineering Video (http://www-me.engr.ccny.cuny.edu/GSOE/video/)
[43] Bernard and Anne Spitzer School of Architecture at the City College of New York. (http://www1.ccny.cuny.edu/prospective/architecture/index.cfm)
[44] Hughes, C. J. (April 22, 2009). City College's Architecture School Snares $25 Million Gift. *Architectural Record*. (http://archrecord.construction.com/news/daily/archives/090422citycollege.asp)
[45] "Free Academy Building (1849-1927)" (http://origin.admin.ccny.cuny.edu/library/exhibitions/lostworld/freeacademy.html), *The "The Lost World of CCNY: Architectural Gems of Our Past*, CCNY Libraries
[46] "Early CCNY picture" (http //www.ccny.cuny.edu/library/exhibitions/images/full/Fletcher'sNYCpage.jpg), *CCNY in Souvenirs, 1900-1947*, CCNY Libraries
[47] "Early CCNY picture postcard" (http://www.ccny.cuny.edu/library/exhibitions/images/full/CCNYpostcard3.jpg), *CCNY in Souvenirs, 1900-1947*, CCNY Libraries
[48] "General View of The College of the City of New York (c.1906)" (http://web.archive.org/web/20060218224053/http://www.ccny.cuny.edu/public_safety/ccny-convent-old.jpg) (archived 2006)
[49] "Panoramic View of The College of The City of New York" (c.1906)" (http://web.archive.org/web/20060218224056/http://www.ccny.cuny.edu/public_safety/Graphics/panoramic.jpg) (archived 2006)
[50] "Early CCNY picture postcard: Shepard Hall" (http://www.ccny.cuny.edu/library/exhibitions/images/full/CCNYpostcard16.jpg), *CCNY in Souvenirs, 1900-1947*, CCNY Libraries]
[51] "Great Hall CCNY" (http://www.nycago.org/Organs/NYC/img/CCNY_GreatHallInt.jpg), *NYC Chapter of the American Guild of Organists* website
[52] Weiner, Mina Rieur, (editor), *Edwin Howland Blashfield: Master American Muralist*, New York : W.W. Norton, 2009. ISBN 9780393732818
[53] "New Book on Edwin Blashfield features CCNY Mural" (http://www1.ccny.cuny.edu/advancement/pr/New-Book-on-Edwin-Blashfield-Features-CCNY-Mural.cfm), Press Release, City College of New York, Thursday, Sep 17, 2009
[54] "Old Photograph of Townsend Harris Hall" (http://web.archive.org/web/20080414140919/http://www.ccny.cuny.edu/public_safety/harris-hall.jpg) (archived 2008)
[55] "Modern View of Wingate Hall entrance" (http://www.liberty-stone.com/Images/wingate.jpg)
[56] "Modern Photograph of Wingate Hall" (http://www.ccny.cuny.edu/aboutus/campus/campuspictssmall/wingatehall.jpg) - CCNY website

[57] "Old postcard of Wingate Hall/Harris Hall" (http://web.archive.org/web/20080414140919/http://www.ccny.cuny.edu/public_safety/shep-wingate.jpg)
[58] "Old Postcard: College of the City of New York: Chemical Building (Baskerville Hall)" (http://web.archive.org/web/20080414140919/http://www.ccny.cuny.edu/public_safety/BASKERVILLE.GIF) (archived 2008)
[59] "Old Postcard: College of the City of New York: Mechanical Arts Building (Compton Goethals Hall)" (http://www.ccny.cuny.edu/library/exhibitions/images/full/CCNYpostcard15.jpg) (archived 2008)
[60] "Compton Goethals Hall Remodeling Project" (http://www.lhparch.com/project.aspx?cat=5&id=19), Lee Harris Pomeroy Architects website
[61] Kadinsky, Sergey (November 23, 2005). "The Hidden Architecture of CCNY" (http://www.ccnycampus.com/home/index.cfm?event=displayArticle&ustory_id=9b9979b7-7a1b-4fdd-9723-b4ee1361718b). *CCNY Campus Newspaper*. . Retrieved November 23, 2005.
[62] "Image of a stone grotesque on a CCNY building from 1906, holding a model of Shepard Hall" (http://www1.cuny.edu/portal_ur/news/cuny_matters/april_06/images/architectural_janus_top.jpg), *CUNY Matters* magazine, Spring 2006
[63] Rosenfeld, Neill S., Architectural JANUS: CUNY Preserves the Past, Builds for the Future" (http://www1.cuny.edu/portal_ur/news/cuny_matters/archives/2006/cm_legislative_lowres.pdf), *CUNY Matters* magazine, Spring 2006, pp.7-11
[64] "Old Postcard: Entrance to Campus Grounds: CCNY 138th Street Gates" (http://web.archive.org/web/20080414140919/http://www.ccny.cuny.edu/public_safety/138-gates-amsterdam-people.jpg)
[65] "Old Postcard: (Lewisohn) Stadium of the City College of New York" (http://www.ccny.cuny.edu/library/exhibitions/images/full/CCNYpostcard12.jpg), CCNY Libraries exhibitions website
[66] "The Lost World of CCNY: Architectural Gems of Our Past: The Bowker/Alumni Library (1929-1957)" (http://origin.admin.ccny.cuny.edu/library/exhibitions/lostworld/bowker.html), CCNY Libraries exhibitions website
[67] "Biography of William H. Hume" (http://www.sah.org/index.php?src=gendocs&ref=BiographiesArchitectsH&category=Resources), Society of Architectural Historians biographies website
[68] "The Lost World of CCNY: Architectural Gems of Our Past: Army Hall (1883-1956)" (http://origin.admin.ccny.cuny.edu/library/exhibitions/lostworld/armyhall.html), CCNY Libraries exhibitions website
[69] Gray, Christopher (August 31, 1997). "An Orphan Asylum and a Fifth Avenue 'Farmhouse'" (http://www.nytimes.com/1997/08/31/realestate/an-orphan-asylum-and-a-fifth-avenue-farmhouse.html). *New York Times*. .
[70] "The Lost World of CCNY: Architectural Gems of Our Past: Paul Klapper Hall (1905-1983)" (http://origin.admin.ccny.cuny.edu/library/exhibitions/lostworld/klapperhall.html), CCNY Libraries exhibitions website
[71] "The Lost World of CCNY: Architectural Gems of Our Past: Architectural model of David B. Steinman Hall by Lorimar and Rose" (http://origin.admin.ccny.cuny.edu/library/exhibitions/lostworld/modelbuild.html), CCNY Libraries exhibitions website, and Archives, City College of New York
[72] "Administration Building CCNY" (http://www.ccny.cuny.edu/aboutus/campus/campuspictssmall/adminwithsondra.jpg)- CCNY website
[73] "The Lost World of CCNY: Architectural Gems of Our Past: The Administration Building which was constructed on the northern portion of Jasper Oval" (http://origin.admin.ccny.cuny.edu/library/exhibitions/lostworld/dsc6.html), CCNY Libraries exhibitions website
[74] "Administration Building Named for Howard E. Wille, '55", 138@Convent, CCNY newsletter, Volume 2, n.1, February 1, 2007, Office of Communications of The City College of New York.
[75] "Old Postcard: CCNY Athletic Field" (http://web.archive.org/web/20080414140919/http://www.ccny.cuny.edu/public_safety/ccny-athletic-old.jpg)
[76] "Old View of CCNY from the Street" (http://origin.admin.ccny.cuny.edu/library/exhibitions/lostworld/images/street.gif)
[77] "Marshak Science Building CCNY" (http://www.ccny.cuny.edu/aboutus/campus/campuspictssmall/sciencebuildingfrombpark2.jpg) - CCNY website
[78] "Sergey Kadinsky: Murals: Dec. 2004: Doors to Knowledge Series: located at The Undergraduate Student Government at CCNY" (http://www.mazeartist.com/usgmurals.htm)
[79] "Aerial view of the South Campus, or Manhattanville Campus, taken prior to 1952" (http://origin.admin.ccny.cuny.edu/library/exhibitions/lostworld/airview.html)
[80] Structural Biology Research Center website (http://www.nysbc.org/)
[81] "The Lost World of CCNY: Architectural Gems of Our Past: Mark Eisner Hall" (http://origin.admin.ccny.cuny.edu/library/exhibitions/lostworld/southcampus1.html), CCNY Libraries Exhibitions website
[82] Mott Hall School website (http://www.motthall.org/)
[83] "The Lost World of CCNY: Architectural Gems of Our Past: John H. Finley Hall" (http://origin.admin.ccny.cuny.edu/library/exhibitions/lostworld/johnhfinley.html), CCNY Libraries Exhibitions website
[84] "The Lost World of CCNY: Architectural Gems of Our Past: Wagner Hall" (http://origin.admin.ccny.cuny.edu/library/exhibitions/lostworld/images/wagnerhall_07.gif), CCNY Libraries Exhibitions website
[85] CCNY Towers website (http://www.ccnytowers.com/)
[86] Fernandez, Manny (August 26, 2006). "Going to College, and Living There, Too" (http://www.nytimes.com/2006/08/26/nyregion/26dorm.html). *New York Times*. .
[87] Photos of the residence hall at the City College of NY (http://www.rkchin.com/ccnytowers/index.html)

[88] "Dormitory Authority of the State of New York: The City College of New York Science Building and The City University of New York Advanced Science Research Center: Phases I and II Project" (http://www.dasny.org/dasny/envaffs/scoping_meetings/FINAL_Legal_Notice.pdf), 2007.

[89] "Draft Environmental Impact Statement for The City College of New York Science Building and The City University of New York Advanced Science Research Center Project, Borough of Manhattan, New York County, New York (December 21, 2007)" (http://www.dasny.org/dasny/envaffs/impact_statements/CCNYSciBldgProj/), The Dormitory Authority of the State of New York, December 21, 2007.

[90] "Fall 2009 CCNY Campus Map with proposed additions" (http://gtn-h.net/IGWCO2010/images/CAMPUS_MAP_L_Fall_09.jpg), Integrated Global Water Cycle Observations (IGWCO) Workshop and Meeting, Feb 23-26, 2010 (http://gtn-h.net/IGWCO2010/index.html) at CCNY.

[91] Townsend Harris Medal Winners (http://www.ccny.cuny.edu/townsend_harris/awards/a_d.htm), CCNY website. Cf. Albert P. D'Andrea entry.

[92] "Albert P. D'Andrea: sculpted relief portrait of Townsend Harris" (http://www.ccny.cuny.edu/library/exhibitions/harris/harris_tablet_pop.html), CCNY Exhibitions website.

[93] CCNY new 2003 logo (http://www1.ccny.cuny.edu/images/CCNY_logo_4.gif)

[94] "The Academic Ranking of World Universities" (http://ed.sjtu.edu.cn/rank/2007/ranking2007.htm) - 2007, published by the Institute of Higher Education, Shanghai Jiao Tong University

[95] "America's Best Colleges" (http://www.forbes.com/lists/2008/94/opinions_college08_CUNY-CCNY_94112.html). Forbes.com. . Retrieved 2009-01-15.

[96] http://colleges.usnews.rankingsandreviews.com/best-colleges/new-york-ny/city-college-2688

[97] "Marty" script (http://www.imsdb.com/scripts/Marty.html) - *Internet Movie Script DataBase*

[98] Hughes, Langston, "Theme for English B" (http://www.eecs.harvard.edu/~keith/poems/English_B.html)

[99] Hughes, Langston; Rampersad, Arnold (ed.), *The Collected Poems of Langston Hughes* (http://books.google.com/books?id=J_nNM6TiNkgC&printsec=frontcover), Vintage; 1st Vintage classics ed edition (October 31, 1995). ISBN 9780679764083. Cf. p.675 (http://books.google.com/books?id=J_nNM6TiNkgC&pg=PA675&lpg=PA675&dq=langston+hughes+poetry+about+ccny&source=bl&ots=&sig=fu5zWBEOuvERd7d6QZrPQ3cbYJE&hl=en&ei=YxGxTbfYMMSftweQ4cCHDA&sa=X&oi=book_result&ct=result&resnum=7&ved=0CEUQ6AEwBg#v=onepage&q=city college of new york&f=false)

[100] Pynchon, Thomas, "V." (http://books.google.com/books?id=jqS2pmUIfOAC&printsec=frontcover&dq=inauthor:"Thomas+Pynchon"&cd=8#v=onepage&q=ccny&f=false). "And the next day she [*Rachel*] would read in the paper where Esther Harvitz, 22, honors graduate of CCNY, has taken a Brody off some bridge, overpass, or high building."

[101] "CUNY Board Appoints Dr. Robert E. Paaswell Interim President of CCNY" (http://www1.cuny.edu/mu/chancellor/2009/09/29/cuny-board-appoints-dr-robert-e-paaswell-interim-president-of-ccny/), *News from the Chancellor*, September 29, 2009

[102] Foderaro, Lisa W., "City College Names a CUNY Alumna President" (http://www.nytimes.com/2010/04/27/nyregion/27cuny.html), *The New York Times*, April 26, 2010

[103] "Temple University Provost Lisa Staiano-Coico Appointed President of The City College of New York" (http://www1.cuny.edu/mu/forum/2010/04/26/temple-university-provost-lisa-staiano-coico-appointed-president-of-the-city-college-of-new-york/), *CUNY Announcement*, April 26, 2010

[104] http://web.archive.org/web/*/http://www.ccny.cuny.edu/plazasite/plazahistory/presidentsccny.htm

References

- Bender, Thomas. *New York Intellect: A History of Intellectual Life in New York City, from 1750 to the Beginnings of Our Own Time*, Knopf, 1987. ISBN 0394550269
- Howe, Irving. *A Margin of Hope: An Intellectual Autobiography*, Harcourt Brace Jovanovich, 1982. ISBN 0-15-157138-4. Cf. Chapter 3, "City College and Beyond", pp. 61–89
- Pearson, Paul David. *The City College of New York: 150 years of academic architecture*, 1997.
- Roff, Sandra S., et al. *From the Free Academy to Cuny: Illustrating Public Higher Education in New York City, 1847-1997* (http://books.google.com/books?id=mzMqUAoAvhYC), 2000.
- Rudy, Willis. *College of the City of New York 1847-1947*, The City College Press, 1949. Reprinted in 1977 by the Arno Press.
- Traub, James. *City on a Hill: Testing the American Dream at City College*, Addison-Wesley: 1994.
- Van Nort, Sydney C. *The City College of New York*, Arcadia Press, February 2007. ISBN 0738549304.

External links

- City College of New York (http://www.ccny.cuny.edu/)
- City College Library Historical CCNY Exhibits (http://www1.ccny.cuny.edu/library/digitalcollections.cfm)
- The Lost World of CCNY exhibit at CCNY Library (http://origin.admin.ccny.cuny.edu/library/exhibitions/lostworld/)
- 100 Years on Hamilton Heights (http://www1.ccny.cuny.edu/ci/centennial/)
- Historic Photographs of City College of New York (http://web.archive.org/web/20080414140919/www.ccny.cuny.edu/public_safety/FUN_STUFF.HTML) (archived 2008)
- The Campus (http://www.ccnycampus.com/) - Student Newspaper
- Arguing the World (http://www.pbs.org/arguing/) - PBS documentary about the "New York Intellectuals," who came of age at City College
- Press release regarding Dr. Andrew Grove's 2005 donation of $26,000,000 to the Engineering School (http://www1.ccny.cuny.edu/advancement/pr/Andrew-Grove-Donation.cfm)
- "Higher education and the poor: The City University of New York" (http://www.economist.com/world/na/displaystory.cfm?story_id=5417329), *The Economist*, January 19, 2006. Economist article on emerging 'elitism' at the City University of New York.
- Some photos of CCNY and Hamilton Heights, the neighborhood in which CCNY is located (http://www.forgotten-ny.com/forgottentour18/tour18.html)
- Special report on preserving CCNY architecture, "Architectural Janus", in the April 2006 issue of CUNY Matters (http://www1.cuny.edu/portal_ur/news/cuny_matters/archives/2006/cm_legislative_lowres.pdf)
- Alumni Association of The City College of New York (http://www.alumniassociationccny.org)
- The City College Fund (http://www.citycollegefund.org)
- CCNY Timeline until 1999 (http://web.archive.org/web/20010306183318/www.citycollegefund.org/ccny/TLSuperSet.html) (archived 2001)

Computer programming

Computer programming (often shortened to **programming** or **coding**) is the process of designing, writing, testing, debugging, and maintaining the source code of computer programs. This source code is written in one or more programming languages. The purpose of programming is to create a program that performs specific operations or exhibits a certain desired behavior. The process of writing source code often requires expertise in many different subjects, including knowledge of the application domain, specialized algorithms and formal logic.

Overview

Within software engineering, programming (the *implementation*) is regarded as one phase in a software development process.

There is an ongoing debate on the extent to which the writing of programs is an art, a craft or an engineering discipline.[1] In general, good programming is considered to be the measured application of all three, with the goal of producing an efficient and evolvable software solution (the criteria for "efficient" and "evolvable" vary considerably). The discipline differs from many other technical professions in that programmers, in general, do not need to be licensed or pass any standardized (or governmentally regulated) certification tests in order to call themselves "programmers" or even "software engineers." Because the discipline covers many areas, which may or may not include critical applications, it is debatable whether licensing is required for the profession as a whole. In most cases, the discipline is self-governed by the entities which require the programming, and sometimes very strict environments are defined (e.g. United States Air Force use of AdaCore and security clearance). However, representing oneself as a "Professional Software Engineer" without a license from an accredited institution is illegal in many parts of the world.

Another ongoing debate is the extent to which the programming language used in writing computer programs affects the form that the final program takes. This debate is analogous to that surrounding the Sapir–Whorf hypothesis[2] in linguistics and cognitive science, which postulates that a particular spoken language's nature influences the habitual thought of its speakers. Different language patterns yield different patterns of thought. This idea challenges the possibility of representing the world perfectly with language, because it acknowledges that the mechanisms of any language condition the thoughts of its speaker community.

History

Wired control panel for an IBM 402 Accounting Machine.

The Antikythera mechanism from ancient Greece was a calculator utilizing gears of various sizes and configuration to determine its operation,[3] which tracked the metonic cycle still used in lunar-to-solar calendars, and which is consistent for calculating the dates of the Olympiads.[4] Al-Jazari built programmable Automata in 1206. One system employed in these devices was the use of pegs and cams placed into a wooden drum at specific locations. which would sequentially trigger levers that in turn operated percussion instruments. The output of this device was a small drummer playing various rhythms and drum patterns.[5] [6] The Jacquard Loom, which Joseph Marie Jacquard developed in 1801, uses a series of pasteboard cards with holes punched in them. The hole pattern represented the pattern that the loom had to follow in weaving cloth. The loom could produce entirely different weaves using different sets of cards. Charles Babbage adopted the use of punched cards around 1830 to control his Analytical Engine. The synthesis of numerical calculation, predetermined operation and output, along with a way to organize and input instructions in a manner relatively easy for humans to conceive and produce, led to the modern development of computer programming. Development of computer programming accelerated through the Industrial Revolution.

In the late 1880s, Herman Hollerith invented the recording of data on a medium that could then be read by a machine. Prior uses of machine readable media, above, had been for control, not data. "After some initial trials with paper tape, he settled on punched cards..."[7] To process these punched cards, first known as "Hollerith cards" he invented the tabulator, and the keypunch machines. These three inventions were the foundation of the modern information processing industry. In 1896 he founded the *Tabulating Machine Company* (which later became the core of IBM). The addition of a control panel (plugboard) to his 1906 Type I Tabulator allowed it to do different jobs without having to be physically rebuilt. By the late 1940s, there were a variety of control panel programmable machines, called unit record equipment, to perform data-processing tasks.

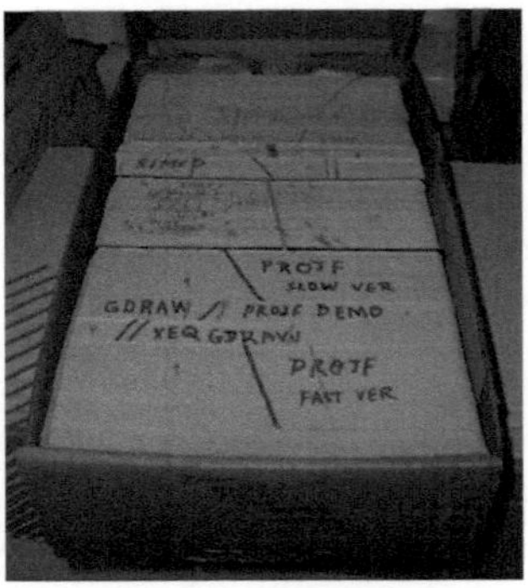

Data and instructions could be stored on external punched cards, which were kept in order and arranged in program decks.

The invention of the von Neumann architecture allowed computer programs to be stored in computer memory. Early programs had to be painstakingly crafted using the instructions (elementary operations) of the particular machine, often in binary notation. Every model of computer would likely use different instructions (machine language) to do the same task. Later, assembly languages were developed that let the programmer specify each instruction in a text format, entering abbreviations for each operation code instead of a number and specifying addresses in symbolic form (e.g., ADD X, TOTAL). Entering a program in assembly language is usually more convenient, faster, and less prone to human error than using machine language, but because an assembly language is little more than a different notation for a machine language, any two machines with different instruction sets also have different assembly languages.

In 1954, FORTRAN was invented; it was the first high level programming language to have a functional implementation, as opposed to just a design on paper.[8] [9] (A high-level language is, in very general terms, any programming language that allows the programmer to write programs in terms that are more abstract than assembly language instructions, i.e. at a level of abstraction "higher" than that of an assembly language.) It allowed programmers to specify calculations by entering a formula directly (e.g. Y = X*2 + 5*X + 9). The program text, or *source*, is converted into machine instructions using a special program called a compiler, which translates the FORTRAN program into machine language. In fact, the name FORTRAN stands for "Formula Translation". Many other languages were developed, including some for commercial programming, such as COBOL. Programs were mostly still entered using punched cards or paper tape. (See computer programming in the punch card era). By the late 1960s, data storage devices and computer terminals became inexpensive enough that programs could be created by typing directly into the computers. Text editors were developed that allowed changes and corrections to be made much more easily than with punched cards. (Usually, an error in punching a card meant that the card had to be discarded and a new one punched to replace it.)

As time has progressed, computers have made giant leaps in the area of processing power. This has brought about newer programming languages that are more abstracted from the underlying hardware. Although these high-level languages usually incur greater overhead, the increase in speed of modern computers has made the use of these languages much more practical than in the past. These increasingly abstracted languages typically are easier to learn and allow the programmer to develop applications much more efficiently and with less source code. However, high-level languages are still impractical for a few programs, such as those where low-level hardware control is necessary or where maximum processing speed is vital.

Throughout the second half of the twentieth century, programming was an attractive career in most developed countries. Some forms of programming have been increasingly subject to offshore outsourcing (importing software and services from other countries, usually at a lower wage), making programming career decisions in developed countries more complicated, while increasing economic opportunities in less developed areas. It is unclear how far this trend will continue and how deeply it will impact programmer wages and opportunities.

Modern programming

Quality requirements

Whatever the approach to software development may be, the final program must satisfy some fundamental properties. The following properties are among the most relevant:

- **Reliability**: how often the results of a program are correct. This depends on conceptual correctness of algorithms, and minimization of programming mistakes, such as mistakes in resource management (e.g., buffer overflows and race conditions) and logic errors (such as division by zero or off-by-one errors).
- **Robustness**: how well a program anticipates problems not due to programmer error. This includes situations such as incorrect, inappropriate or corrupt data, unavailability of needed resources such as memory, operating system services and network connections, and user error.
- **Usability**: the ergonomics of a program: the ease with which a person can use the program for its intended purpose, or in some cases even unanticipated purposes. Such issues can make or break its success even regardless of other issues. This involves a wide range of textual, graphical and sometimes hardware elements that improve the clarity, intuitiveness, cohesiveness and completeness of a program's user interface.
- **Portability**: the range of computer hardware and operating system platforms on which the source code of a program can be compiled/interpreted and run. This depends on differences in the programming facilities provided by the different platforms, including hardware and operating system resources, expected behaviour of the hardware and operating system, and availability of platform specific compilers (and sometimes libraries) for the language of the source code.
- **Maintainability**: the ease with which a program can be modified by its present or future developers in order to make improvements or customizations, fix bugs and security holes, or adapt it to new environments. Good practices during initial development make the difference in this regard. This quality may not be directly apparent to the end user but it can significantly affect the fate of a program over the long term.
- **Efficiency/performance**: the amount of system resources a program consumes (processor time, memory space, slow devices such as disks, network bandwidth and to some extent even user interaction): the less, the better. This also includes correct disposal of some resources, such as cleaning up temporary files and lack of memory leaks.

Readability of source code

In computer programming, readability refers to the ease with which a human reader can comprehend the purpose, control flow, and operation of source code. It affects the aspects of quality above, including portability, usability and most importantly maintainability.

Readability is important because programmers spend the majority of their time reading, trying to understand and modifying existing source code, rather than writing new source code. Unreadable code often leads to bugs, inefficiencies, and duplicated code. A study[10] found that a few simple readability transformations made code shorter and drastically reduced the time to understand it.

Following a consistent programming style often helps readability. However, readability is more than just programming style. Many factors, having little or nothing to do with the ability of the computer to efficiently compile and execute the code, contribute to readability.[11] Some of these factors include:

- Different indentation styles (whitespace)
- Comments
- Decomposition
- Naming conventions for objects (such as variables, classes, procedures, etc.)

Algorithmic complexity

The academic field and the engineering practice of computer programming are both largely concerned with discovering and implementing the most efficient algorithms for a given class of problem. For this purpose, algorithms are classified into *orders* using so-called Big O notation, $O(n)$, which expresses resource use, such as execution time or memory consumption, in terms of the size of an input. Expert programmers are familiar with a variety of well-established algorithms and their respective complexities and use this knowledge to choose algorithms that are best suited to the circumstances.

Methodologies

The first step in most formal software development processes is requirements analysis, followed by testing to determine value modeling, implementation, and failure elimination (debugging). There exist a lot of differing approaches for each of those tasks. One approach popular for requirements analysis is Use Case analysis. Nowadays many programmers use forms of Agile software development where the various stages of formal software development are more integrated together into short cycles that take a few weeks rather than years. There are many approaches to the Software development process.

Popular modeling techniques include Object-Oriented Analysis and Design (OOAD) and Model-Driven Architecture (MDA). The Unified Modeling Language (UML) is a notation used for both the OOAD and MDA.

A similar technique used for database design is Entity-Relationship Modeling (ER Modeling).

Implementation techniques include imperative languages (object-oriented or procedural), functional languages, and logic languages.

Measuring language usage

It is very difficult to determine what are the most popular of modern programming languages. Some languages are very popular for particular kinds of applications (e.g., COBOL is still strong in the corporate data center, often on large mainframes, FORTRAN in engineering applications, scripting languages in web development, and C in embedded applications), while some languages are regularly used to write many different kinds of applications. Also many applications use a mix of several languages in their construction and use.

Methods of measuring programming language popularity include: counting the number of job advertisements that mention the language,[12] the number of books teaching the language that are sold (this overestimates the importance of newer languages), and estimates of the number of existing lines of code written in the language (this underestimates the number of users of business languages such as COBOL).

Debugging

Debugging is a very important task in the software development process, because an incorrect program can have significant consequences for its users. Some languages are more prone to some kinds of faults because their specification does not require compilers to perform as much checking as other languages. Use of a static code analysis tool can help detect some possible problems.

Debugging is often done with IDEs like Eclipse, Kdevelop, NetBeans, Code::Blocks, and Visual Studio. Standalone debuggers like gdb are also used, and these often provide less of a visual environment, usually using a command line.

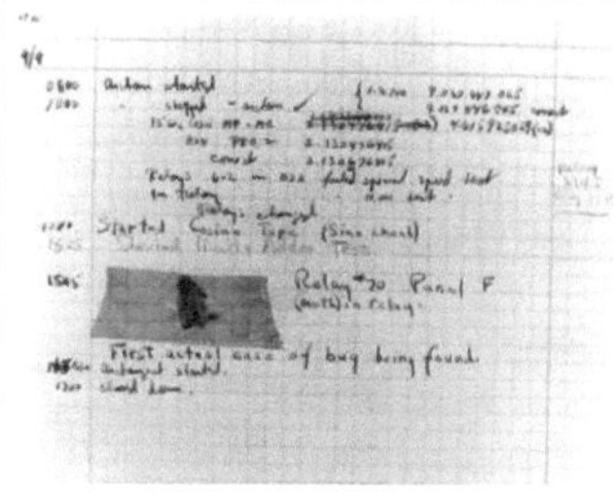

A bug, which was debugged in 1947

Programming languages

Different programming languages support different styles of programming (called *programming paradigms*). The choice of language used is subject to many considerations, such as company policy, suitability to task, availability of third-party packages, or individual preference. Ideally, the programming language best suited for the task at hand will be selected. Trade-offs from this ideal involve finding enough programmers who know the language to build a team, the availability of compilers for that language, and the efficiency with which programs written in a given language execute. Languages form an approximate spectrum from "low-level" to "high-level"; "low-level" languages are typically more machine-oriented and faster to execute, whereas "high-level" languages are more abstract and easier to use but execute less quickly. It is usually easier to code in "high-level" languages than in "low-level" ones.

Allen Downey, in his book *How To Think Like A Computer Scientist*, writes:

> The details look different in different languages, but a few basic instructions appear in just about every language:

- **input**: Get data from the keyboard, a file, or some other device.
- **output**: Display data on the screen or send data to a file or other device.
- **arithmetic**: Perform basic arithmetical operations like addition and multiplication.
- **conditional execution**: Check for certain conditions and execute the appropriate sequence of statements.
- **repetition**: Perform some action repeatedly, usually with some variation.

Many computer languages provide a mechanism to call functions provided by libraries such as in a .so. Provided the functions in a library follow the appropriate run time conventions (e.g., method of passing arguments), then these functions may be written in any other language.

Programmers

Computer programmers are those who write computer software. Their jobs usually involve:

- Coding
- Compilation
- Debugging
- Documentation
- Integration
- Maintenance
- Requirements analysis
- Software architecture

- Software testing
- Specification

See also

- ACCU
- Association for Computing Machinery
- Computer networking
- Computer programming in the punch card era
- Computer science
- Computing
- Hello world program
- Programming paradigms
- Software engineering
- *The Art of Computer Programming*

References

[1] Paul Graham (2003). *Hackers and Painters* (http://www.paulgraham.com/hp.html). . Retrieved 2006-08-22.

[2] Kenneth E. Iverson, the originator of the APL programming language, believed that the Sapir–Whorf hypothesis applied to computer languages (without actually mentioning the hypothesis by name). His Turing award lecture, "Notation as a tool of thought", was devoted to this theme, arguing that more powerful notations aided thinking about computer algorithms. Iverson K.E.," Notation as a tool of thought (http://elliscave.com/APL_J/tool.pdf)", *Communications of the ACM*, 23: 444-465 (August 1980).

[3] " Ancient Greek Computer's Inner Workings Deciphered (http://news.nationalgeographic.com/news/2006/11/061129-ancient-greece.html)". National Geographic News. November 29, 2006.

[4] Freeth, Tony; Jones, Alexander; Steele, John M.; Bitsakis, Yanis (July 31, 2008). "Calendars with Olympiad display and eclipse prediction on the Antikythera Mechanism" (http://www.nature.com/nature/journal/v454/n7204/full/nature07130.html). *Nature* **454** (7204): 614–617. doi:10.1038/nature07130. PMID 18668103. .

[5] A 13th Century Programmable Robot (http://www.shef.ac.uk/marcoms/eview/articles58/robot.html), University of Sheffield

[6] Fowler, Charles B. (October 1967). "The Museum of Music: A History of Mechanical Instruments". *Music Educators Journal* (Music Educators Journal, Vol. 54, No. 2) **54** (2): 45–49. doi:10.2307/3391092. JSTOR 3391092

[7] "Columbia University Computing History - Herman Hollerith" (http://www.columbia.edu/acis/history/hollerith.html). Columbia.edu. . Retrieved 2010-04-25.

[8] 12:10 p.m. ET (2007-03-20). "Fortran creator John Backus dies - Tech and gadgets- msnbc.com" (http://www.msnbc.msn.com/id/17704662/). MSNBC. . Retrieved 2010-04-25.

[9] "CSC-302 99S : Class 02: A Brief History of Programming Languages" (http://www.math.grin.edu/~rebelsky/Courses/CS302/99S/Outlines/outline.02.html). Math.grin.edu. . Retrieved 2010-04-25.

[10] James L. Elshoff , Michael Marcotty, Improving computer program readability to aid modification (http://doi.acm.org/10.1145/358589.358596), Communications of the ACM, v.25 n.8, p.512-521, Aug 1982.

[11] Multiple (wiki). "Readability" (http://docforge.com/wiki/Readability). *Docforge*. . Retrieved 2010-01-30.

[12] Survey of Job advertisements mentioning a given language (http://www.computerweekly.com/Articles/2007/09/11/226631/sslcomputer-weekly-it-salary-survey-finance-boom-drives-it-job.htm)>

Further reading

- Weinberg, Gerald M., *The Psychology of Computer Programming*, New York: Van Nostrand Reinhold, 1971

External links

- Programming Wikia (http://programming.wikia.com/wiki/Main_Page)
- How to Think Like a Computer Scientist (http://openbookproject.net/thinkCSpy) - by Jeffrey Elkner, Allen B. Downey and Chris Meyers

Fortran

The Fortran Automatic Coding System for the IBM 704 (October 15, 1956), the first Programmer's Reference Manual for Fortran

Paradigm(s)	multi-paradigm: structured, imperative (procedural, object-oriented), generic
Appeared in	1957
Designed by	John Backus
Developer	John Backus & IBM
Stable release	Fortran 2008 (ISO/IEC 1539-1:2010) (2010)
Typing discipline	strong, static, manifest
Major implementations	Absoft, Cray, GFortran, G95, IBM, Intel, Lahey/Fujitsu, Open Watcom, Pathscale, PGI, Silverfrost, Oracle, XL Fortran, Visual Fortran, others
Influenced by	Speedcoding
Influenced	ALGOL 58, BASIC, C, PL/I, PACT I, MUMPS, Ratfor
Usual filename extensions	.f, .for, .f90, .f95

Fortran (previously **FORTRAN**) is a general-purpose, procedural, imperative programming language that is especially suited to numeric computation and scientific computing. Originally developed by IBM at their campus in south San Jose, California[1] in the 1950s for scientific and engineering applications, Fortran came to dominate this area of programming early on and has been in continual use for over half a century in computationally intensive areas such as numerical weather prediction, finite element analysis, computational fluid dynamics, computational physics and computational chemistry. It is one of the most popular languages in the area of high-performance computing [2] and is the language used for programs that benchmark and rank the world's fastest supercomputers.

Fortran (a blend derived from *The IBM Mathematical **Formula Translating** System*) encompasses a lineage of versions, each of which evolved to add extensions to the language while usually retaining compatibility with previous versions. Successive versions have added support for processing of character-based data (FORTRAN 77), array programming, modular programming and object-oriented programming (Fortran 90 / 95), and object-oriented and generic programming (Fortran 2003).

The names of earlier versions of the language through FORTRAN 77 were conventionally spelled in all-caps (FORTRAN 77 was the version in which the use of lowercase letters in keywords was strictly nonstandard). The capitalization has been dropped in referring to newer versions beginning with Fortran 90. The official language standards now refer to the language as "Fortran". Because the capitalization was never completely consistent in actual usage, this article adopts the convention of using the all-caps *FORTRAN* in referring to versions of FORTRAN through FORTRAN 77 and the title-caps *Fortran* in referring to versions of Fortran from Fortran 90 onward. This convention is reflected in the capitalization of *FORTRAN* in the ANSI X3.9-1966 (FORTRAN 66) and ANSI X3.9-1978 (FORTRAN 77) standards and the title caps *Fortran* in the ANSI X3.198-1992 (Fortran 90),

ISO/IEC 1539-1:1997 (Fortran 95) and ISO/IEC 1539-1:2004 (Fortran 2003) standards.

History

An IBM 704 mainframe

In late 1953, John W. Backus submitted a proposal to his superiors at IBM to develop a more practical alternative to assembly language for programming their IBM 704 mainframe computer. Backus' historic FORTRAN team consisted of programmers Richard Goldberg, Sheldon F. Best, Harlan Herrick, Peter Sheridan, Roy Nutt, Robert Nelson, Irving Ziller, Lois Haibt, and David Sayre.[3]

A draft specification for *The IBM Mathematical Formula Translating System* was completed by mid-1954. The first manual for FORTRAN appeared in October 1956, with the first FORTRAN compiler delivered in April 1957. This was the first optimizing compiler, because customers were reluctant to use a high-level programming language unless its compiler could generate code whose performance was comparable to that of hand-coded assembly language.[4]

While the community was skeptical that this new method could possibly outperform hand-coding, it reduced the number of programming statements necessary to operate a machine by a factor of 20, and quickly gained acceptance. John Backus said during a 1979 interview with *Think*, the IBM employee magazine, "Much of my work has come from being lazy. I didn't like writing programs, and so, when I was working on the IBM 701, writing programs for computing missile trajectories, I started work on a programming system to make it easier to write programs."[5]

The language was widely adopted by scientists for writing numerically intensive programs, which encouraged compiler writers to produce compilers that could generate faster and more efficient code. The inclusion of a complex number data type in the language made Fortran especially suited to technical applications such as electrical engineering.

By 1960, versions of FORTRAN were available for the IBM 709, 650, 1620, and 7090 computers. Significantly, the increasing popularity of FORTRAN spurred competing computer manufacturers to provide FORTRAN compilers for their machines, so that by 1963 over 40 FORTRAN compilers existed. For these reasons, FORTRAN is considered to be the first widely used programming language supported across a variety of computer architectures.

The development of FORTRAN paralleled the early evolution of compiler technology, and many advances in the theory and design of compilers were specifically motivated by the need to generate efficient code for FORTRAN programs.

FORTRAN

The initial release of FORTRAN for the IBM 704 contained 32 statements, including:

- DIMENSION and EQUIVALENCE statements
- Assignment statements
- Three-way *arithmetic* IF statement.
- IF statements for checking exceptions (ACCUMULATOR OVERFLOW, QUOTIENT OVERFLOW, and DIVIDE CHECK); and IF statements for manipulating sense switches and sense lights
- GOTO, computed GOTO, ASSIGN, and assigned GOTO
- DO loops
- Formatted I/O: FORMAT, READ, READ INPUT TAPE, WRITE, WRITE OUTPUT TAPE, PRINT, and PUNCH
- Unformatted I/O: READ TAPE, READ DRUM, WRITE TAPE, and WRITE DRUM
- Other I/O: END FILE, REWIND, and BACKSPACE
- PAUSE, STOP, and CONTINUE
- FREQUENCY statement (for providing optimization hints to the compiler).

The arithmetic IF statement was similar to a three-way branch instruction on the IBM 704. However, the 704 branch instructions all contained only one destination address (e.g., TZE — Transfer AC Zero, TNZ — Transfer AC Not Zero, TPL — Transfer AC Plus, TMI — Transfer AC Minus). The machine (and its successors in the 700/7000 series) did have a three-way *skip* instruction (CAS — Compare AC with Storage), but using this instruction to implement the IF would consume 4 instruction words, require the constant Zero in a word of storage, and take 3 machine cycles to execute; using the Transfer instructions to implement the IF could be done in 1 to 3 instruction words, required no constants in storage, and take 1 to 3 machine cycles to execute. An optimizing compiler like FORTRAN would most likely select the more compact and usually faster Transfers instead of the Compare (use of Transfers also allowed the FREQUENCY statement to optimize IFs, which could not be done using the Compare). Also the Compare considered –0 and +0 to be different values while the Transfer Zero and Transfer Not Zero considered them to be the same.

The FREQUENCY statement in FORTRAN was used originally and optionally to give branch probabilities for the three branch cases of the Arithmetic IF statement to bias the way code was generated and order of the basic blocks of code generated, in the global optimisation sense, were arranged in memory for optimality. The first FORTRAN compiler used this weighting to do a Monte Carlo simulation of the run-time generated code at compile time. It was very sophisticated for its time. This technique is documented in the original article in 1957 on the first FORTRAN compiler implementation by J. Backus et al. Many years later, the FREQUENCY statement had no effect on the code, and was treated as a comment statement, since the compilers no longer did this kind of compile-time simulation.

Below is a part of the 1957 paper, "The FORTRAN Automatic Coding System" by Backus et al., with this snippet on the FREQUENCY statement and its use in a compile-time Monte Carlo simulation of the run-time to optimise the code generated. Quoting ..

> The fundamental unit of program is the basic block; a basic block is a stretch of program which has a single entry point and a single exit point. The purpose of section 4 is to prepare for section 5 a table of predecessors (PRED table) which enumerates the basic blocks and lists for every basic block each of the basic blocks which can be its immediate predecessor in flow, together with the absolute frequency of each such basic block link. This table is obtained by an actual "execution" of the program in Monte-Carlo fashion, in which the outcome of conditional transfers arising out of IF-type statements and computed GO TO'S is determined by a random number generator suitably weighted according to whatever FREQUENCY statements have been provided.

Fixed layout

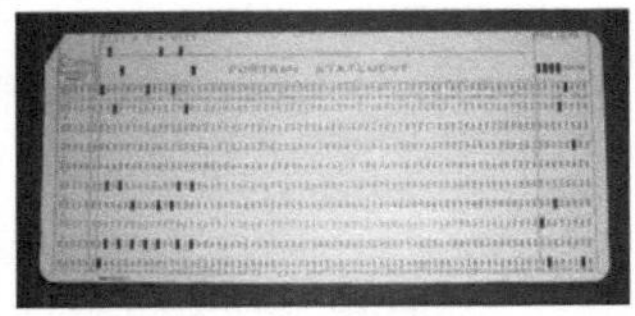

FORTRAN code on a punched card, showing the specialized uses of columns 1-5, 6 and 73-80.

Before the development of disk files, text editors and terminals, programs were most often entered on a keypunch keyboard onto 80 column punched cards, one line to a card. The resulting deck of cards would be fed into a card reader to be compiled. *See Computer programming in the punched card era.*

Originally Fortran programs were written in a fixed column format. Columns 1 to 5 were the label field: a sequence of digits here was taken as a label for the purpose of a GOTO or a FORMAT reference in a WRITE or READ statement. A letter "C" in column 1 caused the entire card to be treated as a comment and ignored by the compiler. Column 6 was a continuation field: a non-blank character here caused the card to be taken as a continuation of the statement on the previous card. Columns 7 to 72 served as the statement field. Columns 73 to 80 were ignored, so they could be used for identification information. One such use was punching a sequence number which could be used to re-order cards if a stack of cards was dropped, though in practice this was reserved for stable, production programs. An IBM 519 could be used to copy a program deck and add sequence numbers. Some early compilers, e.g. the IBM 650's, had additional restrictions.[6] Later compilers relaxed most fixed format restrictions.

Within the statement field, whitespace characters were generally ignored, allowing the programmer to omit space between tokens for brevity, or include spaces within identifiers for clarity (for example, AVG OF X was a valid identifier, and equivalent to AVGOFX).

Recursion

Early FORTRAN compilers did not support recursion in subroutines. Early computer architectures did not support the concept of a stack, and when they did directly support subroutine calls, the return location was often stored in a single fixed location adjacent to the subroutine code, which does not permit a subroutine to be called again before a previous call of the subroutine has returned. Although not specified in Fortran 77, many F77 compilers supported recursion as an option, while it became a standard in Fortran 90.[7]

FORTRAN II

IBM's *FORTRAN II* appeared in 1958. The main enhancement was to support procedural programming by allowing user-written subroutines and functions which returned values, with parameters passed by reference. The COMMON statement provided a way for subroutines to access common (or global) variables. Six new statements were introduced:

- SUBROUTINE, FUNCTION, and END
- CALL and RETURN
- COMMON

Over the next few years, FORTRAN II would also add support for the DOUBLE PRECISION and COMPLEX data types.

Simple FORTRAN II program

This program, for Heron's formula, reads one data card containing three 5-digit integers A, B, and C as input. If A, B, and C cannot represent the sides of a triangle in plane geometry, then the program's execution will end with an error code of "STOP 1". Otherwise, an output line will be printed showing the input values for A, B, and C, followed by the computed AREA of the triangle as a floating-point number with 2 digits after the decimal point.

```
C AREA OF A TRIANGLE WITH A STANDARD SQUARE ROOT FUNCTION
C INPUT - CARD READER UNIT 5, INTEGER INPUT
C OUTPUT - LINE PRINTER UNIT 6, REAL OUTPUT
C INPUT ERROR DISPLAY ERROR OUTPUT CODE 1 IN JOB CONTROL LISTING
      READ INPUT TAPE 5, 501, IA, IB, IC
  501 FORMAT (3I5)
C IA, IB, AND IC MAY NOT BE NEGATIVE
C FURTHERMORE, THE SUM OF TWO SIDES OF A TRIANGLE
C IS GREATER THAN THE THIRD SIDE, SO WE CHECK FOR THAT, TOO
      IF (IA) 777, 777, 701
  701 IF (IB) 777, 777, 702
  702 IF (IC) 777, 777, 703
  703 IF (IA+IB-IC) 777,777,704
  704 IF (IA+IC-IB) 777,777,705
  705 IF (IB+IC-IA) 777,777,799
  777 STOP 1
C USING HERON'S FORMULA WE CALCULATE THE
C AREA OF THE TRIANGLE
  799 S = FLOATF (IA + IB + IC) / 2.0
      AREA = SQRT( S * (S - FLOATF(IA)) * (S - FLOATF(IB)) *
     +     (S - FLOATF(IC)))
      WRITE OUTPUT TAPE 6, 601, IA, IB, IC, AREA
  601 FORMAT (4H A= ,I5,5H  B= ,I5,5H  C= ,I5,8H  AREA= ,F10.2,
     +        13H SQUARE UNITS)
      STOP
      END
```

FORTRAN III

IBM also developed a *FORTRAN III* in 1958 that allowed for inline assembler code among other features; however, this version was never released as a product. Like the 704 FORTRAN and FORTRAN II, FORTRAN III included machine-dependent features that made code written in it unportable from machine to machine. Early versions of FORTRAN provided by other vendors suffered from the same disadvantage.

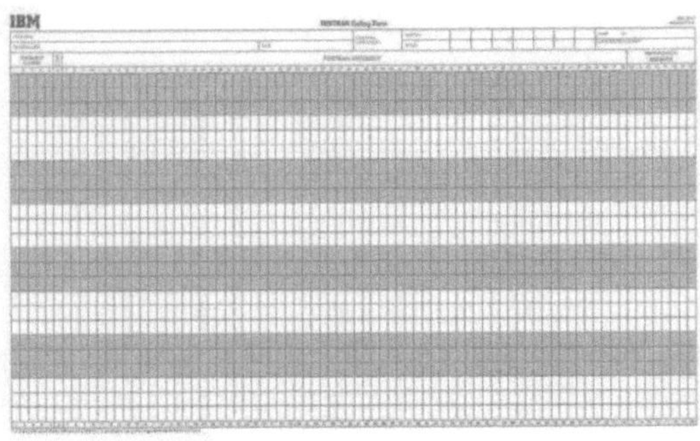

A FORTRAN coding form, printed on paper and intended to be used by programmers to prepare programs for punching onto cards by keypunch operators. Now obsolete.

IBM 1401 FORTRAN

FORTRAN was provided for the IBM 1401 by an innovative 63-pass compiler that ran in only 8k of core. It kept the program in memory and loaded overlays that gradually transformed it, in place, into executable form, as described by Haines et al.[8] The executable form was not machine language; rather it was interpreted, anticipating UCSD Pascal P-code by two decades.

FORTRAN IV

Starting in 1961, as a result of customer demands, IBM began development of a *FORTRAN IV* that removed the machine-dependent features of FORTRAN II (such as READ INPUT TAPE), while adding new features such as a LOGICAL data type, logical Boolean expressions and the *logical IF statement* as an alternative to the *arithmetic IF statement*. FORTRAN IV was eventually released in 1962, first for the IBM 7030 ("Stretch") computer, followed by versions for the IBM 7090 and IBM 7094.

By 1965, Fortran IV was supposed to be the "standard" and in compliance with American Standards Association X3.4.3 FORTRAN Working Group.[9]

FORTRAN 66

Perhaps the most significant development in the early history of FORTRAN was the decision by the *American Standards Association* (now ANSI) to form a committee to develop an "American Standard Fortran." The resulting two standards, approved in March 1966, defined two languages, *FORTRAN* (based on FORTRAN IV, which had served as a *de facto* standard), and *Basic FORTRAN* (based on FORTRAN II, but stripped of its machine-dependent features). The FORTRAN defined by the first standard became known as *FORTRAN 66* (although many continued to refer to it as FORTRAN IV, the language upon which the standard was largely based). FORTRAN 66 effectively became the first "industry-standard" version of FORTRAN. FORTRAN 66 included:

- Main program, SUBROUTINE, FUNCTION, and BLOCK DATA program units
- INTEGER, REAL, DOUBLE PRECISION, COMPLEX, and LOGICAL data types
- COMMON, DIMENSION, and EQUIVALENCE statements
- DATA statement for specifying initial values
- Intrinsic and EXTERNAL (*e.g.*, library) functions
- Assignment statement
- GOTO, assigned GOTO, and computed GOTO statements
- Logical IF and arithmetic (three-way) IF statements

- DO loops
- READ, WRITE, BACKSPACE, REWIND, and ENDFILE statements for sequential I/O
- FORMAT statement
- CALL, RETURN, PAUSE, and STOP statements
- Hollerith constants in DATA and FORMAT statements, and as actual arguments to procedures
- Identifiers of up to six characters in length
- Comment lines

FORTRAN 77

After the release of the FORTRAN 66 standard, compiler vendors introduced a number of extensions to "Standard Fortran", prompting ANSI in 1969 to begin work on revising the 1966 standard. Final drafts of this revised standard circulated in 1977, leading to formal approval of the new FORTRAN standard in April 1978. The new standard, known as *FORTRAN 77*, added a number of significant features to address many of the shortcomings of FORTRAN 66:

- Block IF and END IF statements, with optional ELSE and ELSE IF clauses, to provide improved language support for structured programming
- DO loop extensions, including parameter expressions, negative increments, and zero trip counts
- OPEN, CLOSE, and INQUIRE statements for improved I/O capability
- Direct-access file I/O
- IMPLICIT statement
- CHARACTER data type, with vastly expanded facilities for character input and output and processing of character-based data
- PARAMETER statement for specifying constants
- SAVE statement for persistent local variables
- Generic names for intrinsic functions
- A set of intrinsics (LGE, LGT, LLE, LLT) for lexical comparison of strings, based upon the ASCII collating sequence. (These ASCII functions were demanded by the U.S. Department of Defense, in their conditional approval vote.)

In this revision of the standard, a number of features were removed or altered in a manner that might invalidate previously standard-conforming programs. *(Removal was the only allowable alternative to X3J3 at that time, since the concept of "deprecation" was not yet available for ANSI standards.)* While most of the 24 items in the conflict list (see Appendix A2 of X3.9-1978) addressed loopholes or pathological cases permitted by the previous standard but rarely used, a small number of specific capabilities were deliberately removed, such as:

- Hollerith constants and Hollerith data, such as:

```
GREET = 12HHELLO THERE!
```

- Reading into a H edit (Hollerith field) descriptor in a FORMAT specification.
- Overindexing of array bounds by subscripts.

```
DIMENSION A(10,5)
Y= A(11,1)
```

- Transfer of control into the range of a DO loop (also known as "Extended Range").

Variants: Minnesota FORTRAN

Control Data Corporation computers had another version of FORTRAN 77, called Minnesota FORTRAN (MNF), designed especially for student use, with variations in output constructs, special uses of COMMONs and DATA statements, optimizations code levels for compiling, and detailed error listings, extensive warning messages, and debugs.[10]

Transition to ANSI Standard Fortran

The development of a revised standard to succeed FORTRAN 77 would be repeatedly delayed as the standardization process struggled to keep up with rapid changes in computing and programming practice. In the meantime, as the "Standard FORTRAN" for nearly fifteen years, FORTRAN 77 would become the historically most important dialect.

An important practical extension to FORTRAN 77 was the release of MIL-STD-1753 in 1978.[11] This specification, developed by the U.S. Department of Defense, standardized a number of features implemented by most FORTRAN 77 compilers but not included in the ANSI FORTRAN 77 standard. These features would eventually be incorporated into the Fortran 90 standard.

- DO WHILE and END DO statements
- INCLUDE statement
- IMPLICIT NONE variant of the IMPLICIT statement
- Bit manipulation intrinsic functions, based on similar functions included in Industrial Real-Time Fortran (ANSI/ISA S61.1 (1976))

The IEEE 1003.9 POSIX Standard, released in 1991, provided a simple means for FORTRAN 77 programmers to issue POSIX system calls.[12] Over 100 calls were defined in the document — allowing access to POSIX-compatible process control, signal handling, file system control, device control, procedure pointing, and stream I/O in a portable manner.

Fortran 90

The much delayed successor to FORTRAN 77, informally known as *Fortran 90* (and prior to that, *Fortran 8X*), was finally released as an ISO standard in 1991 and an ANSI Standard in 1992. This major revision added many new features to reflect the significant changes in programming practice that had evolved since the 1978 standard:

- Free-form source input, also with lowercase Fortran keywords
- Identifiers up to 31 characters in length
- Inline comments
- Ability to operate on arrays (or array sections) as a whole, thus greatly simplifying math and engineering computations.
  - whole, partial and masked array assignment statements and array expressions, such as X(1:N)=R(1:N)*COS(A(1:N))
  - WHERE statement for selective array assignment
  - array-valued constants and expressions,
  - user-defined array-valued functions and array constructors.
- RECURSIVE procedures
- Modules, to group related procedures and data together, and make them available to other program units, including the capability to limit the accessibility to only specific parts of the module.
- A vastly improved argument-passing mechanism, allowing interfaces to be checked at compile time
- User-written interfaces for generic procedures
- Operator overloading
- Derived/abstract data types
- New data type declaration syntax, to specify the data type and other attributes of variables

- Dynamic memory allocation by means of the ALLOCATABLE attribute and the ALLOCATE and DEALLOCATE statements
- POINTER attribute, pointer assignment, and NULLIFY statement to facilitate the creation and manipulation of dynamic data structures
- Structured looping constructs, with an END DO statement for loop termination, and EXIT and CYCLE statements for "breaking out" of normal DO loop iterations in an orderly way
- SELECT . . . CASE construct for multi-way selection
- Portable specification of numerical precision under the user's control
- New and enhanced intrinsic procedures.

Obsolescence and deletions

Unlike the previous revision, Fortran 90 did not delete any features. *(Appendix B.1 says, "The list of deleted features in this standard is empty.")* Any standard-conforming FORTRAN 77 program is also standard-conforming under Fortran 90, and either standard should be usable to define its behavior.

A small set of features were identified as "obsolescent" and expected to be removed in a future standard.

Obsolescent feature	Example	Status / Fate in Fortran 95
Arithmetic IF-statement	IF (X) 10, 20, 30	
Non-integer DO parameters or control variables	DO 9 X= 1.7, 1.6, -0.1	Deleted
Shared DO-loop termination or termination with a statement other than END DO or CONTINUE	DO 9 J= 1, 10 DO 9 K= 1, 10 9 L= J + K	
Branching to END IF from outside a block	66 GO TO 77 ; . . . IF (E) THEN ; . . . 77 END IF	Deleted
Alternate return	CALL SUBR(X, Y *100, *200)	
PAUSE statement	PAUSE 600	Deleted
ASSIGN statement and assigned GO TO statement	100 . . . ASSIGN 100 TO H . . . GO TO H . . .	Deleted
Assigned FORMAT specifiers	ASSIGN F TO 606	Deleted
H edit descriptors	606 FORMAT (9H1GOODBYE.)	Deleted
Computed GO TO statement	GO TO (10, 20, 30, 40), index	(obsolete)
Statement functions	FOIL(X, Y)= X**2 + 2*X*Y + Y**2	(obsolete)
DATA statements among executable statements	X= 27.3 DATA A, B, C / 5.0, 12.0. 13.0 / . . .	(obsolete)
CHARACTER* form of CHARACTER declaration	CHARACTER*8 STRING ! Use CHARACTER(8)	(obsolete)
Assumed character length functions		
Fixed form source code	* Column 1 contains * or ! or C for comments. C Column 6 for continuation.	

Fortran 95

Fortran 95 was a minor revision, mostly to resolve some outstanding issues from the Fortran 90 standard. Nevertheless, Fortran 95 also added a number of extensions, notably from the High Performance Fortran specification:

- FORALL and nested WHERE constructs to aid vectorization
- User-defined PURE and ELEMENTAL procedures
- Default initialization of derived type components, including pointer initialization
- Expanded the ability to use initialization expressions for data objects
- Clearly defined that ALLOCATABLE arrays are automatically deallocated when they go out of scope.

A number of intrinsic functions were extended (for example a dim argument was added to the maxloc intrinsic).

Several features noted in Fortran 90 to be deprecated were removed from Fortran 95:

- DO statements using REAL and DOUBLE PRECISION variables
- Branching to an END IF statement from outside its block
- PAUSE statement
- ASSIGN and assigned GOTO statement, and assigned format specifiers
- H edit descriptor.

An important supplement to Fortran 95 was the ISO technical report *TR-15581: Enhanced Data Type Facilities*, informally known as the *Allocatable TR*. This specification defined enhanced use of ALLOCATABLE arrays, prior to the availability of fully Fortran 2003-compliant Fortran compilers. Such uses include ALLOCATABLE arrays as derived type components, in procedure dummy argument lists, and as function return values. (ALLOCATABLE arrays are preferable to POINTER-based arrays because ALLOCATABLE arrays are guaranteed by Fortran 95 to be deallocated automatically when they go out of scope, eliminating the possibility of memory leakage. In addition, aliasing is not an issue for optimization of array references, allowing compilers to generate faster code than in the case of pointers.)

Another important supplement to Fortran 95 was the ISO technical report *TR-15580: Floating-point exception handling*, informally known as the *IEEE TR*. This specification defined support for IEEE floating-point arithmetic and floating point exception handling.

Conditional compilation and varying length strings

In addition to the mandatory "Base language" (defined in ISO/IEC 1539-1 : 1997), the Fortran 95 language also includes two optional modules:

- Varying character strings (ISO/IEC 1539-2 : 2000)
- Conditional compilation (ISO/IEC 1539-3 : 1998)

which, together, comprise the multi-part International Standard (ISO/IEC 1539).

According to the standards developers, "the optional parts describe self-contained features which have been requested by a substantial body of users and/or implementors, but which are not deemed to be of sufficient generality for them to be required in all standard-conforming Fortran compilers." Nevertheless, if a standard-conforming Fortran does provide such options, then they "must be provided in accordance with the description of those facilities in the appropriate Part of the Standard."

Fortran 2003

Fortran 2003 is a major revision introducing many new features. A comprehensive summary of the new features of Fortran 2003 is available at the Fortran Working Group (WG5) official Web site.[13]

From that article, the major enhancements for this revision include:

- Derived type enhancements: parameterized derived types, improved control of accessibility, improved structure constructors, and finalizers.
- Object-oriented programming support: type extension and inheritance, polymorphism, dynamic type allocation, and type-bound procedures.
- Data manipulation enhancements: allocatable components (incorporating TR 15581), deferred type parameters, VOLATILE attribute, explicit type specification in array constructors and allocate statements, pointer enhancements, extended initialization expressions, and enhanced intrinsic procedures.
- Input/output enhancements: asynchronous transfer, stream access, user specified transfer operations for derived types, user specified control of rounding during format conversions, named constants for preconnected units, the FLUSH statement, regularization of keywords, and access to error messages.
- Procedure pointers.
- Support for IEEE floating-point arithmetic and floating point exception handling (incorporating TR 15580).
- Interoperability with the C programming language.
- Support for international usage: access to ISO 10646 4-byte characters and choice of decimal or comma in numeric formatted input/output.
- Enhanced integration with the host operating system: access to command line arguments, environment variables, and processor error messages.

An important supplement to Fortran 2003 was the ISO technical report *TR-19767: Enhanced module facilities in Fortran.* This report provided *submodules,* which make Fortran modules more similar to Modula-2 modules. They are similar to Ada private child subunits. This allows the specification and implementation of a module to be expressed in separate program units, which improves packaging of large libraries, allows preservation of trade secrets while publishing definitive interfaces, and prevents compilation cascades.

Fortran 2008

The most recent standard, ISO/IEC 1539-1:2010, informally known as Fortran 2008, was approved in September 2010.[14] As with Fortran 95, this is a minor upgrade, incorporating clarifications and corrections to Fortran 2003, as well as introducing a select few new capabilities. The new capabilities include:

- Submodules – Additional structuring facilities for modules; supersedes ISO/IEC TR 19767:2005
- Co-array Fortran – a parallel execution model
- The DO CONCURRENT construct – for loop iterations with no interdependencies
- The CONTIGUOUS attribute – to specify storage layout restrictions
- The BLOCK construct – can contain declarations of objects with construct scope
- Recursive allocatable components – as an alternative to recursive pointers in derived types

The Final Draft international Standard (FDIS) is available as document N1830.[15]

Legacy

Since Fortran has been in use for more than fifty years, there is a vast body of Fortran in daily use throughout the scientific and engineering communities. It is the primary language for some of the most intensive supercomputing tasks, such as weather and climate modeling, computational fluid dynamics, computational chemistry, computational economics, animal breeding, plant breeding and computational physics. Even today, half a century later, many of the floating-point benchmarks to gauge the performance of new computer processors are still written in Fortran (*e.g.,*

CFP2006 [16], the floating-point component of the SPEC CPU2006 [17] benchmarks).

Portability

Portability was a problem in the early days because there was no agreed standard—not even IBM's reference manual—and computer companies vied to differentiate their offerings from others by providing incompatible features. Standards have improved portability. The 1966 standard provided a reference syntax and semantics, but vendors continued to provide incompatible extensions. Although careful programmers were coming to realize that use of incompatible extensions caused expensive portability problems, and were therefore using programs such as *The PFORT Verifier,* it was not until after the 1977 standard, when the National Bureau of Standards (now NIST) published *FIPS PUB 69*, that processors purchased by the U.S. Government were required to diagnose extensions of the standard. Rather than offer two processors, essentially every compiler eventually had at least an option to diagnose extensions.

Incompatible extensions were not the only portability problem. For numerical calculations, it is important to take account of the characteristics of the arithmetic. This was addressed by Fox et al. in the context of the 1966 standard by the *PORT* library. The ideas therein became widely used, and were eventually incorporated into the 1990 standard by way of intrinsic inquiry functions. The widespread (now almost universal) adoption of the IEEE 754 standard for binary floating-point arithmetic has essentially removed this problem.

Access to the computing environment (e.g. the program's command line, environment variables, textual explanation of error conditions) remained a problem until it was addressed by the 2003 standard.

Large collections of "library" software that could be described as being loosely related to engineering and scientific calculations, such as graphics libraries, have been written in C, and therefore access to them presented a portability problem. This has been addressed by incorporation of C interoperability into the 2003 standard.

It is now possible (and relatively easy) to write an entirely portable program in Fortran, even without recourse to a preprocessor.

Variants

Fortran 5

Fortran 5 was a programming language marketed by Data General Corp in the late 1970s and early 80s, for the Nova, Eclipse, and MV line of computers. It had an optimizing compiler that was quite good for minicomputers of its time. The language most closely resembles Fortran 66. The name is a pun on the earlier Fortran IV.

Univac also offered a compiler for the 1100 series known as Fortran V. A spinoff of Univac Fortran V was Athena Fortran.

Fortran V

Fortran V was a programming language distributed by Control Data Corporation in 1968 for the CDC 6600 series. The language was based upon Fortran IV.[18]

Fortran 6

Fortran 6 or Visual Fortran 2001 was licensed to Compaq by Microsoft. They have licensed Compaq Visual Fortran and have provided the Visual Studio 5 environment interface for Compaq v6 up to v6.1.[19]

Specific variants

Vendors of high-performance scientific computers (*e.g.,* Burroughs, CDC, Cray, Honeywell, IBM, Texas Instruments, and UNIVAC) added extensions to Fortran to take advantage of special hardware features such as instruction cache, CPU pipelines, and vector arrays. For example, one of IBM's FORTRAN compilers (*H Extended IUP*) had a level of optimization which reordered the machine code instructions to keep multiple internal arithmetic units busy simultaneously. Another example is *CFD*, a special variant of Fortran designed specifically for the ILLIAC IV supercomputer, running at NASA's Ames Research Center. IBM Research Labs also developed an extended FORTRAN-based language called "VECTRAN" for processing of vectors and matrices.

Object-Oriented Fortran was an object-oriented extension of Fortran, in which data items can be grouped into objects, which can be instantiated and executed in parallel. It was available for Sun, Iris, iPSC, and nCUBE, but is no longer supported.

Such machine-specific extensions have either disappeared over time or have had elements incorporated into the main standards; the major remaining extension is OpenMP, which is a cross-platform extension for shared memory programming. One new extension, Co-array Fortran, is intended to support parallel programming.

FOR TRANSIT for the IBM 650

"FOR TRANSIT" was the name of a reduced version of the IBM 704 FORTRAN language, which was implemented for the IBM 650, using a translator program developed at Carnegie [20] in the late 1950s. The following comment appears in the IBM Reference Manual ("FOR TRANSIT Automatic Coding System" C28-4038, Copyright 1957, 1959 by IBM):

> *The FORTRAN system was designed for a more complex machine than the 650, and consequently some of the 32 statements found in the FORTRAN Programmer's Reference Manual are not acceptable to the FOR TRANSIT system. In addition, certain restrictions to the FORTRAN language have been added. However, none of these restrictions make a source program written for FOR TRANSIT incompatible with the FORTRAN system for the 704.*

The permissible statements were:

Arithmetic assignment statements, e.g. a = b

GO to n

GO TO (n_1, n_2, ..., n_m), i

IF (a) n_1, n_2, n_3

PAUSE

STOP

DO n i = m1, m2

CONTINUE

END

READ n, list

PUNCH n, list

DIMENSION V, V, V, ...

EQUIVALENCE (a,b,c), (d,c), ...

Up to ten subroutines could be used in one program.

FOR TRANSIT statements were limited to columns 7 thru 56, only. Punched cards were used for input and output on the IBM 650. Three passes were required to translate source code to the "IT" language, then to compile the IT statements into SOAP assembly language, and finally to produce the object program, which could then be loaded into the machine to run the program (using punched cards for data input, and outputting results onto punched cards).

Two versions existed for the 650s with a 2000 word memory drum: FOR TRANSIT I (S) and FOR TRANSIT II, the latter for machines equipped with indexing registers and automatic floating point decimal (bi-quinary) arithmetic. Appendix A of the manual included wiring diagrams for the IBM 533 control panel.

Fortran-based languages

Prior to FORTRAN 77, a number of preprocessors were commonly used to provide a friendlier language, with the advantage that the preprocessed code could be compiled on any machine with a standard FORTRAN compiler. Popular preprocessors included FLECS, MORTRAN, SFtran, S-Fortran, Ratfor, and Ratfiv. Ratfor and Ratfiv, for example, implemented a C-like language, outputting preprocessed code in standard FORTRAN 66.

LRLTRAN was developed at the Lawrence Radiation Laboratory to provide support for vector arithmetic and dynamic storage, among other extensions to support systems programming. The distribution included the LTSS operating system.

The Fortran-95 Standard includes an optional *Part 3* which defines an optional conditional compilation capability. This capability is often referred to as "CoCo".

Many Fortran compilers have integrated subsets of the C preprocessor into their systems.

SIMSCRIPT is an application specific Fortran preprocessor for modeling and simulating large discrete systems.

The F programming language was designed to be a clean subset of Fortran 95 that attempted to remove the redundant, unstructured, and deprecated features of Fortran, such as the EQUIVALENCE statement. F retains the array features added in Fortran 90, and removes control statements that were obsoleted by structured programming constructs added to both Fortran 77 and Fortran 90. F is described by its creators as "a compiled, structured, array programming language especially well suited to education and scientific computing."[21]

Code examples

The following program illustrates dynamic memory allocation and array-based operations, two features introduced with Fortran 90. Particularly noteworthy is the absence of DO loops and IF/THEN statements in manipulating the array; mathematical operations are applied to the array as a whole. Also apparent is the use of descriptive variable names and general code formatting that conform with contemporary programming style. This example computes an average over data entered interactively.

```
  program average

  ! Read in some numbers and take the average
  ! As written, if there are no data points, an average of zero is
returned
  ! While this may not be desired behavior, it keeps this example
simple
```

```
  implicit none

  real, dimension(:), allocatable :: points
  integer                         :: number_of_points
  real                            :: average_points=0.,
positive_average=0., negative_average=0.

  write (*,*) "Input number of points to average:"
  read  (*,*) number_of_points

  allocate (points(number_of_points))

  write (*,*) "Enter the points to average:"
  read  (*,*) pcints

  ! Take the average by summing points and dividing by number_of_points
  if (number_of_points > 0) average_points = sum(points) /
number_of_points

  ! Now form average over positive and negative points only
  if (count(points > 0.) > 0) then
     positive_average = sum(points, points > 0.) / count(points > 0.)
  end if

  if (count(points < 0.) > 0) then
     negative_average = sum(points, points < 0.) / count(points < 0.)
  end if

  deallocate (points)

  ! Print result to terminal
  write (*,'(a,g12.4)') 'Average = ', average_points
  write (*,'(a,g12.4)') 'Average of positive points = ',
positive_average
  write (*,'(a,g12.4)') 'Average of negative points = ',
negative_average

  end program average
```

Humor

During the same Fortran Standards Committee meeting at which the name "FORTRAN 77" was chosen, a technical proposal was incorporated into the official distribution, bearing the title, "Letter O considered harmful". This proposal purported to address the confusion that sometimes arises between the letter "O" and the numeral zero, by eliminating the letter from allowable variable names. However, the method proposed was to eliminate the letter from the character set entirely (thereby retaining 48 as the number of lexical characters, which the colon had increased to 49). This was considered beneficial in that it would promote structured programming, by making it impossible to use the notorious **GO TO** statement as before. (Troublesome **FORMAT** statements would also be eliminated.) It was noted that this "might invalidate some existing programs" but that most of these "probably were non-conforming, anyway".[22] [23]

During the standards committee battle over whether the "minimum trip count" for the FORTRAN 77 "DO" statement should be zero (allowing no execution of the block) or one (the "plunge-ahead" DO), another facetious alternative was proposed (by Loren Meissner) to have the minimum trip be two—since there is no need for a loop if it is only executed once.

See also

- f2c
- History of compiler writing
- List of Fortran numerical libraries
- List of programming languages
- Matrix representation
- Row-major order

References

[1] "Math 169 Notes - Santa Clara University" (http://math.scu.edu/~dsmolars/ma169/notesfortran.html). .

[2] Eugene Loh (June 18, 2010). "The Ideal HPC Programming Language" (http://queue.acm.org/detail.cfm?id=1820518). *Queue* (Association of Computing Machines) **8** (6). .

[3] Softwarepreservation.org (http://www.softwarepreservation.org/projects/FORTRAN/index.html#By_FORTRAN_project_members)

[4] The Fortran I Compiler (http://polaris.cs.uiuc.edu/publications/c1070.pdf) "The Fortran I compiler was the first major project in code optimization. It tackled problems of crucial importance whose general solution was an important research focus in compiler technology for several decades. Many classical techniques for compiler analysis and optimization can trace their origins and inspiration to the Fortran I compiler."

[5] Fortran creator John Backus dies - Gadgets - MSNBC.com (http://www.msnbc.msn.com/id/17704662/), MSN.com

[6] Bitsavers.org (http://www.bitsavers.org/pdf/ibm/fortran/F28-8074-3_FORTRANII_GenInf.pdf)

[7] Ibibilio.org (http://www.ibiblio.org/pub/languages/fortran/ch1-12.html)

[8] Haines, L. H. (1965). "Serial compilation and the 1401 FORTRAN compiler" (http://domino.research.IBM.com/tchjr/journalindex.nsf/495f80c9d0f539778525681e00724804/cde711e5ad6786e485256bfa00685a03?OpenDocument). *IBM Systems Journal* **4** (1): 73–80. doi:10.1147/sj.41.0073. . This article was reprinted, edited, in both editions of Lee, John A. N. (1967(1st), 1974(2nd)). *Anatomy of a Compiler*. Van Nostrand Reinhold.

[9] McCracken, Daniel D. (1965). "Preface". *A Guide to FORTRAN IV Programming*. New York: Wiley. p. v. ISBN 0-471-58281-6.

[10] Chilton Computing with FORTRAN (http://www.chilton-computing.org.uk/acd/literature/reports/p008.htm), Chilton-computing.org.uk

[11] MIL-STD-1753. *DoD Supplement to X3.9-1978* (http://www.fortran.com/fortran/mil_std_1753.html). United States Government Printing Office. .

[12] POSIX 1003.9-1992. *POSIX FORTRAN 77 Language Interface – Part 1: Binding for System Application Program Interface **API*** (http://standards.ieee.org/reading/ieee/std_public/description/posix/1003.9-1992_desc.html). IEEE. .

[13] Fortran Working Group (WG5) (http://www.nag.co.uk/sc22wg5/). It may also be downloaded as a PDF file (ftp://ftp.nag.co.uk/sc22wg5/N1551-N1600/N1579.pdf) or gzipped PostScript file (ftp://ftp.nag.co.uk/sc22wg5/N1551-N1600/N1579.ps.gz), FTP.nag.co.uk

[14] N1836, Summary of Voting/Table of Replies on ISO/IEC FDIS 1539-1, Information technology - Programming languages - Fortran - Part 1: Base language ftp://ftp.nag.co.uk/sc22wg5/N1801-N1850/N1836.pdfPDF (101 KiB)

[15] N1830, Information technology — Programming languages — Fortran — Part 1: Base language ftp://ftp.nag.co.uk/sc22wg5/N1801-N1850/N1830.pdfPDF (7.9 MiB)

[16] http://www.spec.org/cpu2006/CFP2006/

[17] http://www.spec.org/cpu2006/

[18] Healy, MJR (1968). "Towards FORTRAN VI" (http://hopl.murdoch.edu.au/showlanguage.prx?exp=1092&language=CDC Fortran). *Advanced scientific Fortran by CDC*. CDC. pp. 169–172. . Retrieved 2009-04-10.

[19] "third party release notes for Fortran v6.1" (http://www.cs-software.com/software/fortran/compaq/cvf_relnotes.html#61ver_news). 15 March 2011. .

[20] "Internal Translator (IT) A Compiler for the IBM 650", by A. J. Perlis, J. W. Smith, and H. R. Van Zoeren, Computation Center, Carnegie Institute of Technology

[21] "F Programming Language Homepage" (http://www.fortran.com/F/index.html). .

[22] X3J3 post-meeting distribution for meeting held at Brookhaven National Laboratory in November 1976.
[23] "The obliteration of O", Computer Weekly, March 3, 1977

Further reading

Articles

- Allen, F.E. (September 1981). "A History of Language Processor Technology in IBM" (http://www.research.ibm.com/journal/rd/255/ibmrd2505Q.pdf). *IBM Journal of Research and Development* (IBM) **25** (5).
- Backus, J. W.; H. Stern, I. Ziller, R. A. Hughes, R. Nutt, R. J. Beeber, S. Best, R. Goldberg, L. M. Haibt, H. L. Herrick, R. A. Nelson, D. Sayre, P. B. Sheridan (1957). "The FORTRAN Automatic Coding System". *Western joint computer conference: Techniques for reliability* (Los Angeles, California: Institute of Radio Engineers, American Institute of Electrical Engineers, ACM): 188–198. doi:10.1145/1455567.1455599.
- Chivers, Ian D.; Sleightholme, Jane (2009). "Compiler support for the Fortran 2003 standard" (http://www.fortranplus.co.uk/resources/fortran_2003_2008_compiler_support.pdf). *ACM SIGPLAN Fortran Forum* (ACM) **28** (1): 26–28. doi:10.1145/1520752.1520755. ISSN 10617264.
- Pigott, Diarmuid (2006). "FORTRAN - Backus et al high-level compiler (Computer Language)" (http://hopl.murdoch.edu.au/showlanguage.prx?exp=8&language=FORTRAN). *The Encyclopedia of Computer Languages*. Murdoch University. Retrieved 2010-05-05.
- Roberts, Mark L.; Griffiths, Peter D. (1985). "Design Considerations for IBM Personal Computer Professional FORTRAN, an Optimizing Compiler" (http://www.research.ibm.com/journal/sj/241/ibmsj2401G.pdf). *IBM Systems Journal* (IBM) **24** (1): 49–60. doi:10.1147/sj.241.0049.

"Core" language standards

- ANSI X3.9-1966. *USA Standard FORTRAN* (http://www.fh-jena.de/~kleine/history/languages/ansi-x3dot9-1966-Fortran66.pdf). American National Standards Institute. Informally known as FORTRAN 66.
- ANSI X3.9-1978. *American National Standard – Programming Language FORTRAN* (http://www.fortran.com/fortran/F77_std/rjcnf.html). American National Standards Institute. Also known as ISO 1539-1980, informally known as FORTRAN 77.
- ANSI X3.198-1992 (R1997) / ISO/IEC 1539:1991. *American National Standard – Programming Language Fortran Extended* (http://www.iso.org/iso/en/CatalogueDetailPage.CatalogueDetail?CSNUMBER=17366). American National Standards Institute / ISO/IEC. Informally known as Fortran 90.
- ISO/IEC 1539-1:1997. *Information technology – Programming languages – Fortran – Part 1: Base language* (http://j3-fortran.org/doc/standing/archive/007/97-007r2/pdf/97-007r2.pdf). Informally known as Fortran 95. There are a further two parts to this standard. Part 1 has been formally adopted by ANSI.
- ISO/IEC 1539-1:2004. *Information technology – Programming languages – Fortran – Part 1: Base language* (http://www.dkuug.dk/jtc1/sc22/open/n3661.pdf). Informally known as Fortran 2003.
- ISO/IEC 1539-1:2010 (Final Draft International Standard). *Information technology – Programming languages – Fortran – Part 1: Base language* (ftp://ftp.nag.co.uk/sc22wg5/N1801-N1850/N1830.pdf). Informally known as Fortran 2008.

Related standards

- Kneis, Wilfried (October 1981). "Draft standard Industrial Real-Time FORTRAN". *ACM SIGPLAN Notices* (ACM Press) **16** (7): 45–60. doi:10.1145/947864.947868. ISSN 0362-1340.
- *ISO 8651-1:1988 Information processing systems—Computer graphics—Graphical Kernel System (GKS) language bindings—Part 1: FORTRAN* (http://www.iso.org/iso/catalogue_detail?csnumber=16024). Geneva, Switzerland: ISO. 1988.

Textbooks

- Adams, Jeanne C.; Brainerd, Walter S.; Hendrickson, Richard A.; Maine, Richard E.; Martin, Jeanne T.; Smith, Brian T. (2009). *The Fortran 2003 Handbook* (1st ed.). Springer. ISBN 978-1-84628-378-9.

- Akin, Ed (2003). *Object Oriented Programming via Fortran 90/95* (1st ed.). Cambridge University Press. ISBN 0-521-52408-3.
- Chapman, Stephen J. (2007). *Fortran 95/2003 for Scientists and Engineers* (3rd ed.). McGraw-Hill. ISBN 978-0-07-319157-7.
- Chivers, Ian; Sleightholme, Jane (2006). *Introduction to Programming with Fortran* (1st ed.). Springer. ISBN 1-84628-053-2.
- Etter, D. M. (1990). *Structured FORTRAN 77 for Engineers and Scientists* (3rd ed.). The Benjamin/Cummings Publishing Company, Inc.. ISBN 0-8053-0051-1.
- Ellis, T. M. R.; Phillips, Ivor R.; Lahey, Thomas M. (1994). *Fortran 90 Programming* (1st ed.). Addison Wesley. ISBN 0-201-54446-6.
- Kupferschmid, Michael (2002). *Classical Fortran: Programming for Engineering and Scientific Applications*. Marcel Dekker (CRC Press). ISBN 0-8247-0802-4.
- McCracken, Daniel D. (1961). *A Guide to FORTRAN Programming*. New York: Wiley. LCCN 61016618.
- Metcalf, Michael; John Reid, Malcolm Cohen (2011). *Modern Fortran Explained*. Oxford University Press. ISBN 0-19-960142-9.
- Nyhoff, Larry; Sanford Leestma (1995). *FORTRAN 77 for Engineers and Scientists with an Introduction to Fortran 90* (4th ed.). Prentice Hall. ISBN 0-13-363003-X.
- Page, Clive G. (1988). *Professional Programmer's Guide to Fortran77* (http://www.star.le.ac.uk/~cgp/prof77.html) (7th June 2005 ed.). London: Pitman. ISBN 0-273-02856-1. Retrieved 2010-05-04.
- Press, William H. (1996). *Numerical Recipes in Fortran 90: The Art of Parallel Scientific Computing* (http://www.nrbook.com/a/bookf90pdf.php). Cambridge, UK: Cambridge University Press. ISBN 0-521-57439-0.
- Sleighthome, Jane; Chivers, Ian David (1990). *Interactive Fortran 77: A Hands-On Approach* (http://citeseerx.ist.psu.edu/viewdoc/summary?doi=10.1.1.95.9503). Computers and their applications (2nd ed.). Chichester: E. Horwood. ISBN 0-13-466764-6.

External links

- JTC1/SC22/WG5 (http://www.nag.co.uk/sc22wg5/) — The ISO/IEC Fortran Working Group
- History of Fortran (http://www.softwarepreservation.org/projects/FORTRAN/) at the Computer History Museum's Software Preservation Group
- Bemer, Bob, "Who Was Who in IBM's Programming Research? -- Early FORTRAN Days" (http://www.trailing-edge.com/~bobbemer/PRORES.HTM), January 1957, Computer History Vignettes
- Comprehensive Fortran Standards Documents (http://gcc.gnu.org/wiki/GFortranStandards) from the gfortran project
- Fortran IV - IBM System/360 and System/370 Fortran IV Language - GC28-6515-10 (http://www.fh-jena.de/~kleine/history/languages/GC28-6515-10-FORTRAN-IV-Language.pdf)
- Fortran 77, 90, 95, 2003 Information & Resources (http://www.fortranplus.co.uk/fortran_info.html)
- Fortran 77 4.0 Reference Manual (http://www.physics.ucdavis.edu/~vem/F77_Ref.pdf)
- Fortran 90 Reference Card (http://users.physik.fu-berlin.de/~goerz/blog/2008/12/fortran-90-reference-card/)
- ECMA-9 Fortran Standard (1965) (http://www.ecma-international.org/publications/files/ECMA-ST-WITHDRAWN/ECMA-9, 1st Edition, April 1965.pdf)

Central Washington University

Central Washington University	
Motto	*Docendo Discimus*
Motto in English	By teaching we learn
Established	1891
Type	Public
Endowment	US$13,324,363[1]
President	Dr. James L. Gaudino
Provost	Dr. Marilyn Levine
Admin. staff	1458
Undergraduates	10,400[2]
Postgraduates	498
Location	Ellensburg, Washington, United States of America 47°00′07″N 120°32′24″W
Campus	Rural College Town 380 acres (150 ha)
Former names	Washington State Normal School Central Washington College of Education Central Washington State College
Colors	Crimson & Black
Athletics	NCAA Division II
Sports	13 Varsity Teams
Nickname	Wildcats
Mascot	Wellington P. Wildcat
Website	http://www.cwu.edu/

Central Washington University, often abbreviated **CWU**, is a public university in Ellensburg, Washington in the United States.This location was selected by the state legislature as a consolation prize after Ellensburg lost its bid to be state capital.[3] The university originally opened in the late 19th century as a teacher's college, which is still one of the primary majors taken there. Central Washington University is located about 30 miles (48 km) north of Yakima, Washington on Interstate 82, and 110 miles (180 km) east-southeast of Seattle, Washington on Interstate 90.

Barge Hall, Central Washington University

History

Central Washington University originally opened up as Washington State Normal School in 1891. The school was founded to educate future elementary and junior high teachers. In 1893, the Washington State Normal School's first building was constructed and given the name Barge Hall. Before 1894, classes were held at the Washington Public School in Ellensburg.[4]

The school's name changed to Central Washington College of Education in 1937, Central Washington State College in 1961, and finally to Central Washington University in 1977. It continues to be one of the fastest growing universities in the state of Washington. Dr. James L. Gaudino is the current president, having replaced Dr. Jerilyn S. McIntyre on January 1, 2009 after a yearlong search for a new president.

On April 17, 1974 serial killer Ted Bundy abducted Susan Rancourt from the campus by asking her to help him load books into his Volkswagen Beetle. Two other students reported seeing him around campus in the days leading up to her disappearance.

In 2008, Wildcat softball players Mallory Holtman and Liz Wallace helped carry injured opponent Sara Tucholsky of Western Oregon University around the bases after she hit her first-ever career home run and injured herself running around the bases. CWU lost the game, ending the Wildcats' season. The story received national attention and the trio appeared on the Ellen DeGeneres Show, CBS, CNN, and ESPN. They also won an ESPY award for Best Moment in Sports in 2008, were featured in Sports Illustrated, and are part of a national billboard campaign promoting sportsmanship by the Foundation for A Better Life.

In 1978, CWU began its campus radio station KCWU (88.1 The Burg) that has since flourished into a state-of-the-art broadcast facility.

From 1980 to 2007 the university was home to Washoe, a chimpanzee who was among the first nonhumans to acquire a standarized human language.

University centers

CWU has centers in Des Moines, Lynnwood, Moses Lake, Pierce County, Wenatchee and Yakima, Washington.

Edmonds Community College and Central Washington University-Lynnwood have worked together since 1975 to meet the higher education needs of Snohomish County. After earning a transfer degree online or on campus from Edmonds Community College, students can continue their studies for a bachelor's degree from CWU-Lynnwood in Snoqualmie Hall, a shared facility on the Edmonds CC campus. Snoqualmie Hall has two computer labs for the students to use, as well as a variety of classrooms.

In Des Moines, WA, students can attend Highline Community College, and then continue their education from CWU through the newly-built Higher Education Center. This facility replaces the site in Sea-Tac.

In Yakima, CWU shares a facility with Yakima Valley Community College and Washington State University. The Wenatchee and Moses Lake branches also share facilities with Wenatchee Valley College and Big Bend Community College, respectively.

Research

- The university was home to the signing chimpanzee Washoe from 1980 until her death in October 2007; from 1993 at the university's Chimpanzee and Human Communication Institute. This continues to be only one of the two institutions of its kind in the world.
- The Summer Institute for Theatre Arts [5], formerly the Drama Teacher's Summer Institute, was established in 1996. More than 500 teachers, representing 28 states and six nations, have attended the Institute for over ten years.
- The Science Honors Research Program [6] offers undergraduate students an opportunity to conduct high level research on projects that they design, develop, and implement. The Science Honors Research experience provides CWU undergraduate students an unparalleled opportunity to prepare for graduate school and successful scientific careers

Athletics

CWU students, alumni, and Varsity athletes are known as the "Wildcats" and their colors are Crimson and Black. CWU is part of NCAA Division II and is part of the Great Northwest Athletic Conference. The Wildcats Sports are as follows in seasonal order.

Men's: (Fall) Football, Cross Country, (Winter) Basketball, Swimming (Spring) Baseball, Track & Field.

Women's: (Fall) Soccer, Cross Country, Volleyball (Winter) Basketball, Swimming (Spring) Softball, Track & Field.

Championships:1995 Football NAIA Div 2

The University used to have competitive swimming and wrestling teams. However, the university addressed their budget problems within the athletic department by eliminating these programs in 2004. This was done despite the fact that these programs were two of the least expensive sports in the department. The men's swim team has won four NAIA championships and the women's team won two NAIA championships. The wrestling team also won two NAIA championships of its own and produced 10 national champions as well as 26 All-Americans. Although each of these programs were still competitive forces, the school's athletic department opted to cut the program following the 2003-2004 seasons.

The wrestling team was cut with the University citing a lack of regional competition and a lack of conference affiliation. Despite an outcry by students, alumni and fans, the university stuck with its decision despite being offered a wrestling only membership by the Rocky Mountain Athletic Conference (which is the only Division II conference sponsoring wrestling), and the student body agreeing to increase the schools activity fees to help sponsor the sport, and an abundance of Regional competition at the Division I and NAIA level. Those that still compete on the wrestling team have to try out at the club level which competes in the less prestigious National College Wrestling Association in its three team Northwest Conference.

Football garnered much attention as being one of the most successful NCAA Division II teams in the northwest. In 2006, they moved to the North Central Conference, because the Great Northwest Athletic Conference announced it would discontinue its participation in football following the 2005 season. The football team shares an intense rivalry with Western Washington University (who will also be joining the NCC in 2006). Recently they've been competing in a game called the Battle in Seattle taking place at Seattle's CenturyLink Field before the even more traditional Cascade Cup game, although because of conference scheduling the two games were combined starting 2006. In 2008, The Great Northwest Athletic Conference reinstated football, and Central Washington along with Western Washington rejoined the conference, so the previous format of the Battle in Seattle being played at CenturyLink

Field and the Cascade Cup was contested in Ellensburg. In 2009, Western Washington University disbanded its football team. In 2009, Central Washington University posted a perfect 11-0 record, the only Division II team to post a clean slate in 2009.

Central also offers a variety of club sports, of which, the men's rugby team has had the most success. The University established a men's rugby in 1972. As a club sport, the rugby team has been able to play against bigger university, such as, the University of Washington, Washington State University, University of Oregon, and Oregon State University. Rugby at Central has surprisingly been quite successful against these and other much larger schools, and has gained the University national recognition due to its high level of success in the national playoffs. Several of their most impressive accomplishments include making the Sweet 16 in 1998 and 2001. In 2001, Central defeated North Carolina 52-17 in their Sweet 16 match, and eventually lost to Penn State 14-12 in the Elite 8 (Penn State went on to play in the championship match). In 2007, the men's rugby team was ranked as high as 10th in the nation.

Notable alumni

The following are some notable former Wildcats:

- NFL quarterback Jon Kitna — Seattle Seahawks, Cincinnati Bengals, Detroit Lions, and Dallas Cowboys. Led the team to an NAIA Div. II championship in 1995.
- NFL quarterback Mike Reilly — Pittsburgh Steelers, Green Bay Packers, St. Louis Rams, Seattle Seahawks.
- NFL tight end Jared Bronson — Miami Dolphins
- MLB pitcher Dave Heaverlo — San Francisco Giants, Oakland Athletics, Seattle Mariners
- MLB outfielder Billy North — Chicago Cubs, Oakland Athletics, Los Angeles Dodgers, San Francisco Giants
- NCAA football coach Keith Gilbertson — University of Idaho, University of California, Berkeley, University of Washington. Played football for the Wildcats for one season in 1967, later graduating in 1971[7]
- W. Hudson Kensel, historian of the American West
- USMC General James N. Mattis — United States Marine Corps. Commander of the United States Central Command 2010-Present. Class of 1972.
- Author Stephen L. Nelson — Author "Quicken for Dummies" and 150 other books in the series, over 5 million copies sold worldwide. Named “most prolific computer book writer” by Wall Street Journal.
- Inventor, CPA Roland "Sandy" Wheeler— Inventor of “Bowflex“(NYSE:NLS) in the 1980s he later went on to acquire Nautilus, Stairmaster and Schwinn Fitness.
- Actor Craig T. Nelson — star of sitcom *Coach*[8]
- Ron Sims — Current Deputy Secretary of the United States Department of Housing and Urban Development and former King County Executive.
- Astronaut Dorothy M. Metcalf-Lindenburger Currently, she is assigned to the crew of STS-131, her first expedition.[9]
- U.S. Air National Guard Brigadier General John R. Croft — Chief of Staff of the Wisconsin Air National Guard
- U.S. Air National Guard Brigadier General Myron N. Dobashi — Commander of the Hawaii Air National Guard

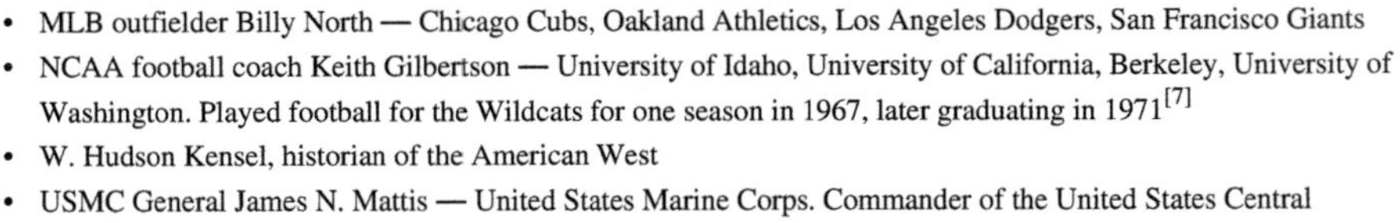

360° panorama of a portion of the Central Washington University campus as seen on an August afternoon. Taken at the southwest corner of campus, buildings, from left to right: Mitchell Hall, current location of most of the school's registrar and general admissions staff; McConnell Hall and auditorium, home of the Theatre Arts department; Barge Hall, financial and administrative center of campus; and Shaw-Smyser Hall, the primary building for the College of

Business.

Student Union and Recreation Center

On April 26, 2006, the school opened a brand new, 228000 sq ft (21200 m^2)., $58 million Student Union and Recreation Center.

The Student Union and Recreation Center is home to a full-sized rock wall, fully equipped gymnasium, and an outdoor recreation office; which rents everything from rafts, to snowshoes and ice axes.

References

[1] "Best Colleges 2010 - Central Washington University" (http://colleges.usnews.rankingsandreviews.com/best-colleges/ellensburg-wa/central-washington-university-3771). *U.S. News & World Report*. . Retrieved April 11, 2010.

[2] "State-Funded Student Enrollments by Site" (http://www.cwu.edu/~ir/translate.php?dir=facts/2009/&xml=enrollmentByAcademicCenter). Central Washington University. October 19, 2009. . Retrieved 2010-01-18.

[3] Ruth Kirk, Carmela Alexander. Exploring Washington's Past: A Road Guide to History. University of Washington Press, 1995. p.124

[4] Historylink.org - Washington State Normal School opens in Ellensburg on September 6, 1891 (http://www.historylink.org/essays/output.cfm?file_id=5093/)

[5] http://www.cwu.edu/~theatre/program/graduate/

[6] http://www.cwu.edu/~cots/scihonors/

[7] "Player Bio: Keith Gilbertson" (http://gohuskies.cstv.com/sports/m-footbl/mtt/gilbertson_keith00.html). Gohuskies.cstv.com. . Retrieved 2010-01-18.

[8] "TV.com - Craig T. Nelson Biography" (http://www.tvguide.com/celebrities/craig-t-nelson/bio/145554). Tvguide.com. . Retrieved 2010-01-18.

[9] http://www.jsc.nasa.gov/Bios/htmlbios/metcalf-lindenburger-dm.html

External links

- Official website (http://http://www.cwu.edu)
- Official Athletics website (http://www.wildcatsports.com/)

General Electric

Type	Public company
Traded as	NYSE: GE [1] Dow Jones Component
Industry	Conglomerate
Founded	Schenectady, New York, US (1892)
Founder(s)	Charles Coffin, Edwin Houston, Elihu Thomson, Thomas Edison
Headquarters	Fairfield, Connecticut, US[2]
Area served	Worldwide
Key people	Jeffrey Immelt (Chairman & CEO)
Products	Appliances, aviation, consumer electronics, electrical distribution, electric motors, energy, entertainment, finance, gas, healthcare, lighting, locomotives, oil, software, water, weapons, wind turbines
Revenue	▼ US$ 150.211 billion (2010)[3]
Operating income	▲ US$ 15.166 billion (2010)[3]
Net income	▲ US$ 12.163 billion (2010)[3]
Total assets	▼ US$ 751.216 billion (2010)[3]
Total equity	▼ US$ 124.198 billion (2010)[3]
Employees	287,000 (2010)[3]
Subsidiaries	GE Capital, GE Energy, GE Home & Business Solutions, GE Technology Infrastructure, NBCUniversal (49%)[4] GE Aviation
Website	www.ge.com [5]

General Electric Company (NYSE: GE [1]), or **GE**, is an American multinational conglomerate corporation incorporated in Schenectady, New York and headquartered in Fairfield, Connecticut, United States.[2] [6] The company operates through four segments: Energy, Technology Infrastructure, Capital Finance and Consumer & Industrial.[7] [8]

Street entrance to GE Headquarters in Fairfield, Connecticut

In 2011, *Fortune* ranked GE the 6th largest firm in the U.S.,[9] as well as the 14th most profitable.[10] Other rankings for 2011 include #7 company for leaders (*Fortune*), #5 best global brand (*Interbrand*), #82 green company (*Newsweek*), #13 most admired company (*Fortune*), and #19 most innovative company (*Fast Company*).[11]

The original version of General Electric's circular logo and trademark. The trademark application was filed on July 24, 1899, and registered on September 18, 1900

History

Further information: General Electric timeline

Formation

By 1890, Thomas Edison had brought together several of his business interests under one corporation to form Edison General Electric. At about the same time, Thomson-Houston Electric Company, under the leadership of Charles Coffin, gained access to a number of key patents through the acquisition of a number of competitors. Subsequently, General Electric was formed by the 1892 merger of Edison General Electric of Schenectady, New York and Thomson-Houston Electric Company of Lynn, Massachusetts and both plants remain in operation under the GE banner to this day.[12] The company was incorporated in New York, with the Schenectady plant as headquarters for many years thereafter. Around the same time, General Electric's Canadian counterpart, Canadian General Electric, was formed.

GE Building in 30 Rock, New York City

Public company

In 1896, General Electric was one of the original 12 companies listed on the newly formed Dow Jones Industrial Average and still remains after 115 years, the only one remaining on the Dow (though it has not continuously been in the DOW index).

23 Ton diesel electric locomotive made at the General Electric Corp. plant in Schenectady, New York

In 1911 the National Electric Lamp Association (NELA) was absorbed into General Electric's existing lighting business. GE then established its lighting division headquarters at Nela Park in East Cleveland, Ohio. Nela Park is still the headquarters for GE's lighting business. In 1935, GE was one of the top 30 companies traded at the London Stock Exchange.[13]

RCA

The Radio Corporation of America (RCA) was founded by GE in 1919 to further international radio. GE used RCA as its retail arm for radio sales from 1919, when GE began production, until separation in 1930.[14] RCA would quickly grow into an industrial giant of its own.

Power generation

GE's long history of working with turbines in the power generation field gave them the engineering know-how to move into the new field of aircraft turbosuperchargers. Led by Sanford Moss, GE introduced the first superchargers during World War I, and continued to develop them during the Interwar period. They became indispensable in the years immediately prior to World War II, and GE was the world leader in exhaust-driven supercharging when the war started. This experience, in turn, made GE a natural selection to develop the Whittle W.1 jet engine that was demonstrated in the United States in 1941. Although their early work with Whittle's designs was later handed to Allison Engine Company, GE Aviation emerged as one of the world's largest engine manufacturers, second only to the well-founded, and older, British company; Rolls-Royce plc, which led the way in innovative, reliable and efficient, high-performance, heavy-duty, jet engine design and manufacture.

In 2002 GE acquired the wind power assets of Enron during its bankruptcy proceedings.[15] Enron Wind was the only surviving U.S. manufacturer of large wind turbines at the time, and GE increased engineering and supplies for the Wind Division and doubled the annual sales to $1.2 billion in 2003.[16] It acquired ScanWind in 2009.[17]

Some consumers boycotted GE light bulbs, refrigerators and other products in the 1980s and 1990s to protest GE's role in nuclear weapons production.[18]

Computing

GE was one of the eight major computer companies through all of the 1960s — with IBM, the largest, called "Snow White" followed by the "Seven Dwarfs": Burroughs, NCR, Control Data Corporation, Honeywell, RCA, UNIVAC and GE.

GE had an extensive line of general purpose and special purpose computers. Among them were the GE 200, GE 400, and GE 600 series general purpose computers, the GE 4010, GE 4020, and GE 4060 real time process control computers, the Datanet 30 and Datanet 355 message switching computers (Datanet 30 and 355 were also used as front end processors for GE mainframe computers). A Datanet 500 computer was designed, but never sold.

In 1962, GE started developing its GECOS (later renamed GCOS) operating system, originally for batch processing, but later extended to timesharing and transaction processing. Versions of GCOS are still in use today.

In 1964–1969, GE and Bell Laboratories (which soon dropped out) joined with MIT to develop the pioneering and influential Multics operating system on the GE 645 mainframe computer. The project took longer than expected and was not a major commercial success, but it demonstrated important concepts such as single level store, dynamic linking, hierarchical file system, and ring-oriented security. Active development of Multics continued until 1985.

It has been said that GE got into computer manufacturing because in the 1950s they were the largest user of computers outside of the United States federal government. However, in 1970, GE sold its computer division to

Honeywell, exiting the computer manufacturing industry, though it retained its timesharing operations for some years afterwards. GE was a major provider of computer timesharing services, through General Electric Information Services (GEIS, now GXS), offering online computing services that included GEnie.

Acquisitions

For a complete list of acquisitions and divestitures, see General Electric timeline

In 1986 GE reacquired RCA, primarily for the NBC television network (also parent of Telemundo Communications Group). The remainder was sold to various companies, including Bertelsmann (Bertelsmann acquired RCA Records) and Thomson SA which traces its roots to Thomson-Houston, one of the original components of GE.

Also in 1986, Kidder, Peabody & Co. a U.S.-based securities firm was sold to GE and following heavy losses was subsequently sold to PaineWebber in 1994.[19]

In 2002 Francisco Partners and Norwest Venture Partners acquired a division of GE called GE Information Systems (GEIS). The new company, named GXS, is based in Gaithersburg, Maryland. GXS is a leading provider of B2B e-Commerce solutions. GE maintains a minority ownership position in GXS.

Also in 2002, GE bought wind turbine manufacturing assets of Enron Wind after the Enron scandals.[20]

In 2004 GE bought 80% of Universal Pictures from Vivendi. Vivendi bought 20% of NBC forming the company NBCUniversal. GE then owned 80% of NBCUniversal and Vivendi owned 20%. As of January 28, 2011 GE owns 49% and Comcast 51%.

In 2004 GE completed the spin-off of most of its mortgage and life insurance assets into an independent company, Genworth Financial, based in Richmond, Virginia.

Genpact formerly known as GE Capital International Services (GECIS) was established by GE in late 1997 as its captive India based BPO. GE sold 60% stake in Genpact to General Atlantic and Oak Hill Capital Partners in 2005 and hived off Genpact into an independent business. GE is still a major client to Genpact getting its services in customer service, finance, information technology and analytics.

GE Plastics was sold in 2007 to SABIC.

In May 2007, GE acquired Smiths Aerospace for $4.8 billion.

In May 2008, GE announced it was exploring options for divesting the bulk of its Consumer and Industrial business.

General Electric's Schenectady, New York facilities (including GE's original headquarters) are assigned the ZIP code 12345. (All Schenectady ZIP codes begin with 123, but no others begin with 1234.)

On December 3, 2009, it was announced that NBCUniversal will become a joint venture between GE and cable television operator Comcast. The cable giant will hold a controlling interest in the company, while GE retains a 49% stake and will buy out shares currently owned by Vivendi.[21]

Vivendi will sell its 20% stake in NBCUniversal to GE for US$5.8 billion. Vivendi will sell 7.66% of NBCUniversal to GE for US$2 billion if the GE/Comcast deal is not completed by September 2010 and then sell the remaining 12.34% stake of NBCUniversal to GE for US$3.8 billion when the deal is completed or to the public via an IPO if the deal is not completed.[22] [23]

On March 1, 2010, General Electric (GE) announced that the company is planning to sell its 20.85% stake in Turkey-based Garanti Bank.[24]

In August 2010, GE Healthcare signed a strategic partnership to bring cardiovascular Computed Tomography (CT) technology from start-up Arineta Ltd. of Israel to the hospital market.[25]

In October 2010, General Electric acquired gas engines manufacture Dresser Inc. for a $3 billion deal and also bought a $1.6 billion portfolio of retail credit cards from Citigroup Inc. This is the first major deal since the start of the financial crisis.[26]

On October 14, 2010, GE announced acquisition of data migration & SCADA simulation specialists Opal Software.[27]

December 2010: For the second times of this year (after Dresser acquisition), General Electric Co. buy oil sector company British Wellstream Holding Plc. an oil drilling pipe maker for 800 million pounds ($1.3 billion).[28]

February 2011: The company has agreed to buy the well-support division of John Wood Group Plc for about $2.8 billion. It is another aggressive moves recently of GE Oil & Gas made GE's acquisition was the largest of oil-service unit world wide in 2010.[29]

March 2011: GE announced it has completed the acquisition of privately-held Lineage Power Holdings, Inc., from The Gores Group, LLC. [30]

GE Capital sold its $2 billion dollar Mexican assets to Santander for $162 million and exit the business in Mexico. Santander will additionally assume the portfolio debts of GE Capital in the country. The transaction will be finished at first half of 2011. GE Capital will focus in the core business and will shed its non-core assets.[31]

Corporate affairs

GE is a multinational conglomerate headquartered in Fairfield, Connecticut. Its New York main offices are located at 30 Rockefeller Plaza in Rockefeller Center, known as the GE Building for the prominent GE logo on the roof. NBC's headquarters and main studios are also located in the building. Through its RCA subsidiary, it has been associated with the Center since its construction in the 1930s.

Classic GE neon sign

The company describes itself as composed of a number of primary business units or "businesses." Each unit is itself a vast enterprise, many of which would, even as a standalone company, rank in the Fortune 500. The list of GE businesses varies over time as the result of acquisitions, divestitures and reorganizations. GE's tax return is the largest return filed in the United States; the 2005 return was approximately 24,000 pages when printed out, and 237 megabytes when submitted electronically.[32] The company also "spends more on U.S. lobbying than any other company."[33]

In 2005 GE launched its "*Ecomagination*" initiative in an attempt to position itself as a "green" company. GE is currently one of the biggest players in the wind power industry, and it is also developing new environment-friendly products such as hybrid locomotives, desalination and water reuse solutions, and photovoltaic cells. The company "plans to build the largest solar-panel-making factory in the U.S.,"[33] and has set goals for its subsidiaries to lower their greenhouse gas emissions.[34]

On May 21, 2007, GE announced it would sell its GE Plastics division to petrochemicals manufacturer SABIC for net proceeds of $11.6 billion. The transaction took place on August 31, 2007, and the company name changed to SABIC Innovative Plastics, with Brian Gladden as CEO.[35]

CEO

Jeffrey Immelt is the current chairman of the board and chief executive officer of GE. He was selected by GE's Board of Directors in 2000 to replace John Francis Welch Jr. (Jack Welch) following his retirement. Previously, Immelt had headed GE's Medical Systems division (now GE Healthcare) as its President and CEO.

His tenure as the Chairman and CEO started at a time of crisis — he took over the role on September 7, 2001[36] four days before the terrorist attacks on the United States, which killed two employees and cost GE's insurance business $600 million — as well as having a direct effect on the company's Aircraft Engines sector. Immelt has also been selected as one of President Obama's financial advisors concerning the economic rescue plan.

Businesses

GE's divisions include GE Capital, GE Energy, GE Technology Infrastructure, and GE Home & Business Solutions

Through these businesses, GE participates in a wide variety of markets including the generation, transmission and distribution of electricity (e.g. nuclear, gas and solar), lighting, industrial automation, medical imaging equipment, motors, railway locomotives, aircraft jet engines, and aviation services. It co-owns NBCUniversal with Comcast. Through GE Commercial Finance, GE Consumer Finance, GE Equipment Services, and GE Insurance it offers a range of financial services as well. It has a presence in over 100 countries.

GE also produces General Imaging digital cameras.[38] In 2010, General Imaging released the Bridge Camera GE X5 with 14MP and 15x optical zoom.[39] In 2011, it is replaced by 16MP GE X500 with optional red color in Japan besides traditional black or white color in world wide.[40]

GE gauges to control a railway locomotive at a museum near Saskatoon, Canada[37]

Since over half of GE's revenue is derived from financial services, it is arguably a financial company with a manufacturing arm. It is also one of the largest lenders in countries other than the United States, such as Japan. Even though the first wave of conglomerates (such as ITT Corporation, Ling-Temco-Vought, Tenneco, etc.) fell by the wayside by the mid-1980s, in the late 1990s, another wave (consisting of Westinghouse, Tyco, and others) tried and failed to emulate GE's success.

It was announced on May 4, 2008 that GE would auction off its appliances business for an expected sale of $5–8 billion.[41] However, this plan fell through as a result of the recession.

Corporate recognition and rankings

In 2011, *Fortune* ranked GE the 6th largest firm in the U.S.,[9] as well as the 14th most profitable.[10] Other rankings for 2011 include the following:[11]

- #7 company for leaders (*Fortune*)
- #5 best global brand (*Interbrand*)
- #82 green company (*Newsweek*)
- #13 most admired company (*Fortune*)
- #19 most innovative company (*Fast Company*).

For 2010, GE's brand was valued at $42.8 billion.[42] CEO Jeffrey Immelt had a set of changes in the presentation of the brand commissioned in 2004, after he took the reins as chairman, to unify the diversified businesses of GE. The changes included a new corporate color palette, small modifications to the GE Logo, a new customized font (GE Inspira), and a new slogan, *"imagination at work"* replacing the longtime slogan *"we bring good things to life"*, composed by David Lucas. The standard requires many headlines to be lowercased and adds visual "white space" to documents and advertising to promote an open and approachable company. The changes were designed by Wolff

Olins and are used extensively on GE's marketing, literature and website.

Recent controversies

During the 2011 Fukushima I Nuclear Power Plant catastrophe it became public that the six reactors in the plant had been designed by General Electric and that critics had opposed GE's design as far back as 1972.[43]

In March 2011, *The New York Times* reported that despite earning $14.2 billion in worldwide profits, including more than $5 billion from U.S. operations, General Electric did not owe taxes in 2010. General Electric had a tax benefit of $3.2 billion. This same article also pointed out that GE has reduced their American workforce by one fifth since 2002.[44]

Environmental record

Pollution

GE has a history of some of its activities giving rise to large-scale air and water pollution. Based on year 2000 data,[45] researchers at the Political Economy Research Institute listed the corporation as the fourth-largest corporate producer of air pollution in the United States, with more than 4.4 million pounds per year (2,000 tons) of toxic chemicals released into the air.[46] GE has also been implicated in the creation of toxic waste. According to EPA documents, only the United States Government, Honeywell, and Chevron Corporation are responsible for producing more Superfund toxic waste sites.[47]

In 1983, New York State Attorney General Robert Abrams filed suit in the United States District Court for the Northern District of New York to compel GE to pay for the cleanup of what was claimed to be more than 100,000 tons of chemicals dumped (legally, at the time) from their plant in Waterford, New York.[48] In 1999, the company agreed to pay a $250 million settlement in connection with claims it polluted the Housatonic River (Pittsfield, Massachusetts) and other sites with polychlorinated biphenyls (PCBs) and other hazardous substances.[49]

From approximately 1947 to 1977, GE discharged as much as 1.3 million pounds of PCBs from its capacitor manufacturing plants at the Hudson Falls and Fort Edward upstate New York facilities into the Hudson River.[50] GE fought a media and political battle to avoid cleaning up the river and countered that dredging the river would actually stir up PCBs.[51] In 2002, GE was ordered to clean up a 40-mile (64 km) stretch of the Hudson River it had contaminated.[52]

In 2003, acting on concerns that the plan proposed by GE did not "provide for adequate protection of public health and the environment," the United States Environmental Protection Agency issued a unilateral administrative order for the company to "address cleanup at the GE site" in Rome, Georgia, also contaminated with PCBs.[53]

The nuclear reactors involved in the 2011 crisis at Fukushima I in Japan are GE designs,[54] and the architectural designs were done by Ebasco,[55] formerly owned by GE. Concerns over the design and safety of these reactors were raised as early as 1975.[56]

Environmental initiatives

On June 6, 2011, GE announced that it has licensed solar thermal technology from California-based eSolar for use in power plants that use both solar and natural gas.[57]

On May 26, 2011, GE unveiled its EV Solar Carport, a carport that incorporates solar panels on its roof, with electric vehicle charging stations under its cover.[58]

In May 2005 GE announced the launch of a program called "Ecomagination," intended, in the words of CEO Jeff Immelt "to develop tomorrow's solutions such as solar energy, hybrid locomotives, fuel cells, lower-emission aircraft engines, lighter and stronger durable materials, efficient lighting, and water purification technology".[59] The announcement prompted an op-ed piece in *The New York Times* to observe that, "while General Electric's increased emphasis on clean technology will probably result in improved products and benefit its bottom line, Mr. Immelt's credibility as a spokesman on national environmental policy is fatally flawed because of his company's intransigence in cleaning up its own toxic legacy."[60]

GE has said that it will invest $1.4 billion in clean technology research and development in 2008 as part of its Ecomagination initiative. As of October 2008, the scheme had resulted in 70 green products being brought to market, ranging from halogen lamps to biogas engines. In 2007, GE raised the annual revenue target for its Ecomagination initiative from $20 billion in 2010 to $25 billion following positive market response to its new product lines.[61] In 2010, GE continued to raise its investment by adding $10 billion into Ecomagination over the next five years.[62]

GE (General Electric) Energy's renewable energy business has expanded greatly, to keep up with growing U.S. and global demand for clean energy. Since entering the renewable energy industry in 2002, GE has invested more than $850 million in renewable energy technology. In August 2008 it acquired Kelman Ltd,[63] a Northern Ireland company specializing in advanced monitoring and diagnostics technologies for transformers used in renewable energy generation, and announced an expansion of its business in Northern Ireland in May 2010.[64] In 2009, GE's renewable energy initiatives, which include solar power, wind power and GE Jenbacher gas engines using renewable and non-renewable methane-based gases,[65] employ more than 4,900 people globally and have created more than 10,000 supporting jobs.[66]

GE Energy and Orion New Zealand Limited (Orion) have announced implementation of the first phase of a GE network management system to help improve power reliability for customers. GE's ENMAC Distribution Management System is the foundation of Orion's initiative. The system of smart grid technologies will significantly improve the network company's ability to manage big network emergencies and help it to restore power faster when outages occur.

GE unveiled a 40W replacement Energy Smart LED bulb, to be available late 2010 or early 2011. The company claims that the new LED bulb will provide a 77% energy savings and produce nearly the same light output as a 40W incandescent bulb, while lasting more than 25 times as long.[67]

Educational initiatives

GE Healthcare is collaborating with The Wayne State University School of Medicine and the Medical University of South Carolina to offer an integrated radiology curriculum during their respective MD Programs led by investigators of the Advanced Diagnostic Ultrasound in Microgravity study.[68] GE has donated over one million dollars of Logiq E Ultrasound equipment to these two institutions.[69]

Legal issues

On August 4, 2009 the SEC fined General Electric $50 million for breaking accounting rules in two separate cases, misleading investors into believing GE would meet or beat earnings expectations.[70]

GE has faced criminal action regarding its defense related operations. GE was convicted in 1990 of defrauding the US Department of Defense, and again in 1992 on charges of corrupt practices in the sale of jet engines to Israel.[71] [72]

Notable appearances in media

GE was the focus of a 1991 short subject Academy Award-winning documentary, *Deadly Deception: General Electric, Nuclear Weapons, and Our Environment* [73],[74] that juxtaposed GE's rosy "We Bring Good Things To Life" commercials with the true stories of workers and neighbors whose lives have been affected by the company's activities involving nuclear weapons.[75]

In the early 1950s Kurt Vonnegut was a writer for General Electric. A number of his novels and stories (notably *Cat's Cradle*) refer to the fictional city of Ilium, which appears to be loosely based on Schenectady, New York. The Ilium Works is the setting for the short story "Deer in the Works".

The NBC sitcom *30 Rock* is set at the NBC Studios in the GE Building at 30 Rockefeller Center (hence the title). All characters in the main cast are NBC (and therefore GE) employees, and one character, Jack Donaghy (Alec Baldwin) is portrayed as having risen through the ranks of GE management to become Vice President of NBC's East Coast operations through the company's microwave oven division.

See also

- Carousel of Progress
- College Bowl
- Edison Engineering Development Program
- GE Building
- GE Global Research
- Knolls Atomic Power Laboratory, Schenectady, NY
- List of assets owned by General Electric
- Phoebus cartel
- Top 100 US Federal Contractors

References

[1] http://www.nyse.com/about/listed/quickquote.html?ticker=ge

[2] "GE Fact Sheet: Businesses, Locations, Awards, Leadership" (http://www.ge.com/company/factsheets/corporate.html). *GE company website.*. Retrieved May 25, 2011.

[3] "2010 Form 10-K, General Electric Company" (http://www.sec.gov/Archives/edgar/data/40545/000119312511047479/d10k.htm#tx37537_11). *U.S. Securities and Exchange Commission.*.

[4] "NBC Universal Transaction – A Comcast-GE Joint Venture" (http://www.comcast.com/nbcutransaction/). *Comcast.*.

[5] http://www.ge.com/

[6] "Company Search, EDGAR System, Securities and Exchange Commission" (http://www.sec.gov/cgi-bin/browse-edgar?action=getcompany&CIK=0000040545&owner=include&count=40). . Retrieved December 22, 2009.

[7] "GE Fact Sheet: Businesses, Locations, Awards, Leadership" (http://www.ge.com/company/factsheets/corporate.html). General Electric. . Retrieved May 10, 2011.

[8] Wald, Matthew L.. "General Electric Company" (http://topics.nytimes.com/top/news/business/companies/general_electric_company/index.html). *The New York Times.*. Retrieved May 10, 2011.

[9] "Fortune 500: GE" (http://money.cnn.com/magazines/fortune/fortune500/2011/snapshots/170.html). Fortune. 2011. . Retrieved 17 December 2010.

[10] "Fortune 20 most profitable companies: IBM" (http://money.cnn.com/galleries/2011/fortune/1104/gallery.fortune500_most_profitable.fortune/14.html). Fortune. 2011. . Retrieved 17 December 2010.

[11] "GE rankings" (http://rankingthebrands.com/Brand-detail.aspx?brandID=82). Ranking the Brands. . Retrieved 17 December 2010.

[12] "Thomas Edison & GE" (http://www.ge.com/company/history/edison.html). GE company web site. . Retrieved December 22, 2009.

[13] FT.com / FT Magazine — The FT30 and how industry has changed (http://www.ft.com/cms/s/2/d35c4056-9527-11df-b2e1-00144feab49a.html)
[14] Mahon, Morgan E. *A Flick of the Switch 1930–1950* (Antiques Electronics Supply, 1990), p.86.
[15] "GE Completes Enron Wind Acquisition; Launches GE Wind Energy" (http://findarticles.com/p/articles/mi_m0EIN/is_2002_May_10/ai_85689772/). Business Wire. May 10, 2002. . Retrieved August 9, 2010.
[16] Fairly, Peter. The Greening of GE (http://spectrum.ieee.org/energy/environment/the-greening-of-ge) *IEEE Spectrum*, July 2005. Retrieved: November 6, 2010.
[17] Arnott, Sarah (March 26, 2010). "GE to build £99m UK wind turbine plant" (http://www.independent.co.uk/news/business/news/ge-to-build-16399m-uk-wind-turbine-plant-1928159.html). *The Independent* (UK). . Retrieved December 20, 2010.
[18] Global Corruption Report 2009, Corruption and the Private Sector (http://www.transparency.org/publications/publications/global_corruption_report/gcr2009) Transparency International 2009 page 148 **(English)**
[19] "Kidder, Peabody & Co." (http://en.wikipedia.org/wiki/Kidder,_Peabody_&_Co.). *Wikipedia*. .
[20] Murphy, Dennis. GE completes Enron Wind acquisition; Launches GE Wind Energy (http://www.desertskywind.com/news05022002.htm) *Desert Sky Wind Farm*, May 10, 2002. Retrieved: May 1, 2010.
[21] Goldman, Davis; Pepitone, Julianne (December 3, 2009). "GE, Comcast announce joint NBC deal" (http://money.cnn.com/2009/12/03/news/companies/comcast_nbc/index.htm). CNNMoney.com. . Retrieved December 22, 2009.
[22] "Vivendi to Sell its Stake in NBCUniversal for US$5.8 billion" (http://www.vivendi.fr/vivendi/Nouvel-article,5902). Vivendi SA. December 3, 2009. . Retrieved December 22, 2009.
[23] "Vivendi To Sell 20% Stake In NBCU To GE For $5.8 Bln" (http://www.bloomberg.com/apps/news?pid=newsarchive&sid=aMoJZHPclWnY). *The Wall Street Journal*. December 3, 2009. . Retrieved December 22, 2009.
[24] "General Electric to sell stake in Garanti Bank" (http://www.newstatesman.com/banking-and-insurance/2010/03/garanti-bank-turkey-stake). March 1, 2010. . Retrieved March 2, 2010.
[25] "GE to get its heart tech from Israel" (http://www.zdnet.com/blog/healthcare/ge-to-get-its-heart-tech-from-israel/3950). August 1, 2010. . Retrieved August 21, 2010.
[26] Comcast.net — GE posts sales slump, rattles recovery hopes (http://www.comcast.net/articles/news-finance/20101006/BUSINESS-US-GE/print/)
[27] "GE Acquires Opal Software — Strengthens Smart Grid Software Portfolio" (http://www.genewscenter.com/content/Detail.aspx?ReleaseID=11178&NewsAreaID=2). GE. . Retrieved October 19, 2010.
[28] NewsDaily: GE to buy UK oil pipe maker Wellstream for $1.3 billion reuters.com (http://www.reuters.com/article/idUSTRE6BC0U920101213)
[29] Businessweek.com (http://www.businessweek.com/news/2011-02-14/ge-agrees-to-buy-2-8-billion-oil-service-unit-shares-surge.html)
[30] Businesswire.com (http://www.businesswire.com/news/home/20110302005457/en/GE-Energy-Completes-Acquisition-Lineage-Power)
[31] GE Capital sells Mexican assets to Santander | Finance News (http://www.financenews.co.uk/fnews/ge-capital-sells-mexican-assets-to-santander/)
[32] "IRS e-file Moves Forward; Successfully Executes Electronic Filing of Nation's Largest Tax Return" (http://www.irs.gov/newsroom/article/0,,id=157845,00.html) (Press release). United States Department of the Treasury— Internal Revenue Service. May 31, 2006. . Retrieved February 1, 2007.
[33] Carney, Timothy (2011-04-07) Want to know how GE paid $0 income taxes? Think green. (http://washingtonexaminer.com/blogs/beltway-confidential/2011/04/want-know-how-ge-paid-0-income-taxes-think-green), *Washington Examiner*
[34] "GE Launches Ecomagination to Develop Environmental Technologies; Company-Wide Focus on Addressing Pressing Challenges" (http://www.businesswire.com/news/home/20050509005663/en) (Press release). General Electric. May 9, 2005. . Retrieved January 15, 2007.
[35] Deutsch, Claudia (May 22, 2007). "General Electric to Sell Plastics Division" (http://www.nytimes.com/2007/05/22/business/22plastics.html?_r=1). *The New York Times*. . Retrieved December 25, 2009.
[36] "Jeff Immelt, CEO" (http://www.ge.com/company/leadership/ceo.html). *Company Biography*. General Electric. . Retrieved December 25, 2009.
[37] "Welcome to Saskrailmuseum.org" (http://www.saskrailmuseum.org/). *Contact Us*. September 11, 2008. . Retrieved October 3, 2008.
[38] VIDEO – General Imaging's blink detection cameras | TG Daily (http://www.tgdaily.com/consumer-electronics-features/35959-video-â-general-imagingâs-blink-detection-cameras)
[39] Walmart.com: GE X5 Black 14MP Digital Camera w/ 15x Optical Zoom, 2.7" LCD: Digital Cameras (http://www.walmart.com/ip/GE-X5-BK/14245324)
[40] http://dandygadget.com/2011/04/19/ge-x500-power-pro-bridge-dslr-camera-added-a-new-color/
[41] "GE confirms it's exiting appliance business" (http://www.msnbc.msn.com/id/24630072). MSNBC. May 16, 2008. . Retrieved December 25, 2009.
[42] "Best Global Brands Ranking for 2010" (http://www.interbrand.com/en/best-global-brands/best-global-brands-2008/best-global-brands-2010.aspx). Interbrand. . Retrieved 15 February 2011.
[43] "Design of G.E.'s Mark 1 Nuclear Reactors Shows Weaknesses" (http://www.nytimes.com/2011/03/16/world/asia/16contain.html?_r=1&scp=2&sq=general electric&st=cse). *The New York Times*. March 15, 2011. .

[44] Kocieniewski, David (March 24, 2011). "G.E.'s Strategies Let It Avoid Taxes Altogether" (http://www.nytimes.com/2011/03/25/business/economy/25tax.html?scp=2&sq=ge&st=cse). *The New York Times.*.

[45] Political Economy Research Institute Toxic 100 Corporate Toxics Information Project Technical Notes (http://web.archive.org/web/20071114225754/http://www.peri.umass.edu/Technical-Notes.264.0.html). Retrieved November 9, 2007.

[46] Political Economy Research Institute (http://web.archive.org/web/20070927204419/http://www.rtknet.org/new/tox100/toxic100.php?database=t1&detail=1&datype=T&reptype=a&company1=&company2=8337&chemfac=fac&advbasic=bas)

[47] EPA Document Lists Firms Tied to Superfund Sites (http://projects.publicintegrity.org/superfund/report.aspx?aid=849) The Center for Public Integrity

[48] The Region; G.E. Plant Accused Of Water Pollution" (http://www.nytimes.com/1983/01/21/nyregion/the-region-ge-plant-accused-of-water-pollution.html?n=Top/Reference/Times Topics/Subjects/W/Water Pollution), *The New York Times*, January 21, 1983

[49] GE agrees to $250 million Settlement to Clean Up PCBs in Housatonic River (http://www.justice.gov/opa/pr/1999/October/471enr.htm), Department of Justice news release, October 7, 1999

[50] Hudson River PCBs (http://www.epa.gov/hudson/)

[51] Historic Hudson River Cleanup to Begin After Years of Delay, But Will General Electric Finish the Job? *Under the EPA's unusual agreement with General Electric, the company could escape full responsibility for cleaning up the toxic mess it made in the Hudson River* (http://www.nrdc.org/water/pollution/hhudson.asp)

[52] Old Questions Linger as New PCB Cleanup Starts (http://query.nytimes.com/gst/fullpage.html?res=9403EFD7133EF932A35756C0A9619C8B63) *The New York Times* May 1, 2007

[53] EPA issues unilateral administrative order to General Eletric Company in Rome, Georgia (http://yosemite.epa.gov/opa/admpress.nsf/e51aa292bac25b0b85257359003d925f/5592f5848c70b2858525731b00674e9c!OpenDocument) United States Environmental Protection Agency

[54] General Electric-designed reactors in Fukushima have 23 sisters in U.S. (http://openchannel.msnbc.msn.com/_news/2011/03/13/6256121-general-electric-designed-reactors-in-fukushima-have-23-sisters-in-us)

[55] Nuclear Reactor Maps: Fukushima-Daiichi (http://nuctrans.org/Nuc_Trans/locations/daiichi/daiichi.htm)

[56] Fukushima: Mark 1 Nuclear Reactor Design Caused GE Scientist To Quit In Protest (http://abcnews.go.com/Blotter/fukushima-mark-nuclear-reactor-design-caused-ge-scientist/story?id=13141287)

[57] Martin LaMonica, CNET. " GE invests in eSolar for combined solar, gas plants (http://news.cnet.com/8301-11128_3-20069472-54/ge-invests-in-esolar-for-combined-solar-gas-plants/?part=rss&subj=news&tag=2547-1_3-0-20)." Jun 6, 2011. Retrieved Jun 6, 2011.

[58] Candace Lombardi, CNET. " Solar power carport charges cars in Connecticut (http://news.cnet.com/8301-11128_3-20066460-54.html?part=rss&subj=news&tag=2547-1_3-0-20)." May 26, 2011. Retrieved May 26, 2011.

[59] "Ecomagination: Inside GE's Power Play" (http://www.worldchanging.com/archives/002669.html)

[60] "Talking Green, Acting Dirty." *The New York Times* June 12, 2005 (http://www.nytimes.com/2005/06/12/opinion/nyregionopinions/12WEsullivan.html)

[61] GE cleantech sales to top $17 billion this year (http://www.businessgreen.com/bg/news/1804493/ge-cleantech-sales-usd17bn)

[62] VentureBeat, Camille Ricketts. " GE Pumps 10B More Into Green Technology R&D (http://venturebeat.com/2010/06/24/ge-pumps-10b-more-into-green-technology-rd/)." June 24, 2010.

[63] GE Energy Acquires Kelman Limited (http://www.renewableenergyworld.com/rea/news/article/2008/08/ge-energy-acquires-kelman-limited-53356)

[64] GE to create 104 jobs in Lisburn (http://www.insideireland.ie/index.cfm/section/news/ext/generalelectric001/category/1084)

[65] GE's ecomagination™ (http://www.gepower.com/about/press/en/2008_press/120208e.htm) Certified Clarke Energy Jenbacher Power Plant Commissioned at Australian Coal Mine to Help Reduce Greenhouse Gas Emissions, 2008, www.gepower.com, Accessed April 14, 2011

[66] GE illustrates broad spectrum of alternative energy projects (http://www.reliableplant.com/Read/17126/ge-illustrates-broad-spectrum-of-alternative-energy-projects)

[67] GE makes LED replacement for 40-watt bulb | Green Tech — CNET News (http://news.cnet.com/8301-11128_3-20002001-54.html)

[68] Jultrasoundmet.org (http://www.jultrasoundmed.org/cgi/content/abstract/27/5/745), A Pilot Study of Comprehensive Ultrasound Education at the Wayne State University School of Medicine

[69] (http://www.gehealthcare.com/usen/ultrasound/genimg/products/logiq_e/hryfrdhosp_waynestuni.html)

[70] SEC Fines GE $50 million for Accounting Misdeeds (http://www.businessweek.com/bwdaily/dnflash/content/aug2009/db2009084_567813.htm)

[71] Sam Husseini, Felons On The Air: Does GE's Ownership of NBC Violate the Law? (http://www.fair.org/index.php?page=1254), FAIR.ORG, November/December 1994

[72] Stevenson, Richard W. G.E. Guilty Plea in U.S. Aid to Israel (http://www.nytimes.com/1992/07/23/business/company-news-ge-guilty-plea-in-us-aid-to-israel.html), New York Times, July 23, 1992.

[73] http://www.newday.com/films/DeadlyDeception.html

[74] Deadly Deception: General Electric, Nuclear Weapons, and Our Environment (http://www.newday.com/films/DeadlyDeception.html)

[75] Nuclear Weaponmakers Campaign – Corporate Accountability International – Challenging Abuse, Protecting People – Think Outside the Bottle – challenging the bottled water industry ... (http://web.archive.org/web/20060621082431/http://stopcorporateabuse.org/cms/page1127.cfm)

Further reading

- Carlson, W. Bernard. *Innovation as a Social Process: Elihu Thomson and the Rise of General Electric, 1870–1900* (Cambridge: Cambridge University Press, 1991).
- Woodbury, David O. *Elihu Thomson, Beloved Scientist* (Boston: Museum of Science, 1944)
- Haney, John L. *The Elihu Thomson Collection* American Philosophical Society Yearbook 1944.
- Hammond, John W. *Men and Volts: The Story of General Electric*, published 1941, 436 pages.
- Mill, John M. *Men and Volts at War: The Story of General Electric in World War II*, published 1947.

External links

- General Electric corporate page (http://www.ge.com/)
- Official site for GE Appliances, the corporation's leading consumer product (http://www.geappliances.com/)
- SEC filings including 10-k (http://www.sec.gov/cgi-bin/browse-edgar?action=getcompany&CIK=0000040545&owner=exclude)
- Official site for SABIC Innovative Plastics (http://www.sabic-ip.com/).
- Historic Development of the GE.com website (http://www.vb.com/ge.htm).
- Financial Times article on GE's effort to go green (http://news.ft.com/cms/s/ac5c3e90-e60b-11da-b309-0000779e2340.html)
- GE energy (http://www.gepower.com/)
- G.E. to Double Investments in Renewables to $4B (http://www.greenbiz.com/news/2007/06/04/ge-double-investments-renewables-4b)
- USA Today article about GE's success at creating CEOs at large companies (http://www.usatoday.com/money/companies/management/2008-01-08-ceo-companies_N.htm)

Video clips

- GE Reports YouTube channel (http://www.youtube.com/user/GEreports)

Business data

- General Electric (http://finance.google.com/finance?q=GE) at Google Finance
- General Electric (http://finance.yahoo.com/q?s=GE) at Yahoo! Finance
- General Electric (http://www.hoovers.com//--ID__10634--/free-co-factsheet.xhtml) at Hoover's
- General Electric (http://www.reuters.com/finance/stocks/overview?symbol=GE) at Reuters
- General Electric (http://google.brand.edgar-online.com/?sym=GE) SEC filings at EDGAR Online
- General Electric (http://www.sec.gov/cgi-bin/browse-edgar?action=getcompany&CIK=40545) SEC filings at the Securities and Exchange Commission

United States Atomic Energy Commission

The **United States Atomic Energy Commission** (AEC) was an agency of the United States government established after World War II by Congress to foster and control the peace time development of atomic science and technology. President Harry S. Truman signed the McMahon/Atomic Energy Act on August 1, 1946, transferring the control of atomic energy from military to civilian hands, effective from January 1, 1947.

Shield of the U.S. Atomic Energy Commission

An increasing number of critics during the 1960s charged that the AEC's regulations were insufficiently rigorous in several important areas, including radiation protection standards, nuclear reactor safety, plant siting, and environmental protection. By 1974, the AEC's regulatory programs had come under such strong attack that Congress decided to abolish the agency. The agency was abolished by the Energy Reorganization Act of 1974, which assigned its functions to two new agencies: the Energy Research and Development Administration and the Nuclear Regulatory Commission.[1]

History

In creating the AEC, Congress declared that atomic energy should be employed not only in the form of nuclear weapons for the nation's defense, but also to promote world peace, improve the public welfare and strengthen free competition in private enterprise. At the same time, the McMahon Act which created the AEC also gave it unprecedented powers of regulation over the entire field of nuclear science and technology. It furthermore explicitly prevented technology transfer between the United States and other countries, and required FBI investigations for all scientists or industrial contractors who wished to have access to any AEC controlled nuclear information. The signing was the culmination of long months of intensive debate among politicians, military planners and atomic scientists over the fate of this new energy source and the means by which it would be regulated. President Truman appointed David Lilienthal as the first Chairman of the AEC.

Congress gave the new civilian Commission extraordinary power and considerable independence to carry out its mission. To provide the Commission exceptional freedom in hiring scientists and professionals, Commission employees were exempt from the Civil Service system. Because of the need for great security, all production facilities and nuclear reactors would be government-owned, while all technical information and research results would be under Commission control. The National Laboratory system was established from the facilities created under the Manhattan Project. Argonne National Laboratory was one of the first laboratories authorized under this legislation as a contractor-operated facility dedicated to fulfilling the new Commission's mission.

The AEC was furthermore in charge of developing the United States' nuclear arsenal, taking over these responsibilities from the wartime Manhattan Project. Over the course of its first decade, the AEC oversaw the operation of Los Alamos Scientific Laboratory, devoted primarily to weapons development, and, in 1952, the establishment of a second weapons laboratory in California (the Lawrence Livermore National Laboratory). It also implemented the "crash" program to develop the hydrogen bomb, and played key roles in the prosecution of the Rosenbergs for espionage. It began a program of regular nuclear testing both in the Pacific Proving Grounds and at the continental Nevada Test Site. While it also supported much basic research, the vast majority of its early budget was devoted to atomic weapons development and production.

Within the AEC, high-level scientific and technical advice was provided by the General Advisory Committee, originally headed by J. Robert Oppenheimer. In its early years, the GAC provided a number of controversial decisions, notably its decision against building the hydrogen bomb in 1949. The AEC's connections with the armed services was facilitated by a Military Liaison Committee. Congressional oversight over the AEC was exercised by the Joint Committee on Atomic Energy, which had considerable power in influencing AEC decisions and policy.

The AEC's far-reaching powers and control over subject matter which had far-reaching social, public health, and military implications made it an extremely controversial organization. One of the drafters of the McMahon Act, James R. Newman, famously concluded that the bill made "the field of atomic energy [an] island of socialism in the midst of a free-enterprise economy".

Before the Nuclear Regulatory Commission (NRC) was created, nuclear regulation was the responsibility of the AEC, which Congress first established in the Atomic Energy Act of 1946. Eight years later, Congress replaced that law with the **Atomic Energy Act Amendments** of 1954, which for the first time made the development of commercial nuclear power possible, and resolved a number of other outstanding problems in implementing the first Atomic Energy Act. The act assigned the AEC the functions of both encouraging the use of nuclear power and regulating its safety. The AEC's regulatory programs sought to ensure public health and safety from the hazards of nuclear power without imposing excessive requirements that would inhibit the growth of the industry. This was a difficult goal to achieve, especially in a new industry, and within a short time the AEC's programs stirred considerable controversy. Stephanie Cooke has written that:

> "the AEC had become an oligarchy controlling all facets of the military and civilian sides of nuclear energy, promoting them and at the same time attempting to regulate them, and it had fallen down on the regulatory side ... a growing legion of critics saw too many inbuilt conflicts of interest".[2]

An increasing number of critics during the 1960s charged that the AEC's regulations were insufficiently rigorous in several important areas, including radiation protection standards, nuclear reactor safety, plant siting, and environmental protection.

In 1973, the AEC predicted that, by the turn of the century, one thousand reactors would be producing electricity for homes and businesses across the United States. But after 1973, reactor orders declined sharply as electricity demand fell and construction costs rose. Many orders and partially completed plants were cancelled.[3]

By 1974, the AEC's regulatory programs had come under such strong attack that Congress decided to abolish the agency. Supporters and critics of nuclear power agreed that the promotional and regulatory duties of the AEC should be assigned to different agencies. The Energy Reorganization Act of 1974 put the regulatory functions of the AEC into the new NRC, which began operations on January 19, 1975 and placed the promotional functions within the Energy Research and Development Administration, which was later incorporated into the United States Department of Energy.

AEC Chairperson

Term	Name	President(s) served
1946–1950	David E. Lilienthal	Harry S. Truman
1950–1953	Gordon Dean	Harry S. Truman
1953–1958	Lewis Strauss	Dwight D. Eisenhower
1958–1960	John A. McCone	Dwight D. Eisenhower
1961–1971	Glenn T. Seaborg	John F. Kennedy, Lyndon Johnson, Richard Nixon
1971–1973	James R. Schlesinger	Richard Nixon
1973–1974	Dixy Lee Ray	Richard Nixon

See also

- Human experimentation in the United States
- Kenneth Nichols (first General Manager of AEC)
- Anti-nuclear movement in the United States
- Calvert Cliffs Coordinating Committee
- Nuclear engineering
- Nuclear physics
- Nuclear power plant
- Oppenheimer security hearing
- Operation Plowshare
- Plutonium
- Price-Anderson Nuclear Industries Indemnity Act
- Alvin Radkowsky (Chief Scientist, Office of Naval Reactors from 1950 to 1972)
- The Cult of the Atom: The Secret Papers of the Atomic Energy Commission
- United States Department of Energy
- Uranium
- Harold Hodge, head of the United States Atomic Energy Commission's (AEC) Division of Pharmacology and Toxicology for the Manhattan Project, where he studied on the effects of the inhalation of uranium and beryllium through the "Rochester Chamber".

References

[1] "Atomic Energy Commission" (http://www.nrc.gov/reading-rm/basic-ref/glossary/atomic-energy-commission.html). Nuclear Regulatory Commission. . Retrieved 2009-11-16.
[2] Stephanie Cooke (2009). *In Mortal Hands: A Cautionary History of the Nuclear Age*, Black Inc., p. 252.
[3] Stephanie Cooke (2009). *In Mortal Hands: A Cautionary History of the Nuclear Age*, Black Inc., p. 283.

Further reading

- Buck, Alice L. *A History of the Atomic Energy Commission.* U.S. Department of Energy, DOE/ES-0003. July 1983. PDF file (http://www.atomictraveler.com/HistoryofAEC.pdf)
- Richard G. Hewlett; Oscar E. Anderson. *The New World, 1939-1946.* University Park: Pennsylvania State University Press, 1962.
- Richard G. Hewlett; Francis Duncan. *Atomic Shield, 1947-1952.* University Park: Pennsylvania State University Press, 1969.
- Richard G. Hewlett; Jack M. Holl. *Atoms for Peace and War, 1953-1961: Eisenhower and the Atomic Energy Commission.* Berkeley: University of California Press, 1989.

External links

- Diary of T. Keith Glennan, Dwight D. Eisenhower Presidential Library (http://www.eisenhower.archives.gov/listofholdingshtml/finding_aids_g.html)
- Papers of John A. McCone, Dwight D. Eisenhower Presidential Library (http://www.eisenhower.archives.gov/listofholdingshtml/finding_aids_m.html)

New York University

New York University	
Motto	*Perstare et praestare* (Latin)
Motto in English	To persevere and to excel
Established	1831
Type	Private
Endowment	$2.43 billion[1]
President	John Sexton, Ph.D., J.D.
Academic staff	6,755
Admin. staff	15,286
Students	43,404[2]
Undergraduates	21,638
Postgraduates	21,766
Location	New York, NY, United States
Campus	Urban
Newspaper	*Washington Square News*
Colors	Violet and White
Athletics	NCAA Division III UAA 19 varsity teams
Nickname	Violets
Mascot	Bobcat
Website	NYU.edu [3]

New York University (**NYU**) is a private, nonsectarian research university based in New York City. NYU's main campus is situated in the Greenwich Village section of Manhattan. Founded in 1831, NYU is one of the largest private, nonprofit institutions of higher education in the United States.[4]

NYU is organized into 18 schools, colleges, and institutes,[4] located in six centers throughout Manhattan and Downtown Brooklyn, as well as other sites across the globe. NYU operates study abroad facilities in London, Paris, Florence, Prague, Madrid, Berlin, Accra, Shanghai, Buenos Aires and Tel Aviv in addition to the Singapore campus of the Tisch School of the Arts and a comprehensive liberal-arts campus in Abu Dhabi that opened in September 2010.[5] NYU plans to open a portal degree granting campus in China as part of its Global Network University initiative[6] and plans to open a site in Washington, D.C. and in Sydney in 2012.[7]

With approximately 12,500 residents, NYU has the seventh-largest university housing system in the U.S. and the largest among private schools.[8] Some of the first fraternities in the country were formed at NYU.[9] [10]

NYU's sports teams are called the Violets, the colors being the trademarked hue "NYU Violet," and white. The school mascot is modeled after a bobcat. Almost all sports teams at NYU participate in the NCAA's Division III and the University Athletic Association. While NYU has had All-American football players, it has not had a varsity football team since the 1960s.

NYU is regularly ranked as one of the top academic institutions in the world.[11] [12] The university counts 33 Nobel Prize winners, 3 Abel Prize winners,[13] [14] 10 National Medal of Science recipients,[15] [16] 16 Pulitzer Prize winners,[17] 21 Academy Award winners,[17] [18] [19] and Emmy,[20] Grammy,[21] and Tony Award[22] winners. NYU also has MacArthur and Guggenheim Fellowship holders[23] as well as National Academy of Sciences members among its past and present graduates and faculty.[24] Of the more than 3,000 colleges and universities in America, NYU is one of only 60 member institutions of the distinguished Association of American Universities.[4]

History

Albert Gallatin

Albert Gallatin, Secretary of Treasury under Thomas Jefferson and James Madison, declared his intention to establish "in this immense and fast-growing city ... a system of rational and practical education fitting for all and graciously opened to all." A three-day long "literary and scientific convention" held in City Hall in 1830 and attended by over 100 delegates debated the terms of a plan for a new university. These New Yorkers believed the city needed a university designed for young men who would be admitted based on merit, not birthright, status or social class. On April 18, 1831, an institution was established, with the support of a group of prominent New York City residents from the city's landed class of merchants, bankers, and traders. Albert Gallatin was elected as the institution's first president. On April 21, 1831, the new institution received its charter and was incorporated as the University of the City of New York by the New York State Legislature; older documents often refer to it by that name. The university has been popularly known as New York University since its beginning and was officially renamed New York University in 1896. In 1832, NYU held its first classes in rented rooms of four-story Clinton Hall, situated near City Hall.[25] In 1835, the School of Law, NYU's first professional school, was established. Although the impetus to found a new school was partly a reaction by evangelical Presbyterians to what they perceived as the Episcopalianism of Columbia College,[26] NYU was created non-denominational, unlike many American colonial colleges at the time.[25]

The University Heights campus, now home to the Bronx Community College.

Whereas NYU had its Washington Square campus since its founding, the university purchased a campus at University Heights in the Bronx because of overcrowding on the old campus. NYU also had a desire to follow New York City's development further uptown. NYU's move to the Bronx occurred in 1894, spearheaded by the efforts of Chancellor Henry Mitchell MacCracken.[25] The University Heights campus was far more spacious than its predecessor was. As a result, most of the university's operations along with the undergraduate College of Arts and Science and School of Engineering were housed there. NYU's administrative operations were moved to the new campus, but the graduate schools of the university remained at Washington Square.[27] In 1914, Washington Square College was founded as the downtown undergraduate college of NYU. In 1935, NYU opened the "Nassau College-Hofstra Memorial of New York University at Hempstead, Long Island". This extension would later become a fully independent Hofstra University.[28]

In the late 1960s and early 1970s, financial crisis gripped the New York City government and the troubles spread to the city's institutions, including NYU.[29] Feeling the pressures of imminent bankruptcy, NYU President James McNaughton Hester negotiated the sale of the University Heights campus to the City University of New York, which occurred in 1973. After the sale of the Bronx campus, University College merged with Washington Square College. In the 1980s, under the leadership of President John Brademas,[30] NYU launched a billion-dollar campaign that was spent almost entirely on updating facilities.[31] The campaign was set to complete in 15 years, but ended up being completed in 10.[32] In 2003 President John Sexton launched a 2.5-billion dollar campaign for funds to be spent especially on faculty and financial aid resources.[33]

University logo

The university logo, the upheld torch, is derived from the Statue of Liberty, signifying NYU's service to the city of New York. The torch is depicted on both the NYU seal and the more abstract NYU logo, designed in 1965 by renowned graphic designer Tom Geismar of the branding and design firm Chermayeff & Geismar. There are at least two versions of the possible origin of the university color, violet. Some believe that it may have been chosen because violets are said to have grown abundantly in Washington Square and around the buttresses of the Old University Building. Others argue that the color may have been adopted because the violet was the flower associated with Athens, the center of learning in ancient Greece.[24]

Cultural setting

Washington Square and Greenwich Village have been hubs of cultural life in New York City since the early nineteenth century. Much of this culture has intersected with NYU at various points in its history. Artists of the Hudson River School, the United States' first prominent school of painters, settled around Washington Square. Samuel F.B. Morse, the first chair of Painting and Sculpture at NYU, and Daniel Huntington were early tenants of the Old University Building in the mid-nineteenth century. (The University rented out studio space and residential apartments within the "academic" building.) Artists and intellectuals such as Edgar Allan Poe, Mark Twain, Herman Melville and Walt Whitman contributed to the artistic scene near NYU. As a result, they had notable interaction with the cultural and academic life of the University.[29]

In the 1870s, sculptors Augustus Saint-Gaudens and Daniel Chester French lived and worked near the Square. By the 1920s, Washington Square Park was nationally recognized as a focal point for artistic and moral rebellion. As such, the Washington Square campus became more diverse and bustled with urban energy, contributing to academic change at NYU.[29] Famed residents of this time include Eugene O'Neill, John Sloan, and Maurice Prendergast. In the 1930s, the abstract expressionists Jackson Pollock and Willem de Kooning, and the realists Edward Hopper and

Thomas Hart Benton had studios around Washington Square. In the 1960s the area became one of the centers of the beat and folk generation, when Allen Ginsberg and Bob Dylan settled there. This led to tension with the University, which at the time was in the midst of an aggressive facilities expansion phase.[29] In 1975 the University opened The Grey Art Gallery at 100 Washington Square East, housing the New York University art collection and featuring museum quality exhibitions.[34] [35]

Campus

Most of NYU's buildings are located across a roughly 229 acre area bounded by Houston Street to the south, Broadway to the east, 14th Street to the north, and Sixth Avenue (Avenue of the Americas) to the west. The core of NYU consists of buildings that surround Washington Square Park.

Washington Square campus

Since the late 1970s, the central part of NYU has been its Washington Square campus in the heart of Greenwich Village. The Washington Square Arch is an unofficial symbol of NYU. Until 2007, NYU had held its commencement ceremonies in Washington Square Park, but moved the ceremonies to Yankee Stadium in 2008 because of renovations to Washington Square.[36]

The Silver Center circa 1900

In the 1990s, NYU became a "two square" university by building a second community around Union Square, in close proximity to Washington Square. NYU's Union Square community primarily consists of the priority residence halls of Carlyle Court, Palladium Residence Hall, Alumni Hall, Coral Tower, Thirteenth Street Hall, University Hall, Third North Residence Hall, and Founders Hall.

NYU operates theaters and performance facilities that are often used by the University's music conservatory and Tisch School of the Arts. External productions are also occasionally held in NYU's facilities. The largest performance accommodations at NYU are the Skirball Center for Performing Arts (850 seats) at 566 LaGuardia Place, just south of Washington Square South; and the Eisner-Lubin Auditorium (560 seats) in the Kimmel Center. Recently, the Skirball Center hosted important speeches on foreign policy by John Kerry[37] and Al Gore[38] as well as the recording of the third season finale of The Apprentice. The Skirball Center is the largest performing arts facility south of 42nd Street.[39] [40]

Bobst Library

A view of the interior of Bobst

The Elmer Holmes Bobst Library, built between 1967 and 1972, is the largest library at NYU and one of the largest academic libraries in the United States. Designed by Philip Johnson and Richard Foster, the 12-story, 425,000-square-foot (39,000 m^2) structure sits on the southern edge of Washington Square Park (at 70 Washington Square South) and is the flagship of an eight-library, 4.5 million-volume system. Bobst Library offers one Multidisciplinary Reference Center, a Research Commons, 28 miles of open-stacks shelving, and approximately 2,000 seats for student study. The library is visited by more than 6,800 users each day, and circulates more than one million books annually.[41]

Bobst's Avery Fisher Center for Music and Media is one of the world's largest academic media centers, where students and researchers use more than 95,000 audio and video recordings per year. The Digital Studio offers a constantly evolving, leading-edge resource for faculty and student projects and promotes and supports access to digital resources for teaching, learning, research and arts events.

Bobst Library is also home to significant special collections. The Fales Collection houses one of the finest collections of English and American fiction in the United States, the unique Downtown Collection, documenting the New York literary avante-garde arts scene from the 1970s to the present, and the Food and Cookery Collection, which documents American food history with a focus on New York City. Bobst Library also houses the Tamiment Library, one of the finest collections in the world for scholarly research in labor history, socialism, anarchism, communism, and American radicalism. Tamiment includes the Robert F. Wagner Labor Archives, the Archives of Irish America, the Center for the Cold War and the U.S., and the Frederic Ewen Academic Freedom Center.

New facilities

Since the early 2000s, NYU has developed new facilities on and around its Washington Square Campus. The Kimmel Center for University Life was built in 2003 to serve as the primary location for the university's student services offices. The center also houses the Skirball Center for the Performing Arts, the Rosenthal Pavilion, the Eisner & Lubin Auditorium, and the Loeb Student Center. The School of Law built Furman Hall in 2004, incorporating elements of two historic buildings into the new facade, one of which was occupied by poet Edgar Allan Poe.[42]

In 2005, NYU announced the development of a new life science facility on Waverly Place. The facility is the first NYU science building developed since the opening of Meyer Hall in 1971.[43] In November 2005, NYU announced plans to build a 26-floor, 190000-square-foot (18000 m^2) residence hall on 12th Street. The residence hall, named "Founders Hall", accommodates approximately 700 undergraduates and contains a host of other student facilities. It is currently the tallest building in the East Village.[44]

Brooklyn campus

Wunsch Building, a former church

The Polytechnic Institute of New York University, also known as the New York University School of Engineering and Technology, is located in Downtown Brooklyn. It is one of the oldest private technology institutes in the United States,[45] and has a distinguished history in electrical engineering, polymer chemistry, aerospace, and microwave engineering. It is centrally located in the MetroTech Center, and is close to transportation routes and easily accessible from all parts of New York City and Long Island. The institute has state-of-the-art facilities including a brand new library and new facilities for its electrical engineering, computer science and computer engineering programs. The Brooklyn campus offers programs primarily for undergraduate students but also offers opportunities for graduate students, including executive programs for students with related experience.

The Polymer Research Institute was established in 1942 and The Microwave Research Institute was established in 1945. The American Chemical Society designated the Polymer Research Institute as a National Historic Chemical Landmark on September 3, 2003.[46]

Polytechnic Institute played a leadership role in the establishment of the MetroTech Center, one of the largest urban university-corporate parks in the world and the largest in the United States. Today, the 16-acre (65,000 m²), $1 billion complex is home to the institute and several technology-dependent companies, including Securities Industry Automation Corporation (SIAC), New York City Police Department's 911 Center, New York City Fire Department

Headquarters and the U.S. technology and operations functions of JPMorgan Chase. In 1998, a Marriott Hotel was built adjacent to MetroTech. MetroTech has proven to be a case study in effective university, corporate, government and private-developer cooperation. It has resulted in renewing an area that once was characterized more by urban decay.

Wunsch Building houses the school's student union and is used to host many social, cultural, and academic events for the school and community. The building dates back to 1847 and was the first independent black church in Brooklyn. It was also a stop on the Underground Railroad and has been designated a historic landmark since November 24, 1981.

Dibner Library

The Bern Dibner Library of Science and Technology, opened in 1990 in a new building, is Polytechnic's information hub, accessible online from anywhere, on or off campus, 24 hours a day, seven days a week. In addition, wireless networks allow users with notebook computers to access the library's electronic services from anywhere on campus.

The Institute also has campuses in downtown Manhattan, Long Island, Westchester, and in international locations such as Israel, Abu Dhabi, Shanghai, and London.

Other campuses and facilities

The New York University School of Medicine is situated near the East River waterfront at 550 First Avenue between East 30th and East 34th Streets. The campus hosts the medical school, Tisch Hospital, and the Rusk Institute of Rehabilitation Medicine. Other NYU Centers across the city include NYU Hospital for Joint Diseases and the Bellevue Hospital Center. NYU's Silver School of Social Work (formerly Ehrenkranz School of Social Work) manages branch campus programs in Westchester County at Manhattanville College, in Rockland County at St. Thomas Aquinas College, and on Staten Island at the City University of New York's College of Staten Island.

11 West 42nd Street

In Sterling Forest, near Tuxedo, New York, NYU has a research facility that contains institutes, in particular the Nelson Institute of Environmental Medicine. The Midtown Center at 11 West 42nd Street and the Woolworth Building in the financial district are home to NYU's continuing education programs.

NYU has two units located on the Upper East Side. The Institute for the Study of the Ancient World, a discrete entity within New York University, independent of any other school or department of the university, is located on East 84th St, while the New York University Institute of Fine Arts, a graduate school of art history and fine arts, is located at the James B. Duke Building at 1 East 78th St.

NYU has a host of foreign facilities used for study abroad programs. One of the most noteworthy is the 57-acre (m^2) campus of NYU Florence Villa LaPietra in Italy, bequeathed by the late Sir Harold Acton to NYU in 1994.[47] NYU manages undergraduate academic-year and summer study abroad programs in Florence, London, Paris, Prague, Berlin, Accra, and Madrid, and recently started programs in Shanghai and Buenos Aires. On June 1, 2007, NYU announced plans to develop a campus in Israel with Tel Aviv

University. The program is scheduled to begin accepting students for the 2008-9 academic year.[48] The Israel program accepted a small group of students for the spring 2009 semester; however, they were sent to other NYU programs following the Gaza War for safety reasons. Students were able to participate in the program in the 2009-10 school year. Most recently, the government of the United Arab Emirates has announced plans to fund a campus abroad for NYU in the capital city of Abu Dhabi, the first of its kind to be established abroad by a major U.S. research university, which is set to receive students by 2010.[5] The campus construction (estimated at $1 to $1.5 billion) and operational costs will be entirely funded by the Emirati royal family.

La Maison Française

It was announced in 2011 that NYU has plans to open a third portal campus in Shanghai for the Fall semester of 2013. It is set to have about 3,000 undergraduate students, the majority of which will be Chinese. It was approved by the Ministry of Education of the People's Republic of China in Jan 2011.[49]

NYU also has international houses on campus, including the Deutsches Haus, La Maison Française, the Glucksman Ireland House, Casa Italiana, the King Juan Carlos I of Spain Center, the Hagop Kevorkian Center, an Africa House and a China House.

NYU was the founding member of the League of World Universities.

Sustainability

New York University has made the greening of its campus a large priority. For example, NYU has been the largest university purchaser of wind energy in the U.S. since 2009.[50] With this switch to renewable power, NYU is achieving benefits equivalent to removing 12,000 cars from the road or planting 72,000 trees. In May 2008, the N.Y.U. Sustainability Task Force awarded $150,000 in grants to 23 projects that would focus research and efforts toward energy, food, landscape, outreach, procurement, transportation and waste.[51] These projects include a student-led bike-sharing program modeled after Paris' Velib program with 30 bikes free to students, staff, and faculty. NYU received a grade of "B" on the College Sustainability Report Card 2010 from the Sustainable Endowments Institute.[52]

NYU purchased 118 million kilowatt-hours of wind power during the 2006-7 academic year – the largest purchase of wind power by any university in the country and any institution in New York City.[53] For 2007, the university expanded its purchase of wind power to 132 million kilowatt-hours.[54]

The EPA ranked NYU as one of the greenest college in the country in its annual College & University Green Power Challenge.[55]

Residence halls

Washington Square Village, home to NYU faculty and graduate students

With 12,500 residents, NYU has the seventh-largest university housing system in the U.S. and the largest among private schools.[8] NYU's undergraduate housing system consists of 21 buildings. Uniquely, many of NYU's residence halls are converted apartment complexes or old hotels. In general, NYU residence halls receive favorable ratings, and some are opulent. Many rooms are spacious and contain amenities considered rare for individual college residence hall rooms, such as kitchens and living rooms/common areas.[56] The university operates its own transit system to transport its students by bus to its campus.

Undergraduate students are guaranteed housing during their enrollment at NYU. Most freshman residence halls are in the Washington Square area. While nearly all of the residence halls that primarily house sophomores are in the Union Square area, two former residence halls were located in the Financial District and one is still in use in Chinatown. All of NYU's residence halls are governed by the Inter-Residence Hall Council (IRHC), an umbrella student council organization.

In 2007, the National Association of College and University Residence Halls named NYU the National School of the Year for IRHC and NRHH's strong efforts over the past year. In addition, NYU was named the National Program of the Year for UltraViolet Live, the annual inter-hall competition that raises funds for Relay For Life.

Academics

Schools and colleges

New York University comprises 18 colleges, schools, and institutes.[4]

Flags identify NYU buildings in the city. This flag is for the Gallatin School of Individualized Study

- Arts & Science
  - College of Arts and Science (CAS)
  - Liberal Studies (LSP)
  - Graduate School of Arts and Science (GSAS)
- College of Dentistry
- College of Nursing
- Courant Institute of Mathematical Sciences (Courant)
- Gallatin School of Individualized Study (Gallatin)
- Institute of Fine Arts
- Institute for the Study of the Ancient World
- Leonard N. Stern School of Business (Stern)
- NYU Abu Dhabi (NYUAD)
- Polytechnic Institute of New York University (Poly)
- Robert F. Wagner Graduate School of Public Service (Wagner)
- School of Continuing and Professional Studies (SCPS)
- School of Law
- School of Medicine
- Silver School of Social Work
- Steinhardt School of Culture, Education, and Human Development (Steinhardt)
- Tisch School of the Arts (Tisch)

Arts and Science is currently the largest academic unit of the university. It has three subdivisions, which include the College of Arts and Science, the Graduate School of Arts and Science, and Liberal Studies.[57] The College of Arts and Science (CAS) was the first and only school when NYU was founded.

Other undergraduate schools include the Gallatin School of Individualized Study; the School of Social Work; the Preston Robert Tisch Center for Hospitality, Tourism and Sports Management at the New York University School of Continuing and Professional Studies; the Steinhardt School of Culture, Education and Human Development — the first school of education in the United States; the Stern School of Business; and Tisch School of the Arts. In 2008 Polytechnic University merged with the university to become the Polytechnic Institute, providing NYU with an engineering school for the first time in three decades.[58] [59] The university is also planning to open up the Liberal Studies Program to all students for the Fall 2012 term by process of application, rather than by referral (as it has been since 1972).[60] [61] Several schools also offer graduate and professional programs.

NYU's postgraduate schools and divisions include the Gallatin School of Individualized Study, College of Dentistry, the College of Nursing, the Courant Institute of Mathematical Sciences, the Institute of Fine Arts, Institute for the Study of the Ancient World, the Polytechnic Institute, the School of Continuing and Professional Studies, the School of Law, the School of Medicine, Graduate School of Arts and Science, and the Wagner Graduate School of Public Service.

NYU closed its School of Aeronautics in 1973, its College of Veterinary Surgeons in 1922, and merged various previous programs with other schools. For example, its School of Engineering merged with the Polytechnic University of New York in 1973, and NYU's former College Hofstra Memorial became independent in 1937.[62]

Rankings

Only the most recent ranking from each source is listed in the table below.

Ranking System	Rank
Global University Ranking [63][11]	22
HIU World University Rankings [64]	23
MUP Top Research Universities[65]	27
QS World University Rankings[66]	44
SJU Academic Ranking of World Universities: National[67]	23
SJU Academic Ranking of World Universities: World[67]	31
Times Higher Education World University Rankings[68]	44
US News and World Report National University[69]	33
Washington Monthly National University[70]	47
Webometrics Ranking of World Universities	36

NYU is ranked 22nd among all universities in the world by Global University Ranking (maintained by Wuhan University) and as high as 29th in recent years by the Academic Ranking of World Universities (formerly maintained by Shanghai Jiaotong University).[11] [12] Many of NYU's schools and institutes are regularly ranked within the top 10 worldwide.[71] [72] [73] [74] [75] [76] [77] [78]

NYU's philosophy department is ranked #1 among 50 philosophy departments in the English-speaking world.[71] NYU is also ranked #1 in Italian, finance, mathematics, and theater in the U.S. by the Faculty Scholarly Productivity Index, which uses data, such as faculty publications, grants, and honors and awards to rank 104 doctoral programs in

10 academic disciplines based on the research productivity of faculty members.[72]

The Courant Institute of Mathematical Sciences is ranked #1 in applied mathematics in the U.S.,[76] #5 in citation impact worldwide and #12 in citations worldwide.[79] The Academic Ranking of World Universities ranked NYU's math department #16 overall among top universities globally.[80] The Courant Institute of Mathematical Sciences is also known for its research in pure mathematical areas, such as partial differential equations, probability and differential geometry (Professors Peter Lax, S. R. Srinivasa Varadhan and Mikhail Gromov won the 2005, 2007 and 2009 Abel Prize respectively for their research in these areas) as well as applied mathematical areas, such as computational biology and computational neuroscience.

NYU's Stern School of Business undergraduate program is ranked #5 by U.S. News[77] and #15 by Business Week[81] (previous rankings include #12 in 2010 and #8 in 2009). Stern's MBA program is ranked among the top in the U.S. and worldwide: #10 in U.S. News,[82] #15 in Financial Times,[83] #18 in BusinessWeek,[84] #14 in The Economist,[85] and #2 by research contribution.[86]

NYU's Polytechnic Institute was ranked #66 in the graduate program by the 2011 US News Best Colleges, and the graduate computer engineering program was ranked #34 in the nation for the best engineering specialty. The 2011 Best Engineering Colleges By Salary Potential ranked NYU-Poly #5 in the nation, determined by annual pay of bachelors graduates.

NYU's economics department is regularly ranked among the top 10 worldwide, including #6 in an updated Dusansky-Vernon Journal of Economic Literature study which ranked departments in terms of the publications of their faculty in top-five rated journals.[73] [87] NYU was ranked #9 globally in economics/business by the Academic Ranking of World Universities in 2009, one ahead of Yale University.[88]

The School of Law is ranked #6 among law schools in the U.S. by U.S. News and World Report (and has been ranked by the same source as high as #4 in previous years).[78] The law school is particularly noted as the nation's top law school in tax law, international law, and jurisprudence (philosophy of law).[89] [90] [91] Some of NYU's alumni have been appointed justices of the International Court of Justice and International Criminal Court.[92] [93] [94]

In the social sciences, NYU was ranked #10 by the Academic Ranking of World Universities in 2009, and #11 among Shanghai Jiao Tong University's world's top 100 universities.[95] [96] NYU's Steinhardt School of Culture, Education and Human Development has one of the top 15 education programs in the U.S.[97] NYU's Wagner Graduate School of Public Service is ranked 10th nationally by U.S. News and World Report. In addition, several of Wagner's public affairs specializations are ranked in the top 10.[74]

NYU's Tisch School of the Arts has produced more Academy Award winners than any other film institution in the U.S.[98] NYU Tisch members are regularly nominated to win Oscars, Emmys, and other awards: in 2011, 15 Tisch members were nominated for Oscars, and 10 Tisch members claimed Emmys.[18] [19]

NYU's Creative Writing Program (GSAS) was included within *The Atlantic's* list of "Top Ten Graduate Programs in Creative Writing," having been selected from a pool of over 250 such programs currently active in the United States.[75]

From 2004 to 2007, NYU was ranked by the Princeton Review as America's #1 "dream school" among high school seniors.[99] In 2008 however, NYU slipped to 4th place in the Princeton Review poll, led only by Harvard, Yale, and Stanford, citing better financial aid among Ivy Leagues and using additional parental ratings.[100] In 2006, NYU was named by Kaplan as one of the "New Ivies".[101]

According to data compiled by *Forbes Magazine* in 2008, NYU ranks 7th among universities that have produced the largest number of living billionaires.[102]

Admissions and enrollment

NYU has a large, diverse student population representing all 50 states and more than 130 countries.[58] About 25–30% of NYU's incoming freshmen are from New York, New Jersey, and Connecticut, while the remaining 70–75% are from outside the Tri-State Area. Ten percent of the students are from one of New York City's five boroughs and 20% are from the surrounding tri-state area. NYU's main feeder schools reflect a heavy Northeastern U.S. presence, and particularly a strong New York City influence. Among NYU's top feeder schools are prestigious high schools including Stuyvesant High School, Brooklyn Technical High School, Bronx High School of Science, and several top private schools in the northeast.

Out of the 42,242 applicants for the undergraduate class of 2015, around 30% were offered admission (when including admission statistics for the Liberal Studies Program). Out of the acceptances, 38% consisted of early decision applicants, who together form 23% of the undergraduate class. 4,650 new freshmen are set to begin studies at NYU in Fall 2011. In 2008, NYU achieved a record low admission rate of 24% of applicants.[103] [104]

Admission to NYU is extremely selective. The middle 50% of SAT scores for the class of 2015 was in the 630-730 range for critical reading, 650-750 for math, and 660-750 for writing, with mean scores falling within the top percentiles. The middle 50% of ACT scores for the class of 2015 fell between 29 and 31. The average GPA corresponds with an A-range letter grade, and most incoming students were in the top 10% of their class.[103]

On June 21, 2010, NYU announced the profile of the first freshman class of NYU Abu Dhabi, which calls itself the "World's Honors College". The class includes 150 students, 36% of whom are from the United States. The average SAT score was 1470 and the acceptance rate was just 2.1%.[105]

During the admissions process, some institutions at NYU are relatively more selective than others in certain categories, depending on the institution's educational goals. For example, NYU's Abu Dhabi program looks primarily for students who have demonstrated a history of leadership in addition to gifted intellectual ability (the average SAT scores of admitted students are 715 for verbal and 730 for math), whereas NYU's Tisch School of the Arts - while still requiring very high SAT/ACT scores - focuses much more on artistic and creative prowess (demonstrable via a portfolio) than do other schools at NYU.[106]

NYU is among the top 15 universities in the U.S. in the number of National Merit Scholars in the first-year undergraduate student body.[107]

Budget and fundraising

New York University has successfully completed a seven-year, $2.5 billion campaign, surpassing expectations by raising more than $3 billion over the seven-year period, the highest amount ever raised by any university in a completed campaign.[108] Started in 2001, this campaign was the university's largest in its history, as they planned to "raise $1 million per day for scholarships and financial aid, faculty building, new academic initiatives, and enhancing NYU's physical facilities".[109] The campaign included a $50 million gift from the Tisch family (after which one building and the art school are named) and a $60 million gift from six trustees called "The Partners Fund", aimed at hiring new faculty.[109] [110] On October 15, 2007 the university announced that the Silver family donated $50 million to the School of Social Work, which will be renamed as a result.[111] This is the largest donation ever to a school of social work in the United States.[112]

The 2007-8 academic year was the most successful fundraising year to date for NYU, with the school raising $698 million in only the first 11 months of the year, representing a 70% increase in donations from the prior year.[113] The University also recently announced plans for NYU's Call to Action, a new initiative to ask alumni and donors to support financial aid for students at NYU.[114]

The university has announced a 25-year strategic development plan, scheduled to coincide with its bicentennial in 2031. Included in the "NYU 200" plans are increasing resident and academic space, hiring additional exemplary faculty, and involving the New York City community in a transparent planning process. Additionally, NYU hopes to make their buildings more environmentally friendly, which will be facilitated by an evaluation of all campus spaces.[115] As a part of this plan, NYU purchased 118 million kilowatt-hours of wind power during the 2006-7 academic year – the largest purchase of wind power by any university in the country and any institution in New York City.[53] For 2007, the university expanded its purchase of wind power to 132 million kilowatt-hours.[54] As a result, the EPA ranked NYU as one of the greenest college in the country in its annual College & University Green Power Challenge.[55]

Student life

Student government

The Student Senators Council is governing student body at NYU. The SSC has been involved in controversial debates on campus, including a campuswide ban on the sale of Coca-Cola products in 2005[116] [117] and the Graduate Student Organizing Committee unionization in 2001[118] and subsequent strike in 2005.[119] This ban was lifted by the University Senate on February 5, 2009.[120]

Student organizations

NYU has over 450 student clubs and organizations on campus.[121] In addition to the sports teams, fraternities, sororities, and study clubs, there are many organizations on campus that focus on entertainment, arts, and culture. These organizations include various student media clubs: for instance, the daily student newspaper the *Washington Square News*, a daily blog NYU Local, comedy magazine *The Plague*, and the literary journals Washington Square Review and The Minetta Review, as well as student-run event producers such as the NYU Program Board and the Inter-Residence Hall Council. It also operates radio station WNYU-FM 89.1 with a diverse college radio format, transmitting to the entire New York metropolitan area from the original campus, and via booster station WNYU-FM1 which fills in the signal in lower Manhattan from atop one of the Silver Towers, next to the football field at the Washington Square campus.

nyu program board

NYU Program Board logo

A bus system transports students to and from the far ends of campus

During the University Heights era, an apparent rift evolved with some organizations distancing themselves from students from the downtown schools. The exclusive Philomathean Society operated from 1832 to 1888 (formally giving way in 1907 and reconstituted into the Andiron Club). Included among the Andiron's regulations was "Rule No.11: Have no relations save the most casual and informal kind with the downtown schools".[122] The Eucleian Society, rival to the Philomathean Society, was founded in 1832. The Knights of the Lamp was a social organization founded in 1914 at the School of Commerce. This organization met every full moon and had the glowworm as its mascot.[123] The Red Dragon Society, founded in 1898, is thought to be the most selective society at NYU. In addition, NYU's first yearbook was formed by fraternities and "secret societies" at the university.[124]

New York University has traditions which have persisted across campuses. Since the beginning of the 20th century initiation ceremonies have welcomed incoming NYU freshmen. At the Bronx University Heights Campus, seniors used to grab unsuspecting freshmen, take them to a horse-watering trough, and then dunk them head-first into what was known colloquially as "the fountain of knowledge." This underground initiation took place until the 1970s.[125]

Today freshmen take part in university-sponsored activities during what is called "Welcome Week." In addition, throughout the year the university traditionally holds Apple Fest (an apple-themed country fest that began at the University Heights campus), the Violet Ball (a dance in the atrium of Bobst Library), Strawberry Fest (featuring New York City's longest Strawberry Shortcake), and the semi-annual midnight breakfast where Student Affairs administrators serve free breakfast to students before finals.

Greek life

Greek life first formed on the NYU campus in 1837 when Psi Upsilon chartered its Delta Chapter.[9] The first fraternities at NYU were social ones. With their athletic, professional, intellectual, and service activities, later groups sought to attract students who also formed other groups. Since then, Greek letter organizations have proliferated to include 25 social fraternities and sororities. Approximately 7% of NYU students choose to join fraternities or sororities.[126]

Four governing boards oversee Greek life at the university. The Interfraternity Council (IFC) has jurisdiction over all 14 recognized fraternities on campus. Seven sororities are under the jurisdiction of the Panhellenic Council (PhC); four multicultural sororities maintain membership in the Multicultural Greek Council (MGC). All three of the aforementioned boards are managed under the auspices of the Inter-Greek Council.

Greek organizations have historical significance at NYU. Delta Phi Epsilon, Zeta Psi, Alpha Epsilon Pi, Tau Delta Phi,[127] Alpha Kappa Psi and Delta Sigma Pi were founded at NYU. Zeta Psi Fraternity of North America, was chartered in 1847.[10] Delta Sigma Pi, was chartered in 1907.[128] Alpha Epsilon Pi, was chartered in 1913.[129] The NYU Gamma chapter of Delta Phi, founded in 1841, is the longest continuously active fraternity chapter in the world, having never gone inactive since its establishment. Delta Phi is also oldest continuously active fraternity in the United States, being the only organization in the original Union Triad to remain active since its institute. The NYU Gamma chapter of Zeta Beta Tau is the oldest active ZBT chapter in the country. The PhC features four national sororities (ΠΒΦ, ΆΣΤ, ΔΦΈ, and ΑΈΦ) and three local sororities (ΚΨΔ, ΆΦΖ, and ΘΦΒ). Notably, the first chapter of Delta Phi Epsilon was founded at NYU in 1917.[130]

Athletics

NYU's sports teams are referred to as the NYU Violets, the colors being the trademarked hue "NYU Violet", and white. Since 1981, the school mascot has been a bobcat, whose origin can be traced back to the abbreviation then being used by the Bobst Library computerized catalog — short: Bobcat.[131] NYU's sports teams include men's and women's varsity basketball, cross country, fencing, golf, soccer, swimming and diving, tennis, track and field, volleyball, and wrestling.[132] With only two exceptions, all of NYU's sports teams participate in the NCAA's Division III and the University Athletic Association. The exceptions are men's volleyball, which competes in the Division I Eastern Collegiate Volleyball Association, and the fencing team, which also participates in Division I.

NYU Athletic Logo

While NYU has had All-American football players, the school has not had a varsity football team since the 1960s. Notable football players include Hall of Fame Ken Strong (1956) and Ed Smith (1934), the model for the Heisman Trophy.[133] In the 1940 season, before a football game between NYU and Missouri, students protested against the "gentlemen's agreement" to exclude black athletes (at Missouri's request). The protest against this practice is the first time such protests were recorded to have occurred.[134]

A hockey player during a game

Men's volleyball in Coles Sports Center

NYU, within its short history in NCAA Division III, has won two national team championships and many league championships. The basketball program has enjoyed a good deal of success since its return to intercollegiate competition. In 1997, the women's basketball team, led by head coach Janice Quinn, won a national championship over the University of Wisconsin–Eau Claire and in 2007 returned to the Final Four. NYU men's basketball and head coach Joe Nesci appeared in the Division III National Championship game in 1994. In 2006, the Men's cross country team finished 2nd at the NCAA Championship. The following year, led by Jon Phillips, the Men's cross country team won the 2007 NCAA National Cross Country Championship at St. Olaf College in Minnesota.

NYU men's and women's swimming teams captured consecutive (2004–2005) Eastern College Athletic Conference (ECAC) Division III Swimming and Diving Championships. Christian Majdick of the men's track and field team captured the NCAA Division III championship for the triple jump in 2003. Lauren Henkel, one of the most successful athletes in NYU track and field history, and the current assistant coach of the women's track and field team, acquired All-American status three times for High Jump. The men's soccer team won its league ECAC championship in the 2005–2006 season.

The Men's Ice Hockey Team participates in the ACHA (DII) and is in the SECHL. NYU's most successful season for their Ice Hockey team came during the 2003-2004 season, in which the team finished second (2nd) in the nation, losing to Oakland University of Michigan.

The National Intercollegiate Women's Fencing Association (NIWFA) was founded by NYU freshmen Julia Jones and Dorothy Hafner.[135]

It appears from older fight songs that Rutgers University was also NYU's rival at some point.[136]

NYU students also compete in club and intramural sports, including Men's Field Lacrosse, crew, squash, rugby union, badminton, ice hockey, baseball, softball, equestrian, martial arts, ultimate, and triathlon. The Coles Sports and Recreation Center serves as the home base of several of NYU's intercollegiate athletic teams. Many of NYU's varsity teams play their games at various facilities and fields throughout Manhattan because of the scarcity of space for playing fields near campus. In 2002, NYU opened the Palladium Athletic Facility as the second on-campus recreational facility. In the same year, NYU's intramural dance team won the National Championship title at the National Dance Alliance (NDA)Division III competition in Daytona, Florida.

Faculty and alumni

NYU counts 33 Nobel Prize winners by affiliation and 3 winners of the Abel prize; 10 National Medal of Science recipients; 16 Pulitzer Prize winners; 21 Academy Award winners;[18] [98] Emmy, Grammy, and Tony Award winners; and MacArthur and Guggenheim Fellowship holders[23] among its past and present graduates and faculty.[24] NYU has been insistent that its faculty be active in instruction on the undergraduate and graduate level, as well as active in research.[137] [15] [16]

As the largest private non-profit university in the country, NYU has one of the largest alumni bodies in the world. At the end of 2004, NYU had about 350,000 alumni. Of these, at least 17,000 live abroad.[138] The New York University Office for Alumni Affairs oversees the various activities, such as class reunions, local NYU Club gatherings, NYU alumni travel, and Career Services. The Alumni club on campus is the Torch Club. Notable graduating classes include 1941, which graduated three later Nobel Prize laureates (Julius Axelrod, Gertrude B. Elion and Clifford Shull), Olympic Gold Medalist John Woodruff, sportscaster Howard Cosell and sociologist Morris Janowitz; 1957 included Pulitzer Prize winning author Frank McCourt; 1970 included Thomas S. Popkewitz, professor of curriculum theory at the University of Wisconsin-Madison; 1974 included author Warren Farrell, Ph.D. ; and 1977 included: former Fed Chairman Alan Greenspan; IRS Commissioner Mark Everson; INSEAD Dean Gabriel Hawawini; Pulitzer, Oscar and Tony Award winner John Patrick Shanley; NHL Commissioner Gary Bettman; physicist Lewis E. Little; NASDAQ CEO Robert Greifeld; Ma Ying-jeou president of Republic of China (Taiwan); Guillermo Endara president of Republic of Panama, Clive Davis music industry executive, and Cathy Minehan, Federal Reserve Chairman Boston.

Since 1885, the most spirited undergraduate class has been awarded "The Bun". The award consisted of a bun enclosed in a long casket-like enclosure made of silver. The Bun was taken three times: in 1921, 1971, and 1981. The award was last returned in 2002 and currently resides in the Silver Center.[139]

The NYU Club in midtown closed its clubhouse in 1989. Alumni can now join the NYU Club, which is in residence at the Princeton Club across the street.

In film and literature

NYU is often portrayed in a variety of television shows, motion pictures, literature, and other media. Fictional NYU students and faculty include Kramer's intern Darren in *Seinfeld*, who helps him run "Kramerica Industries"; a student reporter in a different episode of Seinfeld who interviews Jerry; Theo Huxtable (Malcolm-Jamal Warner) from *The Cosby Show*, who graduates from NYU in the series finale; Ross Geller (David Schwimmer) from *Friends*, who becomes an NYU professor in Season 6; Character Tom Collins from *Rent*, who taught there; Bud Fox (Charlie Sheen) in the movie *Wall Street* (1987); Finch (Eddie Kaye Thomas) from the *American Pie* films; Paul Tannek (Jason Biggs) in *Loser* (2000); ; Alex Foreman (Scarlett Johansson) in *In Good Company* (2005); Jack Campbell (Nicolas Cage) in *The Family Man* (2000); and Clark Kellogg (Matthew Broderick) in *The Freshman* (1990). In the film version of *Thumbsucker* (2005), the main character, Justin Cobb (Lou Taylor Pucci), secretly applies and is accepted to NYU. In the musical *Bye Bye Birdie*, the struggling songwriter Albert Peterson promises his sweetheart Rosie to start studying at NYU and become an English teacher, so that they can marry. The third season of *Gossip Girl* features NYU prominently with characters Blair Waldorf, Dan Humphrey, Vanessa Abrams and Georgina Sparks attending their freshman year at the university. By fourth season, Blair Waldorf and Georgina Sparks both left the university, but Dan Humphrey and Vanessa Abrams are still said to be attending.

In addition, the campus of NYU has been the backdrop for pieces of fiction: Grace Adler's office in Will & Grace is portrayed in the show as being in the Puck Building, home to NYU's Wagner School; Henry James' novel *Washington Square* is set around the NYU area; *Rose of Washington Square* (1939), *13 Washington Square* (1928), *Annie Hall* (1977), *When Harry Met Sally* (1989), *I Am Legend* (2007), *August Rush* (2007), *Remember Me* (2010), *Step Up 3-D* (2010) and *The Sorcerer's Apprentice* (2010) are centered around the NYU Campus. In Ralph Bakshi's animated feature *Fritz The Cat* (1972), the dormitory that Fritz burns down is clearly supposed to be NYU's Weinstein Hall, located at 5-11 University Place near the northeast corner of Washington Square Park. The WB show *Felicity* was set at the "University of New York", clearly modeled after NYU; and NYU's old University Heights Campus in the Bronx provided the scenery for *Sophie's Choice* (1982), *The Thomas Crown Affair* (1999), *A Beautiful Mind* (2001), *Maid in Manhattan* (2002), and *Mona Lisa Smile* (2003). It's also featured in the TV show Californication.

See also

- Education in New York City

References

[1] "University's endowment improves after 2009 loss Initiative" (http://nyunews.com/news/2010/10/13/14endowment/). Washington Square News. October 14, 2010. . Retrieved 2010-10-14.

[2] "UniversityFacts" (http://www.nyu.edu/about/facts.html). New York University Office of Institutional Research and Program Evaluation. 2008. . Retrieved 2008-12-14.

[3] http://www.nyu.edu/

[4] "About NYU" (http://www.nyu.edu/about.html). New York University. . Retrieved 2010-03-21.

[5] Timm, Jane (September 13, 2010). "NYU Abu Dhabi: the story from concept to classroom" (http://nyunews.com/news/2010/09/13/13abudhabi/). nyunews.com. . Retrieved 2010-11-22.

[6] "NYU to open 1st American campus in Shanghai" (http://news.xinhuanet.com/english2010/culture/2011-01/21/c_13701018.htm). xinhuane news. . Retrieved 2011-02-01.

[7] "NYU > A&S > NYU-DC Center" (http://as.nyu.edu/page/NYUDC). New York University. . Retrieved 2009-05-06.

[8] "Top Ten Residence Hall Systems" (http://web.archive.org/web/20070305034155/http://www.housing.umich.edu/general/topten.html). University of Michigan Housing. Archived from the original (http://www.housing.umich.edu/general/topten.html) on March 5, 2007. . Retrieved 2007-07-16.

[9] "Psi Upsilon History" (http://web.archive.org/web/20070414185849/http://www.psiu.org/fr/history.html). Psi Upsilon Fraternity. 2006. Archived from the original (http://www.psiu.org/fr/history.html) on April 14, 2007. . Retrieved 2007-07-17.

[10] Sunshine, Jared (2007). "History" (http://web.archive.org/web/20070729224238/http://www.zetapsi.org/history.php). Zeta Psi Fraternity of North America, Inc.. Archived from the original (http://www.zetapsi.org/history.php) on July 29, 2007. . Retrieved 2007-07-17.

[11] http://www.globaluniversitiesranking.org/images/banners/top-100(eng).pdf

[12] "Academic Ranking of World Universities" (http://www.arwu.org). ARWU. . Retrieved 2010-12-29.

[13] "2005 Abel Laureate" (http://www.abelprisen.no/en/prisvinnere/2005/index.html). Abel Prize. . Retrieved 2008-12-31.

[14] "2007 Abel Laureate" (http://www.abelprisen.no/en/prisvinnere/2007/index.html). Abel Prize. . Retrieved 2008-12-31.

[15] "New York University" (http://philanthropy.com/employer/New-York-University/125/). The Chronicle of Philanthropy. . Retrieved 2011-10-02.

[16] "NYU Mathematician Varadhan Named Recipient of National Medal of Science" (http://www.nyu.edu/about/news-publications/news/2011/09/27/nyu-mathematician-varadhan-named-recipient-of-national-medal-of-science.html). NYU. . Retrieved 2011-10-02.

[17] *About New York University* (http://www.collegecrunch.org/school-profiles/new-york-university/). College Crunch. . Retrieved 2009-02-27.

[18] "Two NYU Filmmakers Win Oscars!" (http://www.nyu.edu/about/news-publications/news/2011/02/28/two-nyu-filmmakers-win-oscars.html). nyu.edu. . Retrieved 2011-03-02.

[19] "Tisch Community Claim Emmys®!" (http://www.tisch.nyu.edu/object/2011_creative-primetime_emmy_winners.html). NYU Tisch. . Retrieved 2011-10-02.

[20] *NYU Alumni Score Big at the 2007 Emmys* (http://www.nyu.edu/nyutoday/article/787). **21**. NYU Today. 2007. . Retrieved 2009-02-05.

[21] *Jazz Studies Professor and Trumpeter Brian Lynch Wins Grammy Award for Album Simpático* (http://www.nyu.edu/nyutoday/article/505). **20**. NYU Today. 2006. . Retrieved 2009-02-05.

[22] "Tisch Wins at the 2004 Tony Awards" (http://alumni.tisch.nyu.edu/object/tsoa_tonyawards.html). Tisch School of the Arts. 2004. . Retrieved 2009-02-05.

[23] "Two NYU Professors Win Guggenheim Fellowships" (http://www.nyu.edu/public.affairs/releases/detail/469). NYU Office of Public Affairs. April 14, 2005. . Retrieved 2007-09-17.

[24] "Faculty Handbook" (http://www.nyu.edu/oaa/FacHbk2008.pdf) (PDF). NYU Office of Academic Appointments. 2008. . Retrieved 2009-02-05.

[25] Friss, Evan J.. "Window into the Past: NYU in Retrospect" (http://www.nyu.edu/library/bobst/research/arch/thenandnow/). New York University Archives. . Retrieved 2007-07-17.

[26] Burrows, Edwin G. & Wallace, Mike (1999). *Gotham: A History of New York City to 1898*. New York: Oxford University Press. ISBN 0195116348. pp. 531-532

[27] "175 Facts About NYU" (http://www.nyu.edu/library/bobst/research/arch/175/pages/heights.htm). NYU.edu. . Retrieved 2010-12-29.

[28] "Capital Campaign" (http://www.hofstra.edu/alumni/support/devcc/devcc_growth.html). Hofstra University. . Retrieved 2009-02-22.

[29] "NYU and the Village: History" (http://www.nyu.edu/library/bobst/collections/exhibits/bobst/washsq/history/history.html). New York University Archives. . Retrieved 2007-07-17.

[30] Laura Turegano. "Fundraising Beyond U.S. Borders - NYU: A Success Story". *onPhilantrophy*, December 13, 2001. http://www.onphilanthropy.com/prof_inter/pi2001-12-13a.html

[31] Weiss, Kenneth R. (March 22, 2000). "NYU Earns Respect" (http://www.nyu.edu/financial.aid/latimes2000-03-22.pdf) (PDF). *Los Angeles Times*. . Retrieved 2007-10-11.

[32] Honan, William H. (1995-03-20). "Buying Excellence: How N.Y.U. Rebuilt Itself -- A special report.; Decade and $1 Billion Put N.Y.U. With the Elite" (http://query.nytimes.com/gst/fullpage.html?res=990CE6DE1F3BF933A15750C0A963958260&sec=&spon=&pagewanted=1). The New York Times. . Retrieved 2008-03-05.

[33] "NYU Kicks Off $2.5 Billion Campaign" (http://www.nyu.edu/alumni/newsletter/0105/campaign.html). NYU Office for University Development and Alumni relations. January 2005. . Retrieved 2007-07-15.

[34] Grey Art Gallery art collection (http://www.nyu.edu/greyart/collection/collection.html) Retrieved March 5, 2011

[35] The Grey Art Gallery (http://www.nyu.edu/greyart/) Retrieved March 5, 2011

[36] "Commencement ceremony" (http://www.nyu.edu/commencement/ceremony.html). NYU. . Retrieved 2010-04-17.

[37] "Speech at New York University" (http://www.globalsecurity.org/wmd/library/news/iraq/2004/09/iraq-040920-kerry01.htm). GlobalSecurity.org. April 20, 2004. . Retrieved 2007-07-15.

[38] "Former Vice President Al Gore Remarks to MoveOn.org" (http://www.moveon.org/gore-speech.html). MoveOn.org. August 7, 2003. . Retrieved 2007-07-15.

[39] "The Skirball Center for the Performing Arts" (http://www.nyu.edu/kimmel/perf_arts.shtml). NYU Office for University Development and Alumni Relations. . Retrieved 2007-07-15.

[40] "Helen and Martin Kimmel Center for University Life, NYU" (http://www.krjda.com/text/projectDetail.cfm?id=100). Kevin Roche John Dinkeloo and Associates LLC - Architects. . Retrieved 2007-07-15.

[41] "About the NYU Libraries" (http://library.nyu.edu/about/about.html). NYU Libraries. June 2007. . Retrieved 2007-07-15.

[42] Amateau, Albert (January 14–20, 2004). "N.Y.U. opens new building for law school" (http://www.thevillager.com/villager_37/nyuopensnew.html). *The Villager* **73** (37). . Retrieved 2007-10-11.

[43] Anderson, Lincoln (November 17–22, 2004). "N.Y.U. to use Waverly buildings for its new life sciences center" (http://www.thevillager.com/villager_81/nyutousewaverly.html). *The Villager* **74** (28). . Retrieved 2007-10-11.

[44] Skalka, Liz (November 8, 2005). "New dorm coming in 2009: 26-story residence hall to be built on 12th Street" (http://nyunews.com/2005/11/08/9/). *Washington Square News*. . Retrieved 2007-10-11.

[45] "About Poly" (http://www.poly.edu/about/). Polytechnic University of NYU. . Retrieved 2008-12-24.

[46] "Polymer Research Institute" (http://portal.acs.org/portal/acs/corg/content?_nfpb=true&_pageLabel=PP_ARTICLEMAIN&node_id=930&content_id=CTP_004592&use_sec=true&sec_url_var=region1&__uuid=1cd6888c-c9c1-46e0-8b39-8782953586bd). Portal.acs.org. . Retrieved 2011-04-05.

[47] "NYU marks years of successful restoration at La Pietra" (http://www.nyu.edu/nyutoday/archives/16/01/Stories/LaPietra.html). *NYU Today* **16** (1). September 5, 2002. . Retrieved 2007-07-16.

[48] "NYU Announces Plans to Open Study Abroad Site in Israel" (http://www.nyu.edu/public.affairs/releases/detail/1641). NYU Office of Public Affairs. June 1, 2007. . Retrieved 2007-07-16.

[49] "China's Education Ministry Approves NYU Portal Campus in Shanghai" (http://nyulocal.com/on-campus/2011/01/21/chinas-education-ministry-approves-nyu-portal-campus-in-shanghai/). NYU Local. January 21, 2011. . Retrieved 2011-04-21.

[50] Sustainability>About Sustainability>Fast Facts"> "NYU Sustainability Fast Facts" (http://www.nyu.edu/sustainability/about.sustainability/fast.facts.html). New York University. . Retrieved 2009-06-08.

[51] "At New York University, green is the new violet" (http://www.nyu.edu/sustainability/about.sustainability/fast.facts.html). The Villager. . Retrieved 2009-06-08.

[52] "College Sustainability Report Card 2010" (http://www.greenreportcard.org/report-card-2010/f). Sustainable Endowments Institute. .

[53] "NYU, Ivy Leagues Top Schools for Green Power" (http://www.greenbiz.com/news/news_third.cfm?NewsID=34925). GreenBiz.com. April 19, 2007. . Retrieved 2007-09-12.

[54] "NYU buys more wind power credit" (http://media.www.nyunews.com/media/storage/paper869/news/2007/11/15/UniversityNews/Nyu-Buys.More.Wind.Power.Credit-3103146.shtml). Washington Square News. November 15, 2007. . Retrieved 2008-07-22.

[55] "NYU to Purchase Wind-Generated Power As Part of New Sustainability Initiative" (http://www.nyu.edu/public.affairs/releases/detail/1235). NYU Office of Public Affairs. October 5, 2006. . Retrieved 2007-09-12.

[56] Turley, Meredith (July 1, 2006). *New York University: Off the Record*. College Prowler. p. 161. ISBN 978-1427401021.

[57] "Arts & Science" (http://as.nyu.edu/page/asHome). As.nyu.edu. . Retrieved 2010-07-11.

[58] "About NYU" (http://www.nyu.edu/about/facts.html). New York University Office of Institutional Research and Program Evaluation. . Retrieved 2007-07-16.

[59] "Statement by NYU Provost David Mclaughlin On Regents' Vote On NYU and Poly" (http://www.nyu.edu/public.affairs/releases/detail/2180). Nyu.edu. . Retrieved 2011-04-05.

[60] http://nyunews.com/opinion/2010/11/01/02obrien/

[61] http://ls.nyu.edu/page/faq

[62] Blair, Cynthia. "1935: Hofstra University Founded" (http://web.archive.org/web/20071017202401/http://newsday.com/other/special/ny-iholi0905story,0,4371488.htmlstoryp). *It Happened on Long Island.* Newsday.com. Archived from the original (http://www.newsday.com/other/special/ny-iholi0905story,0,4371488.htmlstoryp) on 2007-10-17. . Retrieved 2007-07-15.

[63] http://globaluniversitiesranking.org

[64] "High Impact Universities - World University Rankings - Results for 2010" (http://www.highimpactuniversities.com/rpi.html). High Impact Universities. . Retrieved 2011-04-22.

[65] "The Top American Research Universities" (http://mup.asu.edu/research2009.pdf). The Center for Measuring University Performance. . Retrieved 2011-04-22.

[66] {{cite web|url=http://www.topuniversities.com/university-rankings/world-university-rankings/2011

[67] "ARWU 2010" (http://www.arwu.org/ARWU2010.jsp). Arwu.org. . Retrieved 2011-04-05.

[68] "Top 400 - The Times Higher Education World University Rankings 2011-2012" (http://www.timeshighereducation.co.uk/world-university-rankings/2011-2012/top-400.html). Timeshighereducation.co.uk. . Retrieved 2011-10-8.

[69] "New York University | Overall Rankings | Best College | US News" (http://colleges.usnews.rankingsandreviews.com/best-colleges/new-york-university-193900/overall-rankings). Colleges.usnews.rankingsandreviews.com. . Retrieved 2011-04-05.

[70] "National University Rankings 2010" (http://www.washingtonmonthly.com/college_guide/rankings_2010/national_university_rank.php). Washington Monthly. . Retrieved 2011-04-05.

[71] "The Philosophical Gourmet Report" (http://www.philosophicalgourmet.com/overall.asp). Brian Leiter. 2006. . Retrieved 2007-07-16.

[72] Fogg, Piper (January 12, 2007). "A New Standard for Measuring Doctoral Programs" (http://chronicle.com/free/v53/i19/19a00801.htm). *The Chronicle of Higher Education* **53** (19): pp. A8. .

[73] Kalaitzidakis, Pantelis (June 2003). "Rankings of Academic Journals and Institutions in Economics" (http://www.uoguelph.ca/~tstengos/eearank93.pdf) (PDF). . Retrieved 2007-07-16.

[74] "The NYU Wagner Education" (http://wagner.nyu.edu/academics/). NYU Wagner. . Retrieved 2007-07-16.

[75] *The Best of the Best: A Guide to Graduate Programs in Creative Writing* (http://www.theatlantic.com/doc/200708/mfa-programs). The Atlantic. 2007. .

[76] "America's Best Graduate Schools 2010" (http://grad-schools.usnews.rankingsandreviews.com/grad/mat/applied_math). USNews & World Report. 2010. .

[77] "Best Undergraduate Business Schools" (http://colleges.usnews.rankingsandreviews.com/college/spec-business). U.S. News. 2008. . Retrieved 2008-12-31.

[78] "America's Best Graduate Schools 2010" (http://grad-schools.usnews.rankingsandreviews.com/grad/law/search). USNews & World Report. 2010. .

[79] "Mathematics Research: Institutions Ranked by Citations and Citation Impact" (http://www.sciencewatch.com/may-june2002/sw_may-june2002_page2.htm). *Science Watch* **13** (3). May/June 2002. . Retrieved 2007-07-16.

[80] "ARWU SUBJECT 2009 Mathematics" (http://www.arwu.org/SubjectMathematics2009.jsp). Arwu.org. . Retrieved 2010-12-29.

[81] "The Top Undergraduate Business Programs" (http://www.businessweek.com/interactive_reports/bs_ugrank_tab_0303.html). Business Week. 2011. .

[82] "America's Best Graduate Schools 2010" (http://grad-schools.usnews.rankingsandreviews.com/grad/mba/search). USNews & World Report. 2010. .

[83] "Global MBA Rankings 2011" (http://rankings.ft.com/businessschoolrankings/global-mba-rankings-2011). Financial Times. 2011. . Retrieved 2011-05-21.

[84] "2010 Full-Time MBA Program Rankings" (http://www.businessweek.com/bschools/content/nov2010/bs20101110_255552.htm). BusinessWeek. 2010. . Retrieved 2011-05-21.

[85] "Best Full-time MBA Programmes" (http://www.economist.com/whichmba). The Economist. 2010. . Retrieved 2011-05-21.

[86] "The UTD top 100 World Wide Rankings of Business Schools based on Research Contribution 2002-2006" (http://citm.utdallas.edu/utdrankings/RankingWorldwide_static.aspx). The University of Texas at Dallas. 2006. . Retrieved 2007-07-16.

[87] "Rankings of U.S. Economics Departments" (http://163.117.2.172/iue/rankings/3.pdf). American Economic Association. . Retrieved 2011-02-01.

[88] "ARWU SUBJECT 2009 Economics / Business" (http://www.arwu.org/SubjectEcoBus2009.jsp). Arwu.org. . Retrieved 2010-12-29.

[89] "Law Specialty Rankings: Tax Law" (http://grad-schools.usnews.rankingsandreviews.com/grad/law/tax). USNews. . Retrieved 2008-12-30.

[90] "Law Specialty Rankings: International Law" (http://grad-schools.usnews.rankingsandreviews.com/grad/law/internationall). USNews. . Retrieved 2008-12-30.

[91] "Law School Faculty Quality: Who is Up and Who is Down Since 2003" (http://leiterlawschool.typepad.com/leiter/2006/07/law_school_facu.html). Brian Leiter. . Retrieved 2008-12-30.

[92] "Notable NYU School of Law Alumni" (http://www3.law.nyu.edu/alumni/notable.html). NYU School of Law. . Retrieved 2007-07-16.

[93] "NYU Law's Owada named to International Court of Justice" (http://www.nyu.edu/nyutoday/archives/16/04/Stories/Law.html). *NYU Today* **16** (4). December 10, 2002. . Retrieved 2007-07-16.

[94] "International Criminal Court: Judge Nsereko" (http://www.icc-cpi.int/chambers/judges/Nsereko_David.html). . Retrieved 2008-10-16.

[95] "ARWU FIELD 2009 Social Sciences" (http://www.arwu.org/FieldSOC2009.jsp). Arwu.org. . Retrieved 2010-12-29.

[96] "Top 100 world universities in Social Sciences" (http://ed.sjtu.edu.cn/ARWU-FIELD2007/SOC.htm). Institute of Higher Education, Shanghai Jiao Tong University. 2007. . Retrieved 2007-07-16.

[97] "America's Best Graduate Schools 2010" (http://www.usnews.com/usnews/edu/grad/rankings/edu/brief/edurank_brief.php). USNews & World Report. 2010. .

[98] "NYU Celebrates its 175th Anniversary" (http://www.nyu.edu/alumni/news/AlumSpring06/NewsFeatures/175-anniversary.html). *NYU Alumni News* **12** (1). Spring 2006. . Retrieved 2007-07-24.

[99] O'Neill, James M. (March 28, 2007). *NYU Tops Harvard for Fourth Year as Dream School' for Students* (http://www.bloomberg.com/apps/news?pid=20601103&sid=a00xg.dB1eQI&refer=us). Bloomberg. . Retrieved 2007-07-16.

[100] Platt, Eric (March 31, 2008). *After 4 years on top, NYU dreamy no more* (http://media.www.nyunews.com/media/storage/paper869/news/2008/03/31/University/After.4.Years.On.Top.Nyu.Dreamy.No.More-3291425.shtml). Washington Square News. . Retrieved 2008-03-31.

[101] "America's 25 New Elite 'Ivies'" (http://web.archive.org/web/20070708135928/http://www.msnbc.msn.com/id/14325172/site/newsweek/). Newsweek. August 21–28, 2006. Archived from the original (http://www.msnbc.msn.com/id/14325172/site/newsweek/) on 2007-07-08. . Retrieved 2007-07-16.

[102] "The Billionaire Universities 2008" (http://www.forbes.com/2008/05/19/billionaires-harvard-education-biz-billies-cx_af_0519billieu.html). *Forbes*. 2008. . Retrieved 2008-04-19.

[103] "Just The Facts" (http://www.nyu.edu/admissions/undergraduate-admissions/is-nyu-right-for-you/faqs.html). New York University. . Retrieved 2011-04-22.

[104] "Admission rate drops to 24%, lowest in years" (http://www.nyunews.com/2008/04/02/11/). *Washington Square News*. April 2, 2008. . Retrieved October 12, 2011.

[105] Redden, Elizabeth (2010-06-21). "NYU admits first class for its new Abu Dhabi campus" (http://www.usatoday.com/news/education/2010-06-21-IHE-NYU-Abu-Dhabi21_ST_N.htm?csp=34news&utm_source=feedburner&utm_medium=feed&utm_campaign=Feed:+usatoday-NewsTopStories+(News+-+Top+Stories)). *USA Today*. . Retrieved 2010-07-11.

[106] Foderaro, Lisa W. (June 20, 2010). "N.Y.U. Abu Dhabi Scours Globe for Top Students" (http://www.nytimes.com/2010/06/21/education/21nyu.html?adxnnl=1&ref=homepage&src=me&adxnnlx=1277128960-M5DpEmMP8216O4R/A/b+7w). *The New York Times*. . Retrieved 2010-06-21.

[107] "Recognizing Our Nation's Intellectual Talent: 2005–06 Annual Report" (http://nationalmerit.org/06_annual_report.pdf). National Merit Scholarship Corporation. 2006. . Retrieved 2007-07-16.

[108] Masterson, Kathryn (2008). "NYU Sets Record With $3.1-Billion Campaign" (http://chronicle.com/news/article/5430/nyu-sets-record-with-31-billion-campaign). . Retrieved 2008-11-01.

[109] Beckman, John (April 28, 2004). *New York University Kick Off $2.5 Billion Fundraising Campaign* (http://www.nyu.edu/publicaffairs/newsreleases/b_nyu_campaign_09282004.shtml). NYU Office Public Affairs. . Retrieved 2007-09-04.

[110] "The Campaign for NYU" (http://web.archive.org/web/20070822075608/http://campaign.nyu.edu/). NYU Office for University Development & Alumni Relations. Archived from the original (http://campaign.nyu.edu/) on August 22, 2007. . Retrieved 2007-09-04.

[111] *NYU Alumni Constance & Martin Silver Donate $50 Million to University's School of Social Work* (http://www.nyu.edu/public.affairs/releases/detail/1790). NYU Office Public Affairs. October 15, 2007. . Retrieved 2007-10-17.

[112] Jaschik, Scott (October 17, 2007). *Quick Takes* (http://www.insidehighered.com/news/2007/10/17/qt). Inside Higher Ed. . Retrieved 2007-10-17.

[113] Souccar, Miriam (2008). "Local universities report banner fundraising years" (http://www.crainsnewyork.com/apps/pbcs.dll/article?AID=/20080801/FREE/659182051/1046/toc). . Retrieved 2008-08-02.

[114] Platt, Eric (2008). "Over seven years, NYU rakes in $3 billion" (http://nyunews.com/news/university/over_seven_years%2C_nyu_rakes_in_3_billion). . Retrieved 2008-09-09.

[115] Portlock, Sarah (April 24, 2007). "NYU unveils 25-year plan" (http://web.archive.org/web/20070822173414/http://media.www.nyunews.com/media/storage/paper869/news/2007/04/24/News/Nyu-Unveils.25Year.Plan-2876454.shtml). *Washington Square News*. Archived from the original (http://media.www.nyunews.com/media/storage/paper869/news/2007/04/24/News/Nyu-Unveils.25Year.Plan-2876454.shtml) on August 22, 2007. . Retrieved 2007-09-04.

[116] Leonard, Barbara (November 4, 2005). "Coca-Cola given ultimatum" (http://media.www.nyunews.com/media/storage/paper869/news/2005/11/04/NewscampusNews/CocaCola.Given.Ultimatum-2387167.shtml). *Washington Square News*. . Retrieved 2007-10-12.

[117] Woyke, Elizabeth (January 23, 2006). "How NYU Chose Colombia over Coke" (http://www.businessweek.com/magazine/content/06_04/b3968078.htm). *Business Week*. . Retrieved 2007-10-12.

[118] Smallwood, Scott (March 16, 2001 (cached 6/28/07)). "A Big Breakthrough for T.A. Unions" (http://64.233.169.104/search?q=cache:Nf-NgBDA648J:chronicle.com/weekly/v47/i27/27a01001.htm). *The Chronicle of Higher Education*. . Retrieved 2007-10-12.

[119] Coe III, Richard M. (December 6, 2005). "NYU graduate assistants pledge to continue strike" (http://media.www.dailytarheel.com/media/storage/paper885/news/2005/12/06/StateNational/Nyu-Graduate.Assistants.Pledge.To.Continue.Strike-1368324.shtml). *Daily*

Tar Heel. . Retrieved 2007-10-12.

[120] Hernandez, Sergio (February 5, 2009). *Coke ban lifted* (http://www.nyunews.com/news/university/coke_ban_lifted-1.1356379). Washington Square News. . Retrieved 2009-02-08.

[121] "New York University:Housing & Campus Life" (http://collegesearch.collegeboard.com/search/CollegeDetail.jsp?collegeId=3186&profileId=8). College Board. 2007. . Retrieved 2007-10-10.

[122] "Guide to the Andiron Club of New York City" (http://dlib.nyu.edu/eadapp/transform?source=archives/andiron.xml&style=archives/archives.xsl). New York University Archives. . Retrieved 2007-07-17.

[123] "A Window Into the Past: NYU in Retrospect" (http://www.nyu.edu/library/bobst/research/arch/thenandnow/leisure.html). New York University Archives. . Retrieved 2007-07-15.

[124] "175 Facts About NYU" (http://www.nyu.edu/library/bobst/research/arch/test/175/pages/year.htm). New York University Archives. . Retrieved 2007-07-15.

[125] Friss, Evan (September 13, 2004). "Chronicles: A Look at NYU's Past" (http://www.nyu.edu/nyutoday/archives/18/01/Stories/chronicles-18-01.html). *NYU Today* **18** (1). . Retrieved 2007-07-17.

[126] "New York University: Campus Life" (http://colleges.usnews.rankingsandreviews.com/usnews/edu/college/directory/brief/drlife_2785_brief.php). US News & World Report. 2008. . Retrieved 2007-12-28.

[127] "Our History" (http://www.taudeltaphifraternity.org/history.php). Tau Delta Phi Fraternity, Inc.. 2007. . Retrieved 2008-10-20.

[128] "History" (http://web.archive.org/web/20080319093432/http://www.dspnet.org/site/about_us/history.asp). International Business Fraternity of Delta Sigma Pi. 2008. Archived from the original (http://www.dspnet.org/site/about_us/history.asp) on March 19, 2008. . Retrieved 2008-04-25.

[129] "History - Alpha Epsilon Pi" (http://web.archive.org/web/20070523171037/http://www.aepi.org/site/pp.asp?c=geJQIUOwErH&b=2117019). Kintera, Inc.. Archived from the original (http://www.aepi.org/site/pp.asp?c=geJQIUOwErH&b=2117019) on 2007-05-23. . Retrieved 2007-07-17.

[130] "History and Traditions" (http://web.archive.org/web/20070628142321/http://www.dphie.org/general/index.shtml). Delta Phi Epsilon International Sorority. Archived from the original (http://www.dphie.org/general/index.shtml) on June 28, 2007. . Retrieved 2007-07-17.

[131] "History of the Bobcat" (http://web.archive.org/web/20070612225016/http://www.nyu.edu/athletics/clubs/mascots/history.html). New York University. Archived from the original (http://www.nyu.edu/athletics/clubs/mascots/history.html) on 2007-06-12. . Retrieved 2010-12-29.

[132] "NYU Athletics" (http://www.gonyuathletics.com/). New York University. . Retrieved 2011-04-22.

[133] "The Heisman Trophy" (http://www.heisman.com/history/heisman-trophy.html). CSTV Networks, Inc. and Heisman.com.. 2007. . Retrieved 2007-07-17.

[134] "Evelyn Witkin Reflects on Cold Spring Harbor's Golden Age" (http://www.exploratorium.edu/origins/coldspring/dispatch/witkin.html). Exploratorium. . Retrieved 2007-07-15.

[135] "The Organization" (http://www.niwfa.com/). National Intercollegiate Women's Fencing Association. . Retrieved 2007-07-17.

[136] O'Brien, Robert F. (September 30, 1991). *School Songs of America's Colleges and Universities: A Directory*. Greenwood Press. p. 208. ISBN 978-0313278907.

[137] "Populist manifesto" (http://education.guardian.co.uk/egweekly/story/0,5500,949801,00.html). London: Guardian Unlimited. May 6, 2003. . Retrieved 2007-07-16.

[138] "New York University Alumni" (http://www.nyu.edu/alumni/). NYU Office of Development & Alumni Relations. . Retrieved 2007-07-17.

[139] "175 Facts About NYU" (http://www.nyu.edu/library/bobst/research/arch/175/pages/bun.htm). New York University Archives. . Retrieved 2007-07-17.

Further reading

- Dim, Joan (2000). *The Miracle on Washington Square*. Lanham, MD: Lexington Books.
- Frusciano, Tom & Pettit, Marilyn (1997). *New York University and the City, an Illustrated History*. New Brunswick, NJ: Rutgers University Press.
- Gitlow, Abrahm L. (1995). *NYU's Stern School of Business: A Centennial Retrospective*. New York: NYU Press.
- Harris, Luther S. (2003). *Around Washington Square : An Illustrated History of Greenwich Village*. Baltimore, MD: Johns Hopkins University Press.
- Hester, James M. (1971). *New York University; the urban university coming of age*. New York: Newcomen Society in North America. OCLC 140405.
- Jones, Theodore F. (1933). *New York University, 1832-1932*. London: H. Milford, Oxford University Press.
- Lewis, Naphtali (1968). *Greek papyri in the collection of New York University*. Leiden: E.J. Brill.

- Tonne, Herbert A., ed (1981). *Early Leaders in Business Education at New York University*. Reston, Virginia: National Business Education Association.
- Potash, David M. (1991). *The Graduate School of Arts and Sciences at New York University: A History*. New York: NYU Arts and Sciences Publications.

External links

- Official website (http://http://www.nyu.edu)
- New York University Press (http://nyupress.org/)
- Official NYU Athletics website (http://www.gonyuathletics.com/)
- New York University (http://topics.nytimes.com/top/reference/timestopics/organizations/n/new_york_university/) collected news and commentary at *The New York Times*

Courant Institute of Mathematical Sciences

Courant Institute of Mathematical Sciences (CIMS)	
Established	1935
Type	Private
Academic staff	82
Undergraduates	1,500
Postgraduates	600
Location	New York City, New York, USA
Director	Gerard Ben Arous
Website	CIMS.NYU.EDU [1]

Courant Institute of Mathematical Sciences

The **Courant Institute of Mathematical Sciences (CIMS)** is an independent division of New York University (NYU) under the Faculty of Arts & Science that serves as a center for research and advanced training in computer science and mathematics. The Director of the Courant Institute directly reports to New York University's Provost and President and works closely with deans and directors of other NYU colleges and divisions respectively.[2] The Courant Institute is named after Richard Courant, one of the founders of the Courant Institute and also a mathematics professor at New York University from 1936 to 1972.

The Courant Institute of Mathematical Sciences is considered one of the most prestigious and leading mathematics schools and mathematical sciences research centers in the world. The Courant Institute of Mathematical Sciences is ranked #1 in applied mathematical research,[3] #5 in citation impact worldwide, and #12 in citation worldwide. On the Faculty Scholarly Productivity Index, it is ranked #3 with an index of 1.84.[4] It is also known for its extensive research in pure mathematical areas, such as partial differential equations, probability and geometry, as well as applied mathematical areas, such as computational biology, computational neuroscience, and mathematical finance. The Mathematics Department of the Courant Institute has 18 members of the National Academy of Sciences (more than any other mathematics department in the U.S.) and five members of the National Academy of Engineering. Four faculty members have been awarded the National Medal of Science, one was honored with the prestigious Kyoto Prize, and nine have received career awards from the National Science Foundation. Courant Institute professors Peter Lax, S. R. Srinivasa Varadhan, Mikhail Gromov won the 2005, 2007 and 2009 Abel Prize respectively for their research in partial differential equations, probability and geometry.[5]

Although run independently by the Courant Institute, the undergraduate programs and graduate programs at the Courant Institute are formally associated with the NYU College of Arts and Science and NYU Graduate School of Arts and Science respectively.

Academics

Rankings

The Courant Institute specializes in applied mathematics, mathematical analysis and scientific computation. There is emphasis on partial differential equations and their applications. The mathematics department is constantly ranked in the United States as #1 in applied mathematics.[3] Other strong points are analysis (currently #5)[6] and geometry (currently #10).[7] Within the field of computer science, CIMS concentrates in theory, programming languages, computer graphics and parallel computing. The computer science program is ranked 28th among computer science programs in the US.[8]

Admissions

View of Warren Weaver Hall, Courant Institute of Mathematical Sciences from the Ground Floor of Gould Plaza

The Courant Institute offers Bachelors of Arts, Bachelors of Science, Master of Science and Ph.D. degree programs in both mathematics and computer science with program acceptance rates ranging from 3% to 29%.[9] The overall acceptance rate for all CIMS graduate programs is 15%, and program admissions reviews are holistic. A high undergraduate GPA and high GRE score are typically prerequisites to admission to its graduate programs but are not required. Majority of accepted candidates met these standards. However, character and personal qualities and evidence of strong quantitative skills are very important admission factors. Consistent with its scientific breadth, the Institute welcomes applicants whose primary background is in quantitative fields such as economics, engineering, physics, or biology, as well as mathematics. For doctoral programs, research experience is required. Undergraduate program admissions are not directly administrated by CIMS but by the NYU undergraduate admissions office of College of Arts and Science.[10] [11] [12] [13]

Graduate Program

The Department of Mathematics at the Courant Institute offers PhDs in Mathematics, Atmosphere-Ocean Science, and Computational Biology; Masters of Science in Mathematical Finance, Mathematics, and Scientific Computing.

The Graduate Department of Mathematics at the Courant Institute offers balanced training in mathematics and its applications in the broadest sense. The Department occupies a leading position in pure and applied mathematics, especially in ordinary and partial differential equations, probability theory and stochastic processes, differential geometry, numerical analysis and scientific computation, mathematical physics, mathematical finance, material science, fluid dynamics, math biology, Atmosphere and Ocean science, and Computational Biology.[14] [15] The Mathematical Finance program is considered one of the best quantitative finance programs in the US with an acceptance rate of 8% and job placement rate of nearly 100% at time of graduation; it also offers a dual degree program in conjunction with the Stern School of Business.[10] [16] [17] [18] [19]

The Graduate Department of Computer Science offers a PhD in computer science. In addition it offers Master of Science degrees in computer science, information systems (in conjunction with the Stern School of Business), and in scientific computing. For the PhD program, every PhD computer science student must receive a grade of A or A- on the final examination for algorithms, systems, applications, and a PhD-level course chosen by the student that does not satisfy the first three requirements, such as cryptography and numerical methods. Students may take the final exam for any these courses without being enrolled in the course.

Lecture Hall at Warren Weaver Hall

The Computer Science Masters program offers instruction in the fundamental principles, design and applications of computer systems and computer technologies. Students who obtain an MS degree in computer science are qualified to do significant development work in the computer industry or important application areas. Those who receive a doctoral degree are in a position to hold faculty appointments and do research and development work at the forefront of this rapidly changing and expanding field. The emphasis for the MS in Information Systems program is on the use of computer systems in business. For the Master of Science in Scientific Computing, it is designed to provide broad training in areas related to scientific computing using modern computing technology and mathematical modeling arising in various applications. The core of the curriculum for all computer science graduate students consists of courses in algorithms, programming languages, compilers, artificial intelligence, database systems, and operating systems. Advanced courses are offered in many areas such as natural language processing, the theory of computation, computer vision, software engineering, compiler optimization techniques, computer graphics, distributed computing, multimedia, networks, cryptography and security, groupware and computational finance. Adjunct faculty, drawn from outside academia, teach special topics courses in their areas of expertise.[20]

Most Courant PhD students are fully funded and are paid with a 9-month stipend. Doctoral students take advanced courses in their areas of specialization, followed by a period of research and the preparation and defense of the doctoral thesis. Courant Students in Ph.D. programs may earn a master's degree while in progress toward the Ph.D program. Areas where there are special funding opportunities for graduate students include: Mathematics, Mechanics, and Material Sciences, Number Theory, Probability, and Scientific Computing. All PhD candidates are required to take a written comprehensive examination, oral preliminary examination, and create a dissertation defense. Each supported doctoral student has access to his or her own dedicated Unix workstation. Many other research machines provide for abundant access to a variety of computer architectures, including a distributed computing laboratory. [15]

Undergraduate Program

The Courant Institute houses New York University's undergraduate programs in computer science and mathematics. In addition, CIMS provides opportunities and facilities for undergraduate students to do and discuss mathematical research, including a undergraduate math lounge on the 11th floor and a undergraduate computer science lounge on the 3rd floor of Warren Weaver Hall.[21] [22]

The mathematics and computer science undergraduate and graduate programs at the Courant Institute has a strong focus on building quantitative and problem-solving skills through teamwork.[23] [24] An undergraduate computer science course on Computer Vision, for example, requires students to be in small teams to use and apply recently developed algorithms by researchers around the world on their own. One example assignment requires a student to study a paper written by researchers from Microsoft Research Cambridge in order to do an assignment on Segmentation and Graph Cut. To encourage innovation, students in advanced coursework are allowed to use any means to complete their assignment, such as a programming language of their choice and hacking a Kinect through legal means.[25]

Classroom at Warren Weaver Hall

The Courant Institute's undergraduate program also encourages students to engage in research with professors and graduate students. About 30% of undergraduate students participate in academic research through the competitive Research Experiences for Undergraduates program funded by the National Science Foundation or research funded primarily by the Dean's Undergraduate Research Fund. The Courant Institute has one of the highest percentage of undergraduate students doing research within New York University.[26] [27] [28] [29] With permission of their advisers or faculty, undergraduate students may take graduate-level courses. Courant undergraduate students through the years and alumni contribute greatly to the vitality of the Mathematics and Computer Science departments. Some accomplishments by current and former undergraduate Courant students include an Apple Worldwide Developers Conference Scholarship Winner, development of Object Category Recognition Techniques to sort garbage for recycling for the NYC's trash program, placement in 7th out of 42 in the ACM International Collegiate Programming Contest (ICPC), and inventors of the Diaspora_(software) social network. [27]

The undergraduate division of the Department of Mathematics offers a Bachelor of Arts (BA) degree in Mathematics. It consists of a wide variety of courses in pure and applied mathematics taught by a distinguished faculty with a tradition of excellence in teaching and research. Students in advanced coursework often participate in formulating models outside the field of mathematics as well as in analyzing them. For example, an advanced mathematics course in Computers in Medicine and Biology requires a student to construct two computer models selected from the following list: circulation, gas exchange in the lung, control of cell volume, and the renal countercurrent mechanism. The student uses the models to conduct simulated physiological experiments.[30]

The undergraduate division of the Department of Computer Science offers a Bachelor of Arts (BA) degree, two minors (one in computer science, and one in web programming and applications) and a joint minor in computer science/mathematics. The BA degree can also be pursued with honors. Students may combine the degree with other majors within the College of Arts and Science to create a personalized joint major. Two specific combined degrees are the joint major in computer science/economics and the joint major in computer science/mathematics. The Department of Computer Science also offers a BS/BE Dual Degree in computer science and engineering and an accelerated master's program available to qualifying undergraduates in conjunction with NYU-Poly.[31]

The minor in computer science is designed primarily for mathematics and science majors whose work will require basic programming skills. The minor in web programming and applications is designed for humanities and social sciences students who plan to use computer application software such as spreadsheets, desktop publishing, multimedia, and Internet software extensively in their careers.[32]

Graduation

The Courant Institute encourages students at any stage of their studies, including the very early stage, to seek summer employment opportunities at various government and industry facilities. In the past few years, Courant students have taken summer internships at the National Institute of Health, Los Alamos National Laboratory, Lawrence Berkeley National Laboratory, Woods Hole Oceanographic Institution, Lawrence Livermore National Laboratory and NASA, as well as Wall Street firms. Such opportunities can greatly expand students' understanding of the mathematical sciences, offer them possible areas of interest for thesis research, and enhance their career options. Members of the faculty (and in particular the students' academic advisors) can assist students in finding appropriate summer employment. All graduate students are given official advisers while undergraduates are provided mentors from Courant faculty.

Recent CIMS doctoral placements for undergraduate and Master graduates include the following:[33]

- Columbia University
- Columbia Law School
- University of Chicago
- Harvard University
- Carnegie Mellon University
- UC Berkeley
- University of Minnesota
- Ohio State University
- Max Planck Institute for Mathematics
- IBM T.J. Watson Research Center
- Instituto Superior Técnico (Portugal)
- University of Washington
- Caltech
- Rutgers University
- Stony Brook University
- St. John's University

Academic research

The Department of Mathematics at CIMS occupies a leading position in analysis and applied mathematics, including partial differential equations, differential geometry, dynamical systems, probability and stochastic processes, scientific computation, mathematical physics, and fluid dynamics. A special feature of the Courant Institute is its highly interdisciplinary character — with courses, seminars, and active research collaborations in areas such as financial mathematics, materials science, visual neural science, atmosphere/ocean science, cardiac fluid dynamics, plasma physics, and mathematical genomics. Another special feature is the central role of analysis, which provides a natural bridge between pure and applied mathematics. The Department of Computer Science has strengths in multimedia, programming languages and systems, distributed and parallel computing, and the analysis of algorithms.

The Courant Institute along with Microsoft Research are the founders of the Games for Learning Institute.

Since 1948, CIMS has maintained its own research journal, Communications on Pure and Applied Mathematics, which currently has the highest impact factor internationally among mathematics journals.[34] It publishes original research originating from or solicited by the Courant Institute, typically in the fields of applied mathematics, mathematical analysis, or mathematical physics. Its contents over the years amount to a modern history of the theory of partial differential equations. Most articles originate within the Institute or are specially invited. The journal represents the full spectrum of the Institute's mathematical research activity. CIMS publishes its own series of lecture notes. They are based on the research interests of the faculty and visitors of the Courant Institute. These lecture notes originated in advanced graduate courses and mini-courses offered at the Courant Institute.

Resources

Warren Weaver Hall & 715/719 Broadway

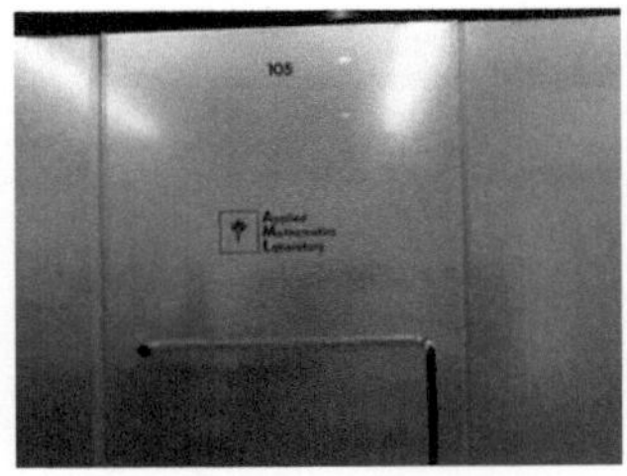

Applied Mathematics Laboratory

CIMS consists of the NYU Departments of Mathematics and Computer Science as well as a variety of research activities. It is housed in Warren Weaver Hall on Mercer Street in NYU's Greenwich Village campus. Unlike many NYU buildings, it does not have an NYU flag. The building contains lecture halls on the first and second floors, two meeting/seminar rooms on every floor from the 3rd floor to the 13th floor, a large common lounge on the 13th floor used for studying and open discussions in topics of mathematics and computer science, and its own extensive Courant library on the 12th floor. It also houses a variety of well-equipped laboratories and offices in Warren Weaver Hall for students and faculty to do research and discuss topics in mathematical sciences. In addition to Warren Weaver Hall, the Computer Science Department is located at 715/719 Broadway, where most of its laboratories and offices are located.[35]

Courant Institute Library

The Courant Institute Library contains one of the United States's most complete mathematics collections with more than 275 journals and 54,000 volumes. Faculty and students at CIMS have access to MathSciNet and Web of Science (also known as the Science Citation Index), and a vast database containing hundred thousands of electronic journals related to mathematics and computer science.[36]

Computing resources

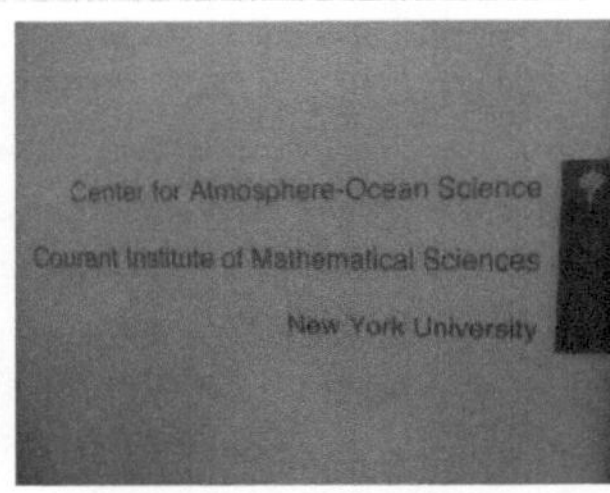

Center for Atmosphere-Ocean Science

CIMS has a IBM eServer BladeCenter system capable of peak performance of 4.5 TeraFlops. According to the TOP500 List, a ranking of supercomputers published at www.top500.org, CIMS's supercomputer is the fastest in New York City and the 117th fastest supercomputer in the world. The acquisition of this supercomputer was funded by IBM and federal funding and is used primarily for research by the faculty and graduate and undergraduate students of CIMS.[37] Computers at CIMS run Windows XP Professional, Solaris, Mac OS X, and Red Hat Enterprise Linux operating systems. There are also many other specialized Linux-based operating systems for research purposes. Every faculty / student office room is fully equipped with scientific software and computer stations. Wi-Fi and X terminals are available in public CIMS locations and every faculty / student office.

All graduate students are provided with an CIMS account to access computers and other resources within the CIMS network upon request. Undergraduate students are only provided CIMS accounts with the approval of their advisor, sponsorship by a CIMS professor, advanced coursework, or for research purposes. CIMS computing resources are not accessible to non-CIMS students without sponsorship by a CIMS professor or approval by either the Department of Mathematics or Department of Computer Science. Faculty, staff, and students with CIMS account have access to free full-featured software provided by the MSDN Academic Alliance and specialized computing resources used primarily for research.[38] [39] [40]

Major research resources

CIMS houses an advanced multi-million-dollar Courant Applied Mathematics Laboratory that opened in 1998, co-founded by Stephen Childress and Michael Shelley, and sponsored by US Department of Energy and the National Science Foundation. It comprises an experimental facility in fluid mechanics and other applied areas and a visualization and simulation facility.[41] The Center for Atmosphere-Ocean Science is also housed at CIMS and is an interdisciplinary research and graduate program within the Courant Institute of Mathematical Sciences.[42]

cSplash and notable student activities

cSplash

Every year, CIMS offers cSplash or Courant Splash, a festival mathematics and computer science program for high school students. It is a one-day festival of classes in the mathematical and computer sciences, designed and taught by graduate and undergraduate students, faculty, and others associated with the Courant Institute of Mathematical Sciences.[43]

Undergraduate Courant student teaching a cSplash course on the ancient history of prime numbers

Extracurricular activities

There are many clubs within the Courant Institute open to undergraduate and graduate students alike. These clubs include the Courant Student Organization, The ACM at NYU, Women-in-Computing (WinC), The Mathematics Society, Masters Association for Computer Science and many more. Additionally, CIMS sponsors and holds seminars and colloquiums almost daily on weekdays on topics of interest, in which some of whom may be held outside of Warren Weaver Hall. Many speakers of these seminars and colloquiums are experienced researchers from corporations from a variety of industries and researchers from private and government research laboratories, top universities, and NYU. Every academic year, CIMS holds award ceremonies, showcases, and parties to celebrate their faculty and undergraduate and graduate students and keep the academic atmosphere fun and enjoyable at CIMS. One such example is the NYU Computer Science Department Showcase held every semester to showcase projects that have been completed in various computer science graduate and undergraduate courses.[44] [45] [46] [47] [48]

History

In 1934, Richard Courant left Göttingen University in Germany to become a visiting professor at NYU. He was given the task of building up the Department of Mathematics at the NYU Graduate School of Arts and Science. He was later joined by Kurt O. Friedrichs and James J. Stoker. In 1946, the department was renamed "Institute for Mathematics and Mechanics". Also in 1946, NYU Professor Morris Kline focused on mathematical problems of electromagnetic wave propagation. This project gave rise to the Institute's Division of Wave Propagation and Applied Mathematics. In 1952, the U.S. Atomic Energy Commission installed one of the first (electronic) computers at New York University, which led to the creation of the Courant Mathematics and Computing Laboratory. The Division of Magnetofluid Dynamics was initiated by a project on plasma fusion by NYU Professor Harold Grad in 1954. The Institute was in the forefront of advanced hardware use, with an early IBM 7094 and the third produced CDC 6600. The Division of Computational Fluid Dynamics was created in 1978, arising from a project of NYU Professor Paul R. Garabedian.

Directors

- Richard Courant (1935–1958)
- James J. Stoker (1958–1966)
- Kurt O. Friedrichs (1966–1967)
- Jürgen Moser (1967–1970)
- Louis Nirenberg (1970–1972)
- Peter Lax (1972–1980)
- S. R. Srinivasa Varadhan (1980–1984)
- Cathleen Synge Morawetz (1984–1988)
- Henry McKean (1988–1994)
- David W. McLaughlin (1994–2002)
- Charles M. Newman (2002–2006)
- Leslie Greengard (2006–2011)
- Gerard Ben Arous (2011–present)

Notable Courant faculty

This is a small selection of Courant's famous faculty over the years and a few of their distinctions:[49]

- Gérard Ben Arous, Davidson Prize
- Marsha Berger, NASA Software of the Year, National Academy of Engineering, National Academy of Sciences
- Sylvain Cappell, Guggenheim Fellowship
- Sourav Chatterjee, Davidson Prize
- Jeff Cheeger, Veblen Prize, Max Planck Research Prize
- Steven Childress, Guggenheim Fellowship, American Physical Society Fellow
- Demetrios Christodoulou, 1993 MacArthur Fellow
- Richard J. Cole, Guggenheim Fellowship
- Martin Davis, Steele Prize
- Percy Deift, George Polya Prize, Guggenheim Fellowship, National Academy of Sciences, American Academy of Arts and Science
- Kurt O. Friedrichs, 1976 National Medal of Science
- Paul Garabedian, NAS Prize in Applied Mathematics, National Academy of Sciences, American Academy of Arts and Science
- Leslie Greengard, Steele Prize, Packard Foundation Fellowship, NSF Presidential Young Investigator, National Academy of Engineering, National Academy of Sciences
- Mikhail Gromov, 2009 Abel Prize, Wolf Prize, Steele Prize, Kyoto Prize, Balzan Prize,
- Helmut Hofer, Ostrowski Prize, National Academy of Sciences
- Fritz John, 1984 MacArthur Fellow
- Joseph B. Keller, 1988 National Medal of Science, Wolf Prize
- Michel Kervaire
- Subhash Khot, 2010 Alan T. Waterman Award
- Morris Kline
- Peter Lax, Abel Prize winner, 1986 National Medal of Science, Steele Prize, Wolf Prize, Norbert Wiener Prize
- Lin Fanghua, Bocher Prize, American Academy of Arts and Science
- Andrew Majda, NAS Prize in Applied Mathematics, John von Neumann Prize (SIAM)
- Henry McKean, National Academy of Science, American Academy of Arts and Science
- David W. McLaughlin, National Academy of Science, American Academy of Arts and Science
- Bud Mishra, Association for Computing Machinery Fellow

- Cathleen Synge Morawetz, 1998 National Medal of Science, Steele Prize, Birkhoff Prize, Noether Lecturer, National Academy of Sciences, American Academy of Arts and Science
- Jürgen Moser, Wolf Prize, James Craig Watson Medal
- Assaf Naor, European Mathematical Society Prize, Packard Fellowship, Salem Prize
- Charles Newman, National Academy of Science, American Academy of Arts and Science
- Louis Nirenberg , 1995 Crafoord Prize, National Medal of Science, Steele Prize, Bocher Prize, American Academy of Arts and Science
- Charles S. Peskin, 1983 MacArthur Fellow, Birkhoff Prize, National Medal of Science,
- Amir Pnueli, National Academy of Engineering, Israel Prize, Turing Award, Association for Computing Machinery Fellow
- Jack Schwartz, who developed the programming language SETL at NYU
- Michael J. Shelley, American Physical Society Fellow, François Naftali Frenkiel Award (APS)
- Jonathan Sondow
- Joel Spencer
- S. R. Srinivasa Varadhan, Abel Prize winner, Steele Prize, National Academy of Sciences, American Academy of Arts and Science, Fellow of the Royal Society
- Akshay Venkatesh, Salem Prize, Packard Fellowship
- Margaret H. Wright, National Academy of Science, National Academy of Engineering
- Lai-Sang Young, National Academy of Science, Satter Prize, Guggenheim Fellowship, American Academy of Arts and Science
- Victor Shoup, who with Ronald Cramer developed the Cramer–Shoup cryptosystem

Notable Courant alumni

This is a small selection of Courant's alumni:

- Anjelina Belakovskaia (Masters in Finance 2001), U.S. Women's Chess Champion.
- Anita Borg (PhD 1981), founding director of the Institute for Women and Technology (IWT)
- Charles Epstein (PhD 1983), hyperbolic geometry
- Corwin Hansch (PhD 1944), statistics
- Joseph B. Keller, 1988 National Medal of Science, Wolf Prize
- Barbara Keyfitz (PhD 1970), Director of the Fields Institute
- David Korn (PhD 1969), creator of the Korn shell,
- Sergiu Klainerman (PhD 1978), Professor at Princeton
- Morris Kline (PhD 1936), NYU Professor (1938–1975),
- Peter Lax (PhD 1949), recipient of the Abel Prize, National Medal of Science, Steele Prize, Wolf Prize, Norbert Wiener Prize
- Chen Li-an, (PhD 1968) Taiwanese Minister of Defence
- Louis Nirenberg (PhD 1949), Crafoord Prize, Bôcher Prize, National Medal of Science
- Brian J. McCartin (PhD 1981), recipient of the 2010 Chauvenet Prize,
- Cathleen Morawetz (PhD 1950), National Medal of Science, Birkhoff Prize, Lifetime Achievement Award from the AMS, professor emeritus at Courant Institute
- Stanley Osher (PhD 1966), Level Set method, professor at University of California, Los Angeles
- George C. Papanicolaou (PhD 1969), professor at Stanford University
- Susan Mary Puglia (BA in Computer Science and Math), Vice President at IBM
- Gary Robinson, software engineer noted for anti-spam algorithms[50] [51]
- Shmuel Weinberger (PhD 1982), topology and geometry, Professor at University of Chicago
- Jacob Wolfowitz (PhD 1942),

See also

- Mikhail Gromov
- Peter Lax
- Amir Pnueli
- S. R. S. Varadhan
- List of New York University people

References

[1] http://www.cims.nyu.edu

[2] "NYU > Courant Institute > About > Courant and NYU" (http://www.cims.nyu.edu/about/courant.html). Cims.nyu.edu. . Retrieved 2011-08-06.

[3] "Best Graduate Schools | Top Graduate Programs | US News Education" (http://grad-schools.usnews.rankingsandreviews.com/grad/mat/applied_math). Grad-schools.usnews.rankingsandreviews.com. . Retrieved 2011-08-06.

[4] "Faculty Scholarly Productivity Index" (http://chronicle.com/stats/productivity/page.php?byinst=true&institution=2478&year=2007). The Chronicle. 2007-11-16. . Retrieved 2011-08-06.

[5] Foderaro, Lisa W. (2009-06-01). "Complex Math, Simple Sum: 3 Awards in 5 Years" (http://www.nytimes.com/2009/06/01/nyregion/01nyu.html). *The New York Times*. .

[6] "Best Mathematical Analysis Programs | Top Math Schools | US News Best Graduate Schools" (http://grad-schools.usnews.rankingsandreviews.com/best-graduate-schools/top-mathematics-programs/mathematical-analysis). Grad-schools.usnews.rankingsandreviews.com. . Retrieved 2011-08-06.

[7] "Best Geometry Programs | Top Math Schools | US News Best Graduate Schools" (http://grad-schools.usnews.rankingsandreviews.com/best-graduate-schools/top-mathematics-programs/geometry). Grad-schools.usnews.rankingsandreviews.com. . Retrieved 2011-08-06.

[8] "Best Computer Science Programs | Top Computer Science Schools | US News Best Graduate Schools" (http://grad-schools.usnews.rankingsandreviews.com/best-graduate-schools/top-science-schools/computer-science-rankings/page+2). Grad-schools.usnews.rankingsandreviews.com. . Retrieved 2011-08-06.

[9] "NYU computer science •" (http://www.thegradcafe.com/survey/index.php?q=NYU+computer+science&t=a&pp=50&o=p). Thegradcafe.com. . Retrieved 2011-08-06

[10] "Courant Institute of Mathematical Sciences NYU" (http://www.math.nyu.edu/financial_mathematics/content/05_prospectiveStudents/04.html). Math.nyu.edu. . Retrieved 2011-08-06.

[11] "Graduate Mathematics Courses" (http://www.math.nyu.edu/degree/phd/application.html). Math.nyu.edu. . Retrieved 2011-08-06.

[12] "NYU Computer Science Department > Graduate Admissions Information" (http://cs.nyu.edu/webapps/content/academic/graduate/admissions/admission). Cs.nyu.edu. . Retrieved 2011-08-06.

[13] "Department of Mathematics Admissions - New York University (Department of Mathematics)" (http://www.petersons.com/graduate-schools/new-york-university-courant-institute-of-mathematical-sciences-department-of-mathematics-admissions-000_10014124_10088.aspx). Petersons.com. . Retrieved 2011-08-06.

[14] "The M.S. Programs" (http://www.math.nyu.edu/degree/ms/). Math.nyu.edu. 2005-09-01. . Retrieved 2011-08-06.

[15] "The Ph.D. Program" (http://www.math.nyu.edu/degree/phd/). Math.nyu.edu. 2005-09-01. . Retrieved 2011-08-06.

[16] Class of 2009 Resume Book (http://math.nyu.edu/financial_mathematics/content/04_current/new/Courant NYU Resume Book Class of 2009.pdf). Retrieved August 2011

[17] "Courant Institute of Mathematical Sciences NYU" (http://www.math.nyu.edu/financial_mathematics/content/06_prospectiveEmployers/02.html). Math.nyu.edu. . Retrieved 2011-08-06.

[18] McEachern, Cristina (2008-07-21). "The Top 10 Quant Schools, According to the Street" (http://www.advancedtrading.com/showArticle.jhtml?articleID=209102204). Advanced Trading. . Retrieved 2011-08-06.

[19] (http://www.nyunews.com/news/university/courant-named-top-10-in-math-finance-1.745668)

[20] "NYU Computer Science Department > Graduate Programs in Computer Science" (http://cs.nyu.edu/webapps/content/academic/graduate/overview). Cs.nyu.edu. . Retrieved 2011-08-06.

[21] "Math Lounge" (http://math.nyu.edu/degree/undergrad/MathLounge.html). Math.nyu.edu. 2005-09-01. . Retrieved 2011-08-06.

[22] "New York University - MSc Mathematics in Finance" (http://www.global-derivatives.com/index.php?Itemid=5&id=91&option=com_content&task=view). Global-derivatives.com. . Retrieved 2011-08-06.

[23] "NYU Computer Science Department > Undergraduate Program" (http://cs.nyu.edu/web/Academic/Undergrad/). Cs.nyu.edu. . Retrieved 2011-08-06.

[24] "Department of Mathematics, Courant Institute" (http://math.nyu.edu/degree/undergrad/). Math.nyu.edu. 2005-09-01. . Retrieved 2011-08-06.

[25] "V22.0480-001" (http://cs.nyu.edu/courses/spring11/V22.0480-001/index.html). Cs.nyu.edu. . Retrieved 2011-08-06.

[26] "NYU > A & S > Dean's Undergraduate Research Fund" (http://cas.nyu.edu/page/ug.DeansResearchFund.html). Cas.nyu.edu. . Retrieved 2011-08-06.

[27] "Undergraduate Student Spotlight - NYU Computer Science Department" (http://cs.nyu.edu/web/Academic/Undergrad/spotlight.html). Cs.nyu.edu. . Retrieved 2011-08-06.

[28] (http://www.quantnet.com/review-nyu-mathematical-finance-program)

[29] "NYU Computer Science Department > Undergraduate Program" (http://cs.nyu.edu/webapps/content/academic/undergrad/). Cs.nyu.edu. . Retrieved 2011-08-06.

[30] "Powered by Google Docs" (http://docs.google.com/viewer?a=v&q=cache:vGj-HafADLoJ:math.nyu.edu/degree/undergrad/Math%20major%20bulletin%202010-11%20Final.pdf+Math+undergraduate+nyu+requirements&hl=en&gl=us&pid=bl&srcid=ADGEESi4x3xv-_X-4B0Xil4BidRNWKCKg9smDHdaXmhcPNv2gRXB173WgH0mNEM6D-RGr6C-oEz4XoRNBZvoWRQ_RWpcHpNzWxe06LDC0 sig=AHIEtbSCuQUYJiy-dq4Yg8t8z5z6AnV2Ig). Docs.google.com. . Retrieved 2011-08-06.

[31] "NYU Computer Science Department > Undergraduate CS Program Overview" (http://cs.nyu.edu/webapps/content/academic/undergrad/overview). Cs.nyu.edu. . Retrieved 2011-08-06.

[32] "NYU Computer Science Department > Computer Science Minors" (http://cs.nyu.edu/webapps/content/academic/undergrad/minors). Cs.nyu.edu. . Retrieved 2011-08-06.

[33] "Department of Mathematics, Courant Institute" (http://www.math.nyu.edu/degree/undergrad/alumni_prof.html). Math.nyu.edu. 2005-09-01. . Retrieved 2011-08-06.

[34] "Wiley Online Library" (http://www3.interscience.wiley.com/journal/78504520/issue). .interscience.wiley.com. . Retrieved 2011-08-06.

[35] "Getting to the Courant Institute" (http://www.cims.nyu.edu/direct.html). Cims.nyu.edu. 2005-09-01. . Retrieved 2011-08-06.

[36] (http://www.petersons.com/gradchannel/code/ProgramVC.asp?sn=New-York-University&mu=Courant-Institute-of-Mathematical-Sciences&pn=Department-of-Mathematics&inunid=46618&sponsor=1&related=true)

[37] "NYU Today" (http://www.nyu.edu/public.affairs/releases/detail/694). Nyu.edu. . Retrieved 2011-08-06.

[38] NYU Computer Science (http://cs.nyu.edu/web/Academic/Graduate/computeracct.html). Retrieved August 2011

[39] "NYU > Courant Institute > Connecting to CIMS FAQ" (http://cims.nyu.edu/webapps/faq/Connecting to CIMS). Cims.nyu.edu. . Retrieved 2011-08-06.

[40] "NYU > Courant Institute > Network Access" (http://cims.nyu.edu/webapps/content/systems/userservices/netaccess). Cims.nyu.edu. . Retrieved 2011-08-06.

[41] "AML" (http://www.math.nyu.edu/aml/index.html). Math.nyu.edu. . Retrieved 2011-08-06.

[42] "Center for Atmosphere Ocean Science | New York University" (http://caos.cims.nyu.edu/page/home). Caos.cims.nyu.edu. . Retrieved 2011-08-06.

[43] "Courant Splash! - cSplash" (http://www.cims.nyu.edu/~csplash/index.php). Cims.nyu.edu. . Retrieved 2011-08-06.

[44] "NYU > Courant Institute > Weekly Bulletin" (http://cims.nyu.edu/events/). Cims.nyu.edu. . Retrieved 2011-08-06.

[45] "New York University - Women in Computing" (http://www.cs.nyu.edu/~wincweb/winc.html). Cs.nyu.edu. . Retrieved 2011-08-06.

[46] "Courant Student Organization:: New York University" (http://www.cims.nyu.edu/~csstu/). Cims.nyu.edu. . Retrieved 2011-08-06.

[47] "NYU Mathematics Society: Home" (http://www.math.nyu.edu/math_club/index.html). Math.nyu.edu. 2010-04-24. . Retrieved 2011-08-06.

[48] "The ACM at NYU" (http://cs.nyu.edu/~acmweb/wordpress/). Cs.nyu.edu. 2011-02-22. . Retrieved 2011-08-06.

[49] "NYU > Courant Institute > About > Scientific Distinction" (http://www.cims.nyu.edu/about/scientific.html). Cims.nyu.edu. 2005-09-01. . Retrieved 2011-08-06.

[50] "Gary Robinson" (http://spambayes.sourceforge.net/). *Google*. 2010-09-18. . Retrieved 2010-09-18. "I make the music recommendation technology at http://www.flyfi.com -- ... Schools I've attended Bard College; Courant Institute of Mathematical Sciences"

[51] Gary Robinson (Mar 01, 2003). "A Statistical Approach to the Spam Problem: Using Bayesian statistics to detect an e-mail's spamminess." (http://www.linuxjournal.com/article/6467). *Linux Journal*. . Retrieved 2010-09-18. "This article discusses one of many possible mathematical foundations for a key aspect of spam filtering—generating ..."

External links

- Courant Institute of Mathematical Sciences (http://www.cims.nyu.edu/)
- Department of Mathematics, New York University (http://www.math.nyu.edu/)
- Applied Mathematics Laboratory (http://www.math.nyu.edu/aml/)
- New York University Computer Science (http://cs.nyu.edu/)
- New York University Mathematics in Finance (http://www.math.nyu.edu/financial_mathematics/)
- New York University Scientific Computing (http://www.math.nyu.edu/degree/ms/scicomputing.html)
- http://www.cims.nyu.edu/~csplash/index.php
- NYU Mathematics Society, New York University (http://www.math.nyu.edu/math_club/)
- http://www.cs.nyu.edu/~wincweb/

- http://www.cs.nyu.edu/~macsweb/
- http://www.cs.nyu.edu/~acmweb/wordpress/

Master of Divinity

In the academic study of theology, the **Master of Divinity** (**M.Div.**, *magister divinitatis* in Latin) is the first professional degree of the pastoral profession in North America. It is the most common academic degree in seminaries and divinity schools.

In many Christian denominations and in some other religions the degree is the standard prerequisite for ordination to the priesthood or pastorship or other appointment, ordination or licensing to professional ministry. At accredited seminaries in the United States this degree requires between 72 and 106 credit hours of study (72 being the minimum determined by academic accrediting agencies and 106 being on the upper end of certain schools that wish to ensure a broader study of the related disciplines).

Christian MDiv programs generally include studies in Christian ministry and theology. Coursework usually includes studies in New Testament Greek, theology, philosophy, church history, pastoral theology, Hebrew Bible (Old Testament), and New Testament studies. Many programs also contain courses in church growth, ecclesiology, evangelism, systematic theology, Christian education, liturgical studies, Latin, Hebrew, canon law, and patristics. The degree may or may not include a thesis.

Contemporary usage

The Master of Divinity has replaced the Bachelor of Divinity in most United States seminaries as the first professional degree, since the former title implied in the American academic system that it was on a par with a Bachelor of Arts or other basic undergraduate education even though a bachelor's degree was and remains a prerequisite for entrance into graduate divinity programs. The Commission on Accrediting of the Association of Theological Schools in the United States and Canada accredits schools in North America and approves the degree programs they offer, including the M.Div.

The M.Div. is a significantly more extensive program than most master's degrees. In the United States the degree usually consists on average of 90 semester hours, as opposed to the usual 36 or 48. Ordination in most mainline Protestant denominations and the Roman Catholic Church thus requires seven or eight years of education past high school: the first four in undergraduate studies leading to a bachelor's degree (which may or may not be in a related field) and then three or four years of seminary or divinity school education leading to the M.Div.

The M.Div. stands in contrast to the Master of Arts (M.A.) in theology and Master of Theological Studies (M.T.S.), the usual academic degrees in the subject (which tend not to include "pastoral" or "practical" courses), and the Bachelor of Sacred Theology (S.T.B.), Licentiate in Sacred Theology (S.T.L.), Master of Theology (M.Th.), Master of Sacred Theology (S.T.M.), and Master of Religion (M.Rel.), which are also academic degrees. Schools with Pontifical faculties in North America often award both the M.Div. and S.T.B. at the same time after a three-year period of graduate studies.

See also

- Graduate programs in religion

Union Theological Seminary in the City of New York

Union Theological Seminary in the City of New York	
 Union Theological Seminary in the City of New York	
Latin: *Seminarii Theologici Unioniensis Novi Eboraci*	
Motto	Unitas, Veritas, Caritas
Motto in English	Unity, Truth, Charity
Established	1836
Type	Private
Endowment	US$ 92,000,000[1]
President	Rev. Dr. Serene Jones
Academic staff	38
Students	300
Location	New York City, New York, USA
Affiliations	Columbia University
Website	www.utsnyc.edu [2]

Union Theological Seminary in the City of New York is a preeminent independent graduate school of theology, located in Manhattan between Claremont Avenue and Broadway, 120th to 122nd Streets. The seminary was founded in 1836 under the Presbyterian Church,[3] and is affiliated with nearby Columbia University.

Side view at Claremont Avenue between 120th and 119th streets (1910)

Campus

The brick and limestone English Gothic architecture, by Francis R. Allen (1844 – 1931) and Collins, completed in 1910, includes the tower (*pictured*), which adapts features of the crossing tower of Durham Cathedral. The Seminary is also adjacent to Teachers College, Barnard College, the Jewish Theological Seminary of America and the Manhattan School of Music and has cross-registration and library access agreements with several of these schools. The building was added to the National Register of Historic Places on April 23, 1980. Some sections of the campus are now on long-term lease to

Columbia University.

Library

The Burke Theological Library, which is the largest theological library in the western hemisphere, contains holdings of over 700,000 items. The Library is recognized as one of the premier theological libraries in the world and includes extensive holdings of unique and special materials including, including Greek census records from 20 CE, a rare twelfth century manuscript of the Life of St. Boniface, a 1520 imprint of Martin Luther's first published writing, and one of the first African-American hymnals, published in Philadelphia in 1818. In 2004 Union's famed Burke Library became fully integrated into the Columbia University Library system which holds over 10 million volumes. The Library is named in honor of Walter Burke, a generous benefactor to the Library who served as Chairman of the Board of Directors of the Seminary from 1976 to 1982.

History

The seminary was founded in 1836, and is one of the most prestigious divinity schools in the country. During the late-19th Century, Union Theological Seminary (UTS) became one of the leading centers of liberal Christianity in the United States. In 1939 the Auburn Theological Seminary moved to its campus.[4]

Among its graduates were the historian of Christianity Arthur McGiffert, biblical scholar James Moffett, Harry Emerson Fosdick, pastor of Riverside Church, who served as professor during his tenure there, and the Socialist leader Norman Thomas. It is home to the **Burke Theological Library**, which is the largest theological library in the Western Hemisphere and serves a national and international field of scholars, pastors, and students. It contains more than 700,000 volumes, periodicals, manuscripts, scores, and rare historic materials.

Union Theological Seminary entrance on Broadway

In 1895, members of the Union Theological Seminary Alumni Club founded Union Settlement Association, one of one of the oldest settlement houses in New York City. After visiting Toynbee Hall in London, and inspired by the example of Hull House in Chicago, the alumni decided to create a settlement house in the area of Manhattan enclosed on the north and south by East 96th and 110th Streets and on the east and west by the East River and Central Park. Known as East Harlem, it was a neighborhood filled with new tenements but devoid of any civic services. The ethos of the settlement house movement called for its workers to "settle" in such neighborhoods in order to learn first-hand the problems of the residents. "It seemed to us that, as early settlers, we had a chance to grow up with the community and affect its development," wrote William Adams Brown, Theology Professor, Union Theological Society (1892–1930) and President, Union Settlement Association (1915–1919).[5] Union Settlement still exists, providing community-based services and programs to support the immigrant and low-income residents of East Harlem. One of East Harlem's largest social service agencies, Union Settlement reaches more than 13,000 people annually at 17 locations throughout East Harlem, through a range of programs, including early childhood education, youth development, senior services, job training, the arts, adult education, nutrition, counseling, a farmers' market, community development and neighborhood cultural events.

On July 1, 2008, feminist theologian Serene Jones became Union's first female president in its 172-year history, succeeding Joseph C. Hough, Jr.[6]

"Union has a distinguished history among graduate theological institutions. Its faculty has always ranked among the best in the world and has included such luminaries as Walter Rauschenbusch, Reinhold Niebuhr, Paul Tillich, Dietrich Bonhoeffer, James Cone, and others. Its students come from around the country and the world. The seminary is known for its progressive understanding of religion in general, and Christianity in particular, and has long been at the forefront of the great social movements in this nation's history."[7]

Faculty

Dr. Serene Jones, the seminary's first female president, was inaugurated in November 2008. Dr. Joseph Hough, UTS' immediate past president, is an important Christian Democratic Socialist. Henry Sloane Coffin was a past president. Dr. James Hal Cone is one of the founders of liberation theology and is especially important in the development of African-American theology. Union has also been home to many prominent Womanist theologians such as Delores Williams. Dr. Gary Dorrien is a leading social ethicist. Dr. James A. Forbes, the former senior pastor of the adjacent Riverside Church, is an adjunct professor at the seminary and had been a full-time, chaired professor before accepting the Riverside post.

Reinhold Niebuhr and Paul Tillich made UTS the center of both liberal and neo-orthodox Protestantism in the post-War period. Prominent public intellectual Dr. Cornel West commenced a promising academic career at UTS in 1977. As liberalism lost ground to conservatism after the 1960s (while neo-orthodoxy dissipated) and thus declined in prestige, UTS ran into financial difficulties, and shrank significantly because of a reduced student base. Eventually, the school agreed to lease some of its buildings to Columbia University and to transfer ownership of and responsibility for the Burke Library to Columbia. These agreements helped stabilize the school's finances, which had been hobbled by increasing library costs and the need for substantial campus repairs.

Degrees

The school confers Master of Arts, Master of Divinity, Master of Sacred Theology, Doctor of Theology, Doctor of Philosophy, and offers joint degree programs with Columbia University. The school has long been associated with ecumenism.

List of founders

- Charles Butler (1802–97)

Notable current faculty

- Mary C. Boys — Skinner and McAlpin Professor of Practical Theology
- Euan K. Cameron — Henry Luce III Professor of Reformation Church History (1958–)
- David M. Carr — Professor of Old Testament; contributed to Genesis in the New Oxford Annotated Bible (New Revised Standard Version)
- James Cone — Charles A. Briggs Distinguished Professor of Systematic Theology – Founder of Black Liberation Theology.
- Gary Dorrien — Reinhold Niebuhr Professor of Social Ethics
- Roger Haight — Visiting Professor of Systematic Theology
- Brigitte Kahl — Professor of New Testament
- Paul F. Knitter — Paul Tillich Professor of Theology
- Chung Hyun Kyung — Associate Professor of Ecumenical Theology
- Barbara Lundblad — Joe R. Engle Associate Professor of Preaching
- Daisy L. Machado — Dean of Academic Affairs and Professor of the History of Christianity; first U.S. Latina ordained in the Christian Church (Disciples of Christ)
- Christopher Morse — Dietrich Bonhoeffer Professor of Theology & Ethics
- John Anthony McGuckin — Professor of Early Church History
- Hal Taussig — Visiting Professor of New Testament

- Ann Belford Ulanov — Christiane Brooks Johnson Memorial Professor of Psychiatry and Religion
- Janet Walton — Professor of Worship

Several of Union's members also teach in the Religious Studies department at Columbia University and at the Teachers College, Columbia University, and the Jewish Theological Seminary of America.

Former theologians and faculty

- William Greenough Thayer Shedd — professor of sacred literature (1863–1874) and of systematic theology (1874–1890).
- Charles Augustus Briggs — professor of Hebrew and cognate languages (1874–1891) and of Biblical theology (1891–1904); an important early leader of the Modernist movement.
- Reinhold Niebuhr (1892–1971) — professor of Applied Christianity – Christian social ethics, author of the influential *The Nature and Destiny of Man* (1941), and the Serenity Prayer (popularized through the Twelve-step program).
- Paul Tillich (1886–1965) — German-American theologian and Christian existentialist philosopher.
- James Cone, Black liberation theologian
- John Macquarrie — professor of Systematic Theology 1962–70, afterwards Lady Margaret Professor of Divinity in the University of Oxford and Canon Residentiary of Christ Church, Oxford 1970–1986.
- Robert Pollack — professor of Science and Religion
- Raymond E. Brown (1928–1998) — One of America's preeminent New Testament scholars and member of Pontificial Bible Commission was professor in UTS for 23 years.
- Edward Robinson, Biblical scholar and discoverer of Robinson's Arch and Hezekiah's Tunnel in Jerusalem.
- Dorothee Soelle Socially-engaged German theologian
- Harry Emerson Fosdick — First minister of Riverside Church and professor of homiletics
- Harry F. Ward, chairman of the ACLU and professor of ethics
- Roger Haight, theologian banned from teaching by the Holy Office.[8]

Notable alumni

- Rubem Alves — Brazilian theologian and writer
- William Scott Ament (Bachelor of Divinity, 1877) — controversial American missionary to China (1877–1909).
- Dietrich Bonhoeffer — German Lutheran theologian and Nazi resister who spent half a year at UTS. Of UTS he wrote: "There is no theology here....they talk a blue streak without the slightest substantive foundation and with no evidence of any criteria. The students....are completely clueless with respect to what dogmatics is really about. They are unfamiliar with even the most basic questions. They become intoxicated with liberal and humanistic phrases, laugh at the fundamentalists, and yet basically are not even up to their level." [9]
- Anton Boisen — founder of Clinical Pastoral Education (CPE) movement
- Marcus Borg — Popular lecturer and writer, Hundere Distinguished Professor of Religion and Culture at Oregon State University
- Frederick Buechner — Writer
- Frederick Buckley Newell (Bachelor of Divinity, 1916) — Bishop of The Methodist Church
- Edwin Otway Burnham (Bachelor of Divinity, 1855) — a rifle shooting Presbyterian missionary in Sioux Indian territory who could bark a squirrel, swing an axe or dispense Gospel with equal ferver and efficiency.
- Walter Brueggemann — William Marcellus McPheeters professor of Old Testament at Columbia Theological Seminary
- Gladwyn M. Childs — Anthropologist and missionary
- Nelson Cruikshank (Master of divinity, 1929) — Labor union activist and strategist responsible for the passage of Medicare

- David Dellinger — Noted American peace activist and member of the Chicago Seven.
- Helen Flanders Dunbar (B.D. 1927) — an important early figure in U.S. psychosomatic medicine.
- Franklin I. Gamwell — Shailer Mathews Professor of Religious Ethics, the Philosophy of Religion, and Theology at the Divinity School of the University of Chicago
- David P. Gushee — Distinguished University Professor of Christian Ethics at Mercer University. Author of 9 books and over 70 articles[10]
- Mark Hanson — current Presiding Bishop of the Evangelical Lutheran Church in America.
- Richard Holloway — Scottish writer and broadcaster and was formerly Bishop of Edinburgh.
- Dwight Hopkins — Professor of Theology at the Divinity School at the University of Chicago
- Myles Horton — Co-founder of the Highlander Center
- William H. Hudnut III — former Mayor of Indianapolis, Indiana (1976–1992)
- Ada Maria Isasi-Diaz — Professor of Ethics and Theology at Drew University
- Mark Juergensmeyer — Professor of Sociology, Religious Studies and Global Studies at the University of California at Santa Barbara. Director of the Orfalea Center for Global and International Studies.
- Norman J. Kansfield – President New Brunswick Theological Seminary 1993–2005. Senior Scholar in Residence, Theological School, Drew University.
- James Franklin Kay – Professor of Homiletics and Liturgics at Princeton Theological Seminary
- James David Manning — chief pastor at the ATLAH World Missionary Church.
- Andrew McLellan — former Moderator of the General Assembly of the Church of Scotland
- Bruce McLeod (PhD) — Moderator of the United Church of Canada
- William P. Merrill — first president on the Church Peace Union, writer of "Rise Up, O Men of God"
- Paul Sherry - President of the United Church of Christ (1989-1999)
- Andrea Smith — Cherokee intellectual and anti-violence activist
- John Sung – A renowned Chinese Christian evangelist who played an instrumental role in the revival movement among the Chinese in Mainland China, Taiwan, and Southeast Asia during the 1920s and 1930s.
- John Stoltenberg — feminist writer
- Norman Thomas — American Socialist
- K. H. Ting — President emeritus of the Three-Self Patriotic Movement and China Christian Council
- George W. Webber (1920–2010), President of the New York Theological Seminary.[11]
- Delores Williams — Womanist theologian
- Lynn de Silva (Master of Sacred Theology) — Sri Lankan theologian, former director of the Ecumenical Institute for Study and Dialogue, Methodist minister, and a pioneer in promoting Buddhist–Christian dialogue
- E.P. Sanders — A principle founder in the New Perspective on Paul movement

References

[1] Joseph C. Hough's Leadership of Union Theological Seminary 1999-2008 (http://www.utsnyc.edu/Page.aspx?pid=935) web site

[2] http://www.utsnyc.edu/

[3] Union Theological Seminary – Timeline, 1836 to 1869 (http://www.utsnyc.edu/NETCOMMUNITY/Page.aspx?&pid=758)

[4] "About Us" (http://www.auburnsem.org/about/welcome.asp?nsectionid=1&pageid=1). *Auburn Theological Seminary web site*.. Retrieved 2010-01-21.

[5] A Teacher and His Times, William Adams Brown, Scribner, 1940.

[6] Union Theological Seminary – Serene Jones, President of the Faculty (http://www.utsnyc.edu/NETCOMMUNITY/Page.aspx?pid=1081&srcid=332)

[7] Columbia Wiki

[8] Commonweal article (http://www.commonwealmagazine.org/blog/?p=2644)

[9] Metaxas, Eric| *Bonhoeffer: Pastor, Martyr, Prophet, Spy* 2010, Thomas Nelson Publishers, p. 101

[10] David P. Gushee's web site (http://www.davidpgushee.com/)

[11] Martin, Douglas. "George W. Webber, Social Activist Minister, Dies at 90" (http://www.nytimes.com/2010/07/13/us/13webber.html), *The New York Times*, July 12, 2010. Accessed July 13, 2010.

External links

- Union Theological Seminary webpage (http://www.utsnyc.edu)
- Union Podcast (http://www.unionpodcast.org/)
- *The WPA Guide to New York City* 1939, reprint 1982.
- Union Theological Seminary in Columbia University's Wiki (http://www.wikicu.com/Union_Theological_Seminary)

Association for Computing Machinery

Association for Computing Machinery	
Formation	1947
Headquarters	New York, NY
Membership	92,000
President	Alain Chesnais
Website	http://www.acm.org

The **Association for Computing Machinery** (**ACM**) is a learned society for computing. It was founded in 1947 as the world's first scientific and educational computing society. Its membership is more than 92,000 as of 2009. Its headquarters are in New York City.

Activities

ACM is organized into over 170 local chapters and 35 Special Interest Groups (SIGs), through which it conducts most of its activities. Additionally, there are over 500 college and university chapters. The first student chapter was founded in 1961 at the University of Louisiana at Lafayette.

Two Penn Plaza site of the ACM headquarters in New York City

Many of the SIGs, like SIGGRAPH, SIGPLAN, SIGCSE and SIGCOMM, sponsor regular conferences which have become famous as the dominant venue for presenting new innovations in certain fields. The groups also publish a large number of specialized journals, magazines, and newsletters.

ACM also sponsors other computer science related events such as the worldwide ACM International Collegiate Programming Contest (ICPC), and has sponsored some other events such as the chess match between Garry Kasparov and the IBM Deep Blue computer.

Services

ACM Press publishes a prestigious academic journal, *Journal of the ACM*, and general magazines for computer professionals, *Communications of the ACM* (also known as *Communications* or *CACM*) and *Queue*. Other publications of the ACM include:

- *ACM XRDS*, formally "Crossroads" and renamed and designed in 2010, the most popular student computing magazine in the US.
- *ACM interactions*, an interdisciplinary HCI publication focused on the connections between experiences, people and technology, and the third largest ACM publication. [1] [2]
- A number of journals, specific to subfields of computer science, titled *ACM Transactions*. Some of the more prominent transactions include:

- *ACM Transactions on Computer Systems* (TOCS)
- *ACM Transactions on Database Systems* (TODS)
- *ACM Transactions on Graphics* (TOG)
- *ACM Transactions on Mathematical Software* (TOMS)
- *ACM Transactions on Programming Languages and Systems* (TOPLAS)

Although *Communications* no longer publishes primary research, and is not considered a prestigious venue, many of the great debates and results in computing history have been published in its pages.

ACM has made almost all of its publications available to paid subscribers online at its Digital Library and also has a Guide to Computing Literature. Individual members additionally have access to Safari Books Online and Books24x7. The ACM also offers insurance, online courses, and other services to its members.

Digital Library

The ACM Digital Library, a part of the ACM Portal, contains a comprehensive archive of the organization's journals, magazines, and conference proceedings. Online services include a forum called Ubiquity and Tech News digest.

ACM requires the copyright of all submissions to be assigned to the organization as a condition of publishing the work.[3] Authors may post the documents on their own websites, but they are required to link back to the digital library's reference page for the paper. Though authors are not allowed to charge for access to copies of their work, downloading a copy from the ACM site requires a paid subscription.

Competition

ACM's primary historical competitor has been the IEEE Computer Society, which is the largest subgroup of the Institute of Electrical and Electronics Engineers. The IEEE focuses more on hardware and standardization issues than theoretical computer science, but there is considerable overlap with ACM's agenda. They occasionally cooperate on projects like developing computing curricula.[4] Some of the major awards in Computer science are given jointly by ACM and the IEEE-CS.[5]

There is also a mounting challenge to the ACM's publication practices coming from the open access movement. Some authors see a centralized peer-review process as less relevant and publish on their home pages or on unreviewed sites like arXiv. Other organizations have sprung up which do their peer review entirely free and online, such as Journal of Artificial Intelligence Research (JAIR), Journal of Machine Learning Research (JMLR) and the Journal of Research and Practice in Information Technology.

Membership grades

In addition to student and regular members, ACM has several advanced membership grades to recognize those with multiple years of membership and "demonstrated performance that sets them apart from their peers".[6]

Fellows

The **ACM Fellows Program** was established by Council of the Association for Computing Machinery in 1993 "to recognize and honor outstanding ACM members for their achievements in computer science and information technology and for their significant contributions to the mission of the ACM."

There are presently about 500 Fellows[7] out of about 60,000 professional members.

Other membership grades

In 2006 ACM began recognizing two additional membership grades. Senior Members have ten or more years of membership and demonstrated performance. Distinguished Engineers and Distinguished Scientists have at least 15 years of membership who "have made a significant impact on the computing field".

Chapters

ACM has three kinds of chapters: Special Interest Groups[8] , Professional Chapters, and Student Chapters. [9]

Special Interest Groups

- SIGACCESS: Accessible Computing
- SIGACT: Algorithms and Computation Theory
- SIGAda: Ada Programming Language
- SIGAPP: Applied Computing
- SIGARCH: Computer Architecture
- SIGART: Artificial Intelligence
- SIGBED: Embedded Systems
- SIGCAS: Computers and Society
- SIGCHI: Computer-Human Interaction
- SIGCOMM: Data Communication
- SIGCSE: Computer Science Education
- SIGDA: Design Automation
- SIGDOC: Design of Communication
- SIGecom: Electronic Commerce
- SIGEVO: Genetic and Evolutionary Computation
- SIGGRAPH: Computer Graphics and Interactive Techniques
- SIGIR: Information Retrieval
- SIGITE: Information Technology Education
- SIGKDD: Knowledge Discovery and Data Mining
- SIGMETRICS: Measurement and Evaluation
- SIGMICRO: Microarchitecture
- SIGMIS: Management Information Systems
- SIGMM: Multimedia
- SIGMOBILE: Mobility of Systems, Users, Data and Computing
- SIGMOD: Management of Data
- SIGOPS: Operating Systems
- SIGPLAN: Programming Languages
- SIGSAC: Security, Audit, and Control
- SIGSAM: Symbolic and Algebraic Manipulation
- SIGSIM: Simulation and Modeling
- SIGSOFT: Software Engineering
- SIGSPATIAL: Spatial Information
- SIGUCCS: University and College Computing Services
- SIGWEB: Hypertext, Hypermedia, and Web

Professional Chapters

As of 2011, ACM has professional chapters in 56 countries.[10]

These chapters include:

- Baltimore ACM Chapter (BACM): official website [11]
- Boston Greater Boston Chapter of the ACM (GBCACM): official website [12]
- District of Columbia ACM Chapter (DCACM): official website [13]

Student Chapters

As of 2011, there exist ACM student chapters in 38 different countries.[14]

These chapters include:

- Birla Institute of Technology Mesra (BIT-ACM): blog [15]
- Birla Institute of Technology and Science (BITS-ACM)
- Brock University: website [16]
- California State University, Long Beach (CSULBACM): official website [17]
- California State University, Sacramento (CSUSACM): official website [18]
- College of Engineering, Guindy, Anna University (AU CEG ACM)
- Cornell University (ACSU), official website [19]
- Georgia Institute of Technology (GTACM) official website [20]
- Indian Institute of Technology, Delhi ACM@IITD : Website [21]
- Johns Hopkins University (JHUACM): official website [22]
- Louisiana State University (ACM@LSU): official website [23]
- New Jersey Institute of Technology: official website [24]
- Peirce College: Official website [25]
- Pennsylvania State University: official website [26]
- Purdue University: official website [27]
- PSG College of Technology (PSG Tech ACM) : official website [28]
- Sardar Vallabhbhai National Institute of Technology, Surat: official Website [29]
- Southern Illinois University Carbondale: official website [30]
- University at Buffalo (UB ACM): official website [31]
- University of Alabama in Huntsville: official website [32]
- University of California, Los Angeles (UCLA ACM): official website [33]
- University of California, San Diego (CSES): official website [34]
- University of California, Santa Barbara (UCSB ACM): official website [35]
- University of California, Santa Cruz (UCSC ACM): official website [36]
- University of Illinois, Chicago (UIC ACM): official website [37]
- University of Illinois, Urbana-Champaign (UIUC ACM): official website [38]
- University of Iowa: official website [39]
- University of Massachusetts Amherst (UMass ACM): official website [40]
- University of Minnesota Twin Cities (UofM): official website [41]
- University of the Philippines (UPACM): official website [42]
- University of Tehran (UTACM): Website [43]
- University of Texas, Austin (UTACM): official website [44]
- Universität Ulm: official website [45]
- Vidyalankar Institute of Technology, Mumbai
- Western Washington University (WWU ACM): official website [46]
- Worcester Polytechnic Institute (WPIACM): official website [47]

- Yeshwantrao Chavan College of Engineering (YCCE): official website [48]

Conferences

The ACM sponsors numerous conferences listed below. Most of the special interest groups also have an annual conference. ACM conferences are often very popular publishing venues and are therefore very competitive. For example, the 2007 SIGGRAPH conference attracted about 30000 visitors, and CIKM only accepted 15% of the long papers that were submitted in 2005.

- CHI: Conference on Human Factors in Computing Systems
- CIKM: Conference on Information and Knowledge Management[49]
- DAC: Design Automation Conference
- FCRC: Federated Computing Research Conference
- GECCO: Genetic and Evolutionary Computation Conference[50]
- SIGGRAPH: International Conference on Computer Graphics and Interactive Techniques
- Hypertext: Conference on Hypertext and Hypermedia[51]
- JCDL: Joint Conference on Digital Libraries[52]
- OOPSLA: Conference on Object-Oriented Programming, Systems, Languages, and Applications
- WWW: World Wide Web Conference

The ACM is a co-presenter and founding partner of the Grace Hopper Celebration of Women in Computing (GHC) with the Anita Borg Institute for Women and Technology.[53]

Leadership

The President of the ACM for 2010–2012[54] is Alain Chesnais, a French citizen living in Toronto where he runs his company named Visual Transitions. He is the successor of Wendy Hall of the University of Southampton.

ACM is led by a Council consisting of the President, Vice-President, Treasurer, Past President, SIG Governing Board Chair, Publications Board Chair, three representatives of the SIG Governing Board, and seven Members-At-Large. This institution is often referred to simply as "Council" in *Communications of the ACM.*

Infrastructure

ACM has five “Boards” that make up various committees and subgroups, to help Headquarters staff maintain quality services and products. These boards are as follows:

1. Publications Board
2. SIG Governing Board
3. Education Board
4. Membership Services Board
5. Professions Board

ACM-W: Association for Computing Machinery Committee on Women

ACM-W, the ACM's committee on women in computing, is set up to support, inform, celebrate, and work with women in computing. Dr. Anita Borg was a great supporter of ACM-W. ACM-W provides various resources for women in computing as well as high school girls interested in the field. ACM-W also reaches out internationally to those women who are involved and interested in computing.

See also

- ACM Classification Scheme
- Association of Information Technology Professionals
- Bernard Galler, former president
- Category:Presidents of the Association for Computing Machinery
- Computer science
- Computing
- Edmund Berkeley, co-founder
- Franz Alt, former president
- Grace Murray Hopper Award, awarded by the ACM
- Ken Kennedy Award, awarded by ACM and the IEEE Computer Society
- Timeline of computing 2400 BC–1949
- Turing Award

References

[1] http://doi.acm.org/10.1145/1897239.1897240
[2] http://delivery.acm.org/10.1145/1900000/1897240/p5-wakkary.html?ip=67.34.143.195&CFID=44596637&CFTOKEN=44967240&__acm__=1316999391_2787abbb2aacb2555d1377d1e08471e5
[3] ACM Copyright Policy (http://www.acm.org/pubs/copyright_policy/)
[4] Joint Task Force of Association for Computing Machinery (ACM), Association for Information Systems (AIS) and IEEE Computer Society (IEEE-CS). "Computing Curricula 2005: The Overview Report" (http://www.acm.org/education/education/curric_vols/CC2005-March06Final.pdf). .
[5] See, e.g., Ken Kennedy Award
[6] ACM Senior Members-An Overview (http://www.acm.org/membership/membership/senior_members/)
[7] List of ACM Fellows (http://fellows.acm.org/)
[8] "ACM Special Interest Groups" (http://www.acm.org/sigs). . Retrieved August 7, 2010.
[9] "ACM Chapters" (http://www.acm.org/chapters/). . Retrieved August 7, 2010.
[10] Professional Chapters http://campus.acm.org/public/chapters/geo_listing/index.cfm?ct=Professional&inus=0
[11] http://balto.acm.org/
[12] http://www.gbcacm.org/
[13] http://www.dcacm.org/
[14] Student Chapters http://campus.acm.org/public/chapters/geo_listing/index.cfm?ct=Student&inus=0
[15] http://wp.acm.org/bitmesra/
[16] http://brockcsc.ca/acm-information
[17] http://csulb.acm.org/
[18] http://www.ecs.csus.edu/acm/
[19] http://acsu.cornell.edu/index.php
[20] http://gtacm.org/
[21] http://www.cse.iitd.ernet.in/~acm
[22] http://www.acm.jhu.edu/
[23] http://acm.lsu.edu/
[24] http://njit.acm.org/
[25] http://www.peirce.edu/
[26] http://psu-acm.org/
[27] http://acm.cs.purdue.edu/
[28] http://psgtech.acm.org

[29] http://www.svnit.ac.in/acm
[30] http://acm.rso.siuc.edu/
[31] http://acm.cse.buffalo.edu/
[32] http://cs.uah.edu/acm/
[33] http://acm.cs.ucla.edu/
[34] http://cses.ucsd.edu/
[35] http://www.acmucsb.com/
[36] http://acm.soe.ucsc.edu/
[37] http://acm.cs.uic.edu/
[38] http://www.acm.uiuc.edu/
[39] http://acm.uiowa.edu/
[40] http://umass.acm.org/
[41] http://acm.umn.edu/
[42] http://www.upacm.org/blog/
[43] http://acm.ut.ac.ir/
[44] http://www.utacm.org/
[45] http://www.informatik.uni-ulm.de/acm/chapter/
[46] http://acm.wwu.edu/
[47] http://www.acm.wpi.edu/
[48] http://www.acmycce.co.nr/
[49] (http://www.cikmconference.org/)
[50] http://www.sigevo.org/gecco-2009/
[51] http://www.ht2009.org/
[52] http://www.jcdl.org/
[53] "Grace Hopper Celebration of Women in Computing, Largest Gathering of Women in Computing, Attracts Researchers, Industry" (http://www.acm.org/press-room/news-releases-2008/hopper-08-preview/). . Retrieved 27 June 2011.
[54] ACM Elects New Leaders Committed to Expanding International Initiatives (http://www.acm.org/press-room/news-releases/2010/acm-leaders-2010)

External links

- Official website (http://http://www.acm.org)
- ACM portal (http://portal.acm.org/) for publications
- ACM Digital Library (http://portal.acm.org/dl.cfm)

Fellow

A **fellow** in the broadest sense is someone who is an equal or a comrade. The term fellow is also used to describe a person, particularly by those in the upper social classes. It is most often used in an academic context: a fellow is often part of an elite group of learned people who are awarded fellowship to work together as peers in the pursuit of knowledge or practice. The fellows may include visiting professors, postdoctoral researchers and doctoral researchers.

Academia

Research fellow

The title of research fellow is used to denote an academic research position at a university or a similar institution.

Teaching fellow

The title of Teaching fellow is used to denote an academic teaching position at a university or similar institution.

Emeritus title in the UK

The title fellow might be given to an academic member of staff upon retirement who continues to be affiliate to a university institution in the United Kingdom.

Oxford, Cambridge and Dublin

At Colleges of the Universities of Oxford, Cambridge, and Trinity College, Dublin, full fellows form the governing body of the college. They may elect a Council to handle day-to-day management. All fellows are entitled to certain privileges within their colleges, which may include dining at High Table (free of charge) and possibly the right to a room in college (free of charge).

There are a number of types of fellow:

- *Research fellows* are researchers, whose salaries or stipends are paid by a college from the income of its endowment. Some of the less affluent colleges do not pay their research fellows a salary, instead award fellowships to researchers already employed by the university.
- At Oxford, *college tutors* are fellows, who are paid to provide small-group teaching to a college's undergraduates. The position is typically a joint appointment (there are a variety of types) with the university.
- At Cambridge, *teaching officers* (lecturers, readers, and professors) are entitled to a college fellowship. For lecturers and readers, the process is competitive – generally the most able academics get fellowships at the richest and most prestigious colleges . Professors are allocated to colleges by a centralised process to ensure fairness. These fellows may or may not provide small-group teaching to undergraduates in the college, for which they would be paid by the hour. College fellows at Cambridge (except for research fellows) have no duties as such and are not paid. They will typically have a salaried post either with their college or the university.
- At Cambridge, a *praelector* is a fellow of a college, who formally presents students during the matriculation and graduation ceremony.

Most Cambridge colleges grant fellowships for life after a qualifying period. Retired academics may therefore remain as fellows. In Oxford upon retirement, a Governing Body fellow would normally be elected a *fellow emeritus* and would leave the Governing Body. Distinguished old members of the college, or its benefactors and friends, might also be elected 'Honorary Fellow', normally for life; but beyond limited dining rights this is merely an honour. Most Oxford colleges have 'Fellows by Special Election' or 'Supernumerary Fellows', who may be members of the teaching staff, but not necessarily members of the Governing Body.

US medical training

In US medical institutions, a fellow refers to someone who has completed residency training (e.g. in internal medicine, pediatrics, general surgery, etc.) and is currently in a 1 to 3 year subspecialty training program (e.g. cardiology, pediatric nephrology, transplant surgery, etc.).

Medical Education Systems in the United Kingdom, Canada, Australia and New Zealand

In these four countries the overarching responsibility of postgraduate specialist medical and surgical education is assigned to a number of Royal colleges. Examples of these colleges are: the Royal College of Surgeons, The Royal College of Physicians and Surgeons of Canada and the Royal Australian and New Zealand College of Psychiatrists. When a graduate medical doctor completes the speciality training/examinations required by one of these colleges he or she is assigned the designation of Fellow of the corresponding college. This designation comes with a post-nominal designation such as FRCS (Fellow of the Royal College of Surgeons), FRCP (C) (Fellow of the Royal College of Physicians of Canada) and FRANZCP (Fellow of the Royal Australian and New Zealand College of Psychiatrists).

Graduate school fellowships

In the context of graduate school in the United States and Canada, a fellow is a recipient of a *fellowship*. Examples are the NSF Graduate Research Fellowship, the National Defense Science and Engineering Graduate Fellowship, the Guggenheim Fellowship, the Rosenthal Fellowship and the Presidential Management Fellowship.

Academia administration

Harvard University

At Harvard and some other universities in the United States, "fellows" are members of the Board of Trustees who hold administrative positions as non-executive trustee rather than academics.

Cambridge and Oxford Colleges

Some senior administrators of a college such as bursars are made fellows, and thereby become members of the governing body, because of their importance to the running of a College.

Secondary education

Teaching fellows in the US

The term used, in the United States, the high school and middle school setting for students or adults that assist a teacher with one or more classes.[1]

Learned or professional societies

Fellows are the highest grade of membership of most professional or learned societies (see for example, the Chartered Institute of Arbitrators. Lower grades are referred to as members (who typically share voting rights with the fellows), or associates (who may or may not, depending on whether "associate" status is a form of full membership).

How a fellowship is acquired varies for each society, but may typically involve some or all of these:

- A qualifying period in a lower grade
- Passing a series of examinations

- Nomination by two existing fellows who know the applicant professionally
- Evidence of continued formal training post-qualification
- Evidence of substantial achievement in the subject area
- Submission of a thesis or portfolio of works which will be examined

Exclusive learned societies such as the Royal Society have Fellow as the only grade of membership, others like the Faculty of Young Musicians (now defunct) have members holding the post of Associate and posts *Honoris Causa*.

Honorary fellow

Appointment as an honorary fellow in a learned or professional society can be either to honour exceptional achievement and/or service within the professional domain of the awarding body or to honour contributions related to the domain from someone who is professionally outside of it. Membership of the awarding body may or may not be a requirement.

Industry / Corporate

Large corporations in research and development-intensive industries (IBM or Sun Microsystems in information technology, Bell Labs or L3 Communications in telecommunications, and Boston Scientific in Medical Devices for example) appoint a small number of senior scientists and engineers as fellows. Fellow is the most senior rank or title one can achieve on a technical career, though some fellows also hold business titles such as vice president or chief technology officer. Examples are:

- IBM Fellows [2].
- Microsoft technical fellows [3].

Nonprofit / Government

The title fellow can be used for participants in a professional development program run by a nonprofit or governmental organization. This type of fellowship is a short term work opportunity (1-2 years)[4] for professionals who already possess some level of academic or professional expertise that will serve the nonprofit mission. Fellows are given a stipend as well as professional experience and leadership training. Examples are:

- White House Fellows [5]
- Supreme Court Fellows Program [6]
- Sample of Nonprofit Leadership Programs [7]

Notes and references

[1] Home - Teaching Fellows (http://www.teachingfellows.org)
[2] http://www.research.ibm.com/resources/awards_fellows.shtml
[3] http://www.microsoft.com/presspass/exec/techfellow/default.mspx
[4] UVM Career Services. "Find Non-Profit Fellowships" (http://www.uvm.edu/~career/?Page=fellowships.html&SM=otherjobsubmenu.html). University of Vermont. . Retrieved 19 July 2011.
[5] http://www.whitehouse.gov/about/fellows
[6] http://www.supremecourt.gov/fellows/default.aspx
[7] http://philanthropy.com/article/A-Sampling-of-Nonprofit/52575/

Computer Professionals for Social Responsibility

Computer Professionals for Social Responsibility	
Abbreviation	CPSR
Motto	Technology is driving the future... it is up to us to do the steering
Formation	1983
Type	NGO
Purpose/focus	impacts of computer technology on society
Headquarters	Seattle, Washington
Website	cpsr.org [1]

Computer Professionals for Social Responsibility (**CPSR**) is a global organization promoting the responsible use of computer technology. CPSR was incorporated [2] in 1983 (following discussions and organizing that began in 1981). It educates policymakers and the public on a wide range of issues. CPSR has incubated numerous projects such as Privaterra, the Public Sphere Project [3], EPIC (the Electronic Privacy Information Center), the 21st Century Project, the Civil Society Project, and the CFP (Computers, Freedom and Privacy) Conference. Originally founded by U.S. computer scientists at Stanford University and Xerox PARC, CPSR now has members in over 30 countries on six continents. CPSR is a non-profit 501.c.3 organization registered in California.

When CPSR was first established it was concerned solely about the use of computers in warfare. This initially was focused on the Strategic Computing Initiative, a US Defense project to use artificial intelligence in military systems, but added opposition to the Strategic Defense Initiative (SDI) shortly after the program was announced. The Boston chapter helped organize a debate related to the software reliability of SDI systems which drew national attention ("Software Seen as Obstacle in Developing 'Star Wars', Philip M. Boffey, (New York Times, September 16, 1986) to these issues. Later, workplace issues, privacy, and community networks were added to CPSR's agenda.

CPSR was originally a chapter-based organization and had chapters in Palo Alto, Boston, Seattle, Austin, Washington, DC, Portland (Oregon) and other US locations as well as a variety of international chapters including Peru and Spain. The chapters often developed innovative projects including a slide show about the dangers of launch on warning (Boston chapter) and the Seattle Community Network [4] (Seattle chapter).

CPSR sponsored two conferences: the Participatory Design Conferences which is held biennially (the most recent, the 11th is being held in Sydney, Australia) and the Directions and Implications of Advanced Computing (DIAC) symposium series which was launched in 1987 in Seattle. The DIAC symposia have been convened roughly every other year since that time (most recently in October , 2010 in Prato Italy in conjunction with the Community Information Research Network (CIRN) annual conference. Four books (*Directions and Implications of Advanced Computing*; *Reinventing Technology, Rediscovering Community*; *Community Practice in the Network Society*; and *Shaping the Network Society*) and two special sections in the Communications of the ACM ("Social Responsibility" and "Social Computing") resulted from the DIAC symposia.

CPSR awards the Norbert Wiener Award for Social and Professional Responsibility. Some notable recipients include David Parnas, Joseph Weizenbaum, Kristen Nygaard, Barbara Simons, Antonia Stone, Peter Neumann, Marc Rotenberg, Mitch Kapor, and Douglas Engelbart.

External links

- Official website [5]
- Documentary film about Norbert Wiener Award winner, Joseph Weizenbaum ("Weizenbaum. Rebel at Work.") [6]
- Computer Professionals for Social Responsibility Records, 1983-1991. [7] Charles Babbage Institute, University of Minnesota.
- Oral history interview with Severo Ornstein and Laura Gould [8], Charles Babbage Institute, University of Minnesota. Oral history interview by Bruce Bruemmer, 1994, discussing the formation and activities of Computer Professionals for Social Responsibility.

References

[1] http://www.cpsr.org
[2] http://www.cpsr.org/about/history
[3] http://www.publicsphereproject.org/
[4] http://www.scn.org
[5] http://www.cpsr.org/
[6] http://www.ilmarefilm.org/W_E_1.htm
[7] http://purl.umn.edu/40803
[8] http://www.cbi.umn.edu/oh/display.phtml?id=179

Golden Key International Honour Society

Golden Key International Honour Society	
Motto	To enable members to realize their potential through the advancement of academics, leadership and service.
Formation	November 29, 1977
Type	Honor society
Headquarters	Atlanta, Georgia
Location	United States
Membership	Over 2 million[1]
Website	http://www.goldenkey.org

The **Golden Key International Honour Society** (formerly **Golden Key National Honor Society**) is an Atlanta, Georgia-based non-profit organization[2] founded in 1977 to recognise academic achievement among college and university students in all disciplines.

Golden Key currently has over 400 chapters at colleges and universities in eight countries: Australia, Canada, India, Malaysia, New Zealand, South Africa, The Bahamas and the United States. Golden Key is the world's largest collegiate honor society. Membership into Golden Key is by invitation only, to the top 15% of college/university 2nd, 3rd and 4th year students and top performing US graduate students in all fields of study, based solely on the criteria of their academic achievements.[3]

History

Golden Key was founded by a group of undergraduate students and faculty members at Georgia State University in Atlanta, Georgia, on November 29, 1977.

In 2001, the society modified its name to Golden Key International Honour Society to reflect its diversity and global presence. The spelling of "Honour" was utilized to observe the more globally accepted spelling.

Activities

Golden Key offers a number of services for its members. These include résumé and graduate program assistance, career planning and opportunities, leadership opportunities, networking, and member discounts. Golden Key claims that it offers more than $1,000,000 annually in scholarships and awards to its members along with a variety of other opportunities, both academic and career.[4] Golden Key's core values include community service and its chapters are involved in a wide variety of volunteer projects in their local communities such as Habitat for Humanity, Terry Fox Run, Make a Difference Day, and various literacy service opportunities.[5] The Golden Key International Honour Society was among 10 organizations to receive the In2Books Community Service Award in 2010.[6]

Golden Key is an active member of several organizations, including the Association of College Honor Societies, an American agency certifying college and university honor societies. Other organizations Golden Key is involved with include:[7]

- National Collegiate Honors Council (NCHC)
- National Association of Student Personnel Administrators (NASPA)
- Association of International Educators (NAFSA)
- National Scholarship Providers Association (NSPA)
- American Association of Collegiate Registrars and Admissions Officers (AACRAO)

Golden Key is governed by an international Board of Directors.[8] Its volunteer advisory structure includes the International Leadership Council, the Council of Advisors[9] and the Council of Student Members.[10]

Controversy

Concerns were raised over a decade ago about the apparently large gap between the amount of money spent on salaries and the amount spent on giving out scholarships. Articles in the University of British Columbia student newspaper the Ubyssey claimed to have examined the society's finances and scholarship practices. Although the society claimed to "return 75 per cent of each membership as benefits and services to local chapters and their members [while the] other 25 per cent is used for administrative expenses," the Ubyssey found that in 1997 salaries, management and general expenses totalled $2,997,827, almost 47 per cent of the $6,430,054 in total expenditures. A second article found that Golden Key spent just $289,461 (US dollars) on scholarships, less than 5 per cent of their total expenditures for the fiscal year ending June 30, 1997. The society now claims to spend approximately $1,000,000 annually on scholarships and awards,[11] though it is unclear whether this allocation has remained proportional since then. All recent financials since 2008 have been made publicly available and audited by third party auditors.

In response to this controversy a decade ago, one Golden Key member recently claimed that $11 of the $80 membership fee goes to the student's local chapter. Each local chapter may use this money as they see fit. A variable amount (minimum $100) of additional funds are allocated for in-house chapter cash scholarships. The amount given for these local scholarships is based on the number of members inducted, which is then distributed by the local chapter in accordance with their determined criteria. Some criteria may include active participation in chapter service projects and meeting attendance. Most chapters divide their available chapter scholarships into three awards; one each for Sophomore, Junior and Senior students. Another Golden Key member stated that this information is anecdotal and not a general practice of the Society today.

An examination of the organization's Form 990[12] from the year 2009 seems to confirm that the organization spends significantly more on salaries and benefits than on scholarships. In the fiscal year ending in 2009, total scholarships (Schedule I, Part III) were $546,291, compared to salaries of over $2 million. Scholarships were less than 6% of the total revenues ($9.4 million). In addition, the organization transferred over $5 million of its assets to a new affiliated foundation.

Honorary members

Honorary members are elected by Golden Key. They do not necessarily endorse the validity of the Golden Key organization or participate in its activities.[13]

Society pin from 1995 when the name was still "Golden Key National Honor Society"

Well-known honorary members include:[14]

1. Roberta Bondar, Canada's First Female Astronaut
2. Adrienne Clarkson, former Governor General of Canada
3. Cooper Randall, Australian Biochemist
4. William J. Clinton, Former US President
5. Ujjal Dev Singh Dosanjh, Canadian lawyer and politician
6. Bill Cosby, Entertainer
7. Archbishop Emeritus Desmond Tutu (Nobel Peace Prize Laureate)
8. Ronald W. Reagan, Former US President
9. Ian Thorpe, Olympic Gold Medalist
10. Elie Wiesel, Nobel Laureate and Author
11. Riaan Manser - Solo adventurer and motivational speaker
12. Clem Sunter - Professional speaker, scenario planner and author
13. Tupac Amaru Shakur - Entertainer
14. Nicol David - No.1 women's squash player in the world
15. Quentin Bryce - Governor General of Australia
16. Professor Patrick McGorry - Australian of the Year 2010
17. Richard Daley - Mayor of Chicago
18. Eddie Sutton - Former Men's Basketball Coach at Oklahoma State
19. Dolly Parton - Entertainer
20. Ted Stevens - Former U.S. Senator
21. Donny Osmond - Entertainer
22. Julian Bond - Civil Rights Activist
23. Joseph P. Kennedy II - Former member of the U.S. House of Representatives
24. Thomas Menino - Mayor of Boston
25. Tim Tebow - Former Heisman Trophy Winner at the University of Florida and current quarterback for the Denver Broncos
26. Tom Allen - Former member of the U.S. House of Representatives
27. Stephen King - Bestselling Author
28. Mike Krzyzewski - Men's Basketball Coach at Duke University
29. Bobby Bowden - Former Head Football Coach at Florida State University
30. Charlie Crist - Former Governor of Florida
31. Jim Perdue - Chairman of Perdue Farms
32. Myron Rolle - Rhodes Scholar and current member of the NFL's Tennessee Titans
33. Margaret Atwood - Canadian Author and Poet

Honorary members are elected by this organization and do not necessarily endorse the validity of the Golden Key organization.

References

[1] "Golden Key International Honour Society website FAQ" (http://www.goldenkey.org/GKIHS/GoldenKeyInDepth/FAQs/). .

[2] IRS Search for Charities (http://www.irs.gov/app/pub-78/searchFromResults.do?nameSearchTypeStarts=true&names=golden+key&nameSearchTypeAll=true&city=&state=All..&country=USA&deductibility=all&dispatchMethod=search&searched.nameSearchTypeStarts=false&searched.names=golden+key&searched.nameSearchTypeAll=false&searched.city=&searched.state=All...&searched.country=USA&searched.deductibility=all&searched.sortColumn=name&searched.indexOfFirstRow=1000&searched.isDescending=false&submitName=Search).

[3] http://www.achsnatl.org/society.asp?society=gk

[4] "Scholarships & Awards" (http://www.goldenkey.org/GKIHS/MemberBenefits/ScholarshipsandAwards/). Golden Key International Honour Society. 2008. . Retrieved 2008-05-27.

[5] http://www.goldenkey.org/GKIHS/MemberBenefits/LiteracyServiceOpportunities/

[6] http://in2books.epals.com/content.aspx?caid=I2BCorp&divid=pressrelease_In2Books

[7] https://www.goldenkey.org/GKIHS/GoldenKeyInDepth/WhatisGoldenKey/

[8] Board of Directors (http://www.goldenkey.org/GKIHS/GoldenKeyInDepth/SocietyLeadership/BoardofDirectors.htm) Golden Key International Honour Society

[9] Council of Advisors (http://www.goldenkey.org/GKIHS/GoldenKeyInDepth/SocietyLeadership/CouncilofAdvisors.htm) Golden Key International Honour Society

[10] Council of Student Members (http://www.goldenkey.org/GKIHS/GoldenKeyInDepth/SocietyLeadership/CouncilofStudentMembers.htm) Golden Key International Honour Society

[11] http://www.goldenkey.org/GKIHS/GoldenKeyInDepth/WhatisGoldenKey/

[12] http://www.guidestar.org/FinDocuments//2009/581/306/2009-581306896-069f4bd9-9.pdf

[13] "What is Golden Key?" (https://www.goldenkey.org/GKIHS/GoldenKeyInDepth/WhatisGoldenKey/). Golden Key International Honour Society. 2008. . Retrieved 2010-12-03.

[14] "What is Golden Key?" (https://www.goldenkey.org/GKIHS/GoldenKeyInDepth/WhatisGoldenKey/). Golden Key International Honour Society. 2008. . Retrieved 2010-12-03.

External links

- Golden Key International Honour Society official website (http://www.goldenkey.org)
- Association of College Honor Societies website (http://www.achsnatl.org/)
- Better Business Bureau website (http://www.bbb.org/atlanta/business-reviews/youth-organizations-and-centers/golden-key-international-honour-society-in-atlanta-ga-4144)

Article Sources and Contributors

Daniel D. McCracken *Source*: http://en.wikipedia.org/w/index.php?title=Daniel_D._McCracken *Contributors*: Aliotra, Auntof6, BrownHairedGirl, Connormah, DanMcCracken, Danny Cotton, Dansteingart, Esmito, G Clark, Horow021, IdahoBackwoods, Janm67, KYPark, Lproven, Park3r, Rms125a@hotmail.com, Robert A West, Royboycrashfan, Rwwww, Satori Son, Schwilgue, Torla42, UnicornTapestry, W Nowicki, W163, Wikiklrsc, William's scraper, 1 anonymous edits

Computer science *Source*: http://en wikipedia.org/w/index.php?title=Computer_science *Contributors*: "alyosha", 144.132.75.xxx, 16@r, 204.96.33.xxx, 211.199.225.xxx, 212.1.96.xxx, 213.253.39.xxx, 216.209.60.xxx, 28bytes, 4jobs, 5 albert square, 7265, 9258fahsflkh917fas, A. B., APH, ARUNKUMAR P.R, Aaronbrick, Abigail-II, Academic Challenger, Acather96, Ackmenm, Aeternus, Agogino, Ahoerstemeier, Ahy1, Airplaneman, Alansohn, Aldie, Alex.g, Allamericanbear, Allan McInnes, Allstarecho, AlphaTwo, Altenmann, Amomam, Anaxial, Ancheta Wis, Andre Engels, Andreas Kaufmann, Android79, Andycjp, Anetode, Angela, Angus Lepper, Anjin-san, Antandrus, Anthony, Apparition11, Applegoddess, Appraiser, ArchStanton69, ArglebargleIV, Aruton, Arvind Singh, Ashish Gaikwad, Astew10, Austin Henderson, Aviroop Ghosh, Avs5221, AxelBoldt, AzraelUK, B4hand, BBB, BMF81, BRG, BRUTE, Bachmann1234, Backslash Forwardslash, Bact, Balaji7, Barcelova, Barfooz, Barneca, Bedwanimas214, Beefyt, Ben Tillman, Bender235, Bensmith, Bergbra, Bethenco, Betterusername, Bevo, Bfigura's puppy, BigMatty93, BigMattyO, Bijuro, Billposer, Blaisorblade, Blix1ms0ns, Bluemask, Bmeguru, Bobo192, Bobthesmiley, BokicaK, Bongwarrior, Bookandcoffee, Bookinvestor, Bookofjude, Borislav, Bovineone, BozMo, Branril209, Brian Pearson, Brick Thrower, Brighterorange, Brion VIBBER, Briséis, Bruchowski, Brycedrm, Bryson1410, Bshankaran, Bubba73, Bumm13, Buridan, Buscalade, Bveedu, Bwfrank, CBM, CES1596, CRGreathouse, CSgroup7, Cadsuane Melaidhrin, Caesura, CalaD33, Calltech, Camembert, CameronHarris, Can't sleep, clown will eat me, Carbuncle, Careercornerstone, CarlHewitt, Cburnett, Ceas webmaster, Charles Matthews, Chocoforfriends, Chris Roy, ChrisHamburg, Chrislk02, Christian Storm, Christian75, Chun-hian, Ckatz, Claygate, Cleduc, ClosedEyesSeeing, CloudNine, Cnkids, Cntras, Coder Dan, CommonsDelinker, Conversion script, Coolcaesar, Corti, Courcelles, Crippled Sloth, Cromoser, Cryoboy, Cupat07, Cyan, Cyanoa Crylate, Cybercobra, D. Recorder, D.h, DARTH SIDIOUS 2, DVD R W, DanKeshet, Daniel Quinlan, Danno uk, Dante Alighieri, Danushka99999, Darkstar56, Daven200520, Dawn Bard, Dawnseeker2000, Dbabbitt, Ddawson, Deadbeatatdawn, Debuggar, Decumanus, Delirium, Demize, Denny, Derek Ross, Dfarrell07, Dfletter, Dgreen34, Dhall1245, Dhp1080, Diana cionoiu, Diderot, Diderot's dreams, Dilaksan, Dimoes, Discospinster, Docu, DoesPHalt, Donhalcon, Dontknoa, Doulos Christos, Download, Dreadstar, Dream Focus, DrewT2, Druiloor, Dullhunk, Dysprosia, Dzenanz, Dzonatas, E rulez, E. H.-A. Gerbracht, ESkog, ESpublic013, EagleOne, Ed g2s, Edenphd, Edivorce, Eequor, Eiserlohpp, Ekrub-ntyh, EllenPetersen, Elsendero, Emerybob, EnglishEfternamn, Epbr123, Epolk, Eray, Erc, Eridani, Erik Zachte, Erkan Yilmaz, Erstats, Esanchez7587, Espen, Evanx, Everyking, Everything counts, Farmerchris, Farzan mc, Favonian, FayssalF, Fennec, Ferengi, Fireduck, Flcelloguy, Flewis, Fluri, Fossum, Fourchannel, Fredrik, Fubar Obfusco, Furkhaocean, Fuzzie, Fvilim, Fyver528, Gaius Cornelius, Galoubet, Garik, Gbali, Ghyll, Giants27, Giftlite, GlasGhost, Glenn, Gnabi82, GraemeL, Grafen, Graham87, GreenEdu, Grim23, Grunt, Guaka, Guanaco, Guppy, Gusisgay, Guy Peters, Gwern, Gwernol, Haakon, Hadal, HaeB, Hahamhanuka, HairyFotr, Ham Pastrami, Hannes Hirzel, Hans Adler, HappyDog, Harryboyles, Hdt83, Headbomb, Hellhound, Hellotoast, Hennessey, Patrick, Henry Flower, HenryLi, Hephaestos, Hermel, Hersfold, Hezarfenn, Hide&Reason, Hobbes, Hon-3s-T, Honta, Hu, Hu12, Hubbard rox 2008, Hughleat, Hunan131, Hunhot, Husond, Hyad, IAENG, IRP, Iain.mcclatchie, Ibbn, Ideogram, Igoldste, InShaneee, Indon, Ino5hiro, Insanity Incarnate, Intgr, Iridescence, Iridescent, IronGargoyle, Itsmesid, J-Wiki, J.delanoy, JCLately, JHunterJ, JaGa, Jackfork, JakeVortex, Jakraay, JamesBWatson, Jason Davies, Jauhienij, Jaxl, Jay, Jay-Sebastos, Jayme, Jcrwaford5, Jdforrester, Jeffhoy, JeremyA, Jerryobject, Jersey Devil, JetLover, Jevansen, Jhballard, Jiang, Jim Mahoney, Jimothytrotter, Jitse Niesen, Jiule0, Jk2q3jrklse, Jkimdgu, Jkominek, Jlenthe, Jmcangas, Jnivekk, John Nevard, John.legal, JohnC1987, JohnOwens, Johnnyw, Jonik, Jonovision, Joseph Solis in Australia, Josephgrossberg, Joshua bigamo, Jpbowen, Jpvinall, Jstrater, Julcia, JulesH, Junglecat, Just Another Dan, Jwalls, Jwdietrich2, Jzcool, K-UNIT, Katefan0, Kayvan45622, Kazuo Moriwaka, Kbh3rd, Kdano, Keeper76, Keith Cascio, Kenny sh, Keraunoscopia, Kgfleischmann, Khalfani khaldun, Khendon, Kiefer.Wolfowitz, Kjetil r, Klausness, Kntg, Kozuch, Kralja, Kungfuadam, Kuru, Kvikeg, Kwekubo, Kwertii, Kwharris, LA2, LC, La Pianista, Ladies gifts, LaggedOnUser, Lake Greifen, Lambiam, Lee Daniel Crocker, Leibniz, Leire Sánchez, Leithp, Leujohn, Levin, Liao, Light current, Lightdarkend, Lightmouse, Lilgip01, Linn, Little Mountain 5, Loisel, Lotje, Loul, Louis Waweru, Lowellian, Lucid, Luminique, Luna Santin, Lupin, Lupo, Lysander89, MCB, MCR789, MIT Trekkie, MOiRe, MTizz1, Mac010382, MacMed, Machine Elf 1735, Maimai009, Makkuro, Mani1, MarSch, Marasmusine, Marc Girod, Mark Renier, Mark Shaw, Markan, MartinSpamer, Masterpiece2000, Materdaddy, Materialscientist, MathMartin, Matt Britt, Matt Crypto, Matteh, Matthe20, Mattingly23, Maurice Carbonaro, Maureen, Mav, Max the tenken, Maxime.Debosschere, Maximus Rex, Mayumashu, Mayuri.sandhanshiv, McGeddon, Mcasswidmeyer, Mdd, Meaghan, Meisterkoch, Merovingian, Metalmaniac69, Metamusing, Methcub, Mgnbar, Mic, Michael Hardy, Michael Zimmermann, MichaelMcGuffin, Michaeln, Mihai.stefanache, Mihas, Mikeeg555, Mikez80, Mineminemine, Minesweeper, Mipadi, Miquonranger03, Mirv, MisterCharlie, Miym, Mkehrt, Mmeri, Mohammadshamma, Mori Riyo, Morwen, Mouhanad alramli, Mpeisenbr, MrOllie, Msc44, Mttcmbs, Muhandes, Mxn, Myasuda, NHRHS2010, Naddy, Nakos2208, Namastheg, NattyBumppo, Nazgul533, Ndenison, Necklace, Neil Dodgson, Neilc, Nerval, Netoholic, Neurolysis, Neutral current, NewEnglandYankee, Newton2, Niaz, Nighthawk19, Nikai, Nikevich, Nikola Smolenski, Noformation, Notinasnaid, Novacatz, Nympheta, OMouse, Ohnoitsjamie, Old Moonraker, Oldwes, Ole Aamot, Oleg Alexandrov, Olexandr Kravchuk, Olivier, Olorin28, Omicronpersei8, Onestone, Oo64eva, OrgasGirl, Orz, Ott, Oxymoron83, PCHS-NJROTC, Pacdude9, Palaeovia, Pasha11, Passw0rd, Pavel Jelinek, Pcb21, Pearle, Pedrito, Pegasus1138, Pengo, Perl guy, Persoid, Peterlin, Petr.adamek, Pfuchs722, Phantomsteve, Philip Trueman, Phoe6, Physis, Piano non troppo, Piecemealcranky, Piet Delport, Pimpedshortie99, Pinar, Pinethicket, Pjoef, Poindexter Propellerhead, Poisoncarter, Polyphilo, Poor Yorick, Popsracer, Porco-esphino, Poshzombie, Poweroid, Powo, Pps, Prashant Dey, Pratapy, Project2501a, Ps ttf, Pumpmeup, Quackor, Quux, Qwertyus, R000t, R3m0t, Raanoo, RadicalBender, Raj Wijesinghe, Ralfipedia, RandomStringOfCharacters, Raul654, Readams, Recognizance, RedWolf, Rednas1234, Regenspaziergang, Reisio, Relix, Remshad, Requestion, Revolver, Rfc1394, Richard001, RichardF, RickiRich, Rivertorch, Rjwilmsi, Rob Hooft, Robert K S, Robert Merkel, Robin klein, Rodhilton, Roxxyroxursox, RoyBoy, Royote, Rrelf, Rror, Rstevens27, Rtc, Rtyq2, Ruud Koot, S.K., S.Örvarr.S, Sajibcse, Saketmitra, Salem F, Salesvery1, Salsa Shark, Sam Korn, Samuel.Jones, Sandeepgupta, Sango123, Sannse, Sanscrit1234, Savie Kumara, Saywhatman, Sbwoodside, Schneelocke, SchreyP, Sciprecision, Scotty16-2007, Sdedeo, Seaphoto, Sebastjanmm, Sega381, SergeyJ, Sfisher, Sheldrake, Sheliak, Shenme, Shepshep, Shimei, Shinjiman, Shirik, Shizhao, Shmitra, Si23mk4n32i, Sickdartzepic, Siebrand, Sigma 7, SilverStar, Simeon, SimonP, SimonW, SixWingedSeraph, Slakr, Slashme, Smimram, SocratesJedi, Soilguy2, SolKarma, Some jerk on the Internet, Somewherepurple, Soultacc, Sovereigna, Spacepotato, Sparkz08, Sparkzy, SpectrumDT, Spellchecker, Spikey, Spitfire, SpuriousQ, Srikant.sharma, Srshetty94, Stan Shebs, Star-Syrup, StaticGull, Steave77, Stephenb, Stevertigo, Superzohar, Systemetsys, T-Solo202, TakuyaMurata, Talbg, Tarquin, Taw, Technotaoist, Tee Owe, TexasDex, Texture, The Anome, The Divine Fluffalizer, The Fish, The Original Wildbear, The Rambling Man, The Thing That Should Not Be, The Transhumanist (AWB), The wub, TheDJ, TheVenerableBede, Thefakeeditor, ThereIsNoSteve, Thiaguwin, Thijswijs, Thingg, Thoreaulylazy, Thray, Thv, Tide rolls, Tigershrike, Tijfo098, Timwi, Tinytn, Tms9980, Tommy2010, Tompsci, Tomsega, Tonywchen, ToxicOranges, Tparameter, Traroth, TreveX, Treyt021, Troworld, Trusilver, Turnipface, Tuxisuau, Tv316, Uncle G, Uncle Milty, Unknown483, User77764, Vanished User 0001, Velblod, Velella, Verbal, Vpovilaitis, Vranak, Vsion, WDavis1911, Waiwai933, Wakka, Wald, Walkerma, Weedwhacker128, Wernher, West.andrew.g, Weylinp, WikHead, WikiNSK, Wikieditor06, Wikipelli, Wilycoder, Wimt, Wmahan, Wolfrock, Woohookitty, Wrathchild, Wtmitchell, Xiaogaozi, Xionbox, Xsmith, Yk Yk Yk, Yondonjamts, Yym, Zanter, Zhou Yu, Zigger, Zito ta xania, Zondor, Zow, Zvika, Иъ Лю Ха, Лев Дубовой, 1694 anonymous edits

City College of New York *Source*: http://en.wikipedia.org/w/index.php?title=City_College_of_New_York *Contributors*: 1122334455, 172, 24.44.230.xxx, 64.26.98.xxx, A bit iffy, Alan W, Almosthonest06, AndreasKQ, Andrew Schaaf, Andy Marchbanks, Anthony Appleyard, ArnoldReinhold, Artyoung, AshcroftIleum, Aspects, Astuishin, Aude, BRG, Babajobu, Baboo, Beginning, Bender235, Benuski, Billy Hathorn, Bkh2107, Bobak, Bobblewik, BostonRed, Brian1979, CALR, CComMack, CapitalR, Carlosferry, Charles Matthews, Conversion script, Curps, D Monack, D6, DOAsaturn, DanBoothCohen, Daniel Yates, Danlurie, Darkcore, DavidLevinson, Dgweiler, Dinopup, Dogears, Dr berman, EagleOne, Edwardx, Efghij, El Mayimbe, ElKevbo, EoGuy, Epeefleche, ExplorerCDT, FeelsLikeHome, Firsfron, Fourchette, FrankEldonDixon, Fuzzy510, Gabbe, Gaius Cornelius, Gamgee, Gar3th, GeorgeLouis, Gioto, Greenshed, Gregfitzy, Grkp511, Ground Zero, Grsz11, Hayupoo2, Hindusauce, Hocusa, Howardjp, Igor alexandrov, Iohannes Animosus, Isnow, Iss246, JASpencer, James Nettles, Jim.henderson, Jmkleeberg, Jonathan71, Josh02138, JustAGal, Jzcool, Knickeditor, Kollision, Kroschka Ru, Kurykh, LaszloWalrus, Lenamarvin, LilHelpa, Llamabr, Lnolan, LtNOWIS, MER-C, MONGO, Madmedea, Malepheasant, Mandarax, Marc Shepherd, Mark83, Marty42, Masonpatriot, Maximus Rex, Mazeartist, MegX, Mentifisto, Metropolitan90, Mhym, Mintleaf, MortalConviction, MovieMadness, Mrbluesky, Mudvaine357, Mystache, Nakon, Ncosmob, Noeticsage, Nogood, Optikos, PTosh, PaulLev, PhilipR, Phoe, Plasticspork, Playtime, Postcard Cathy, Postdlf, Prgcc, Ptricky, Pubdog, Rich Farmbrough, Rikipedia8, Rilkeblake, Rlquall, Rwboa22, S1967isaket, SFTVLGUY2, Sampo Torgo, Santhoshmanam, Satmandu, Sayeth, Scm83x, Sgreen210, ShelfSkewed, Sisaket, Sjzukrow, Slo-mo, SportsMaster, Suandsoe, SuperStroke, Superflush, TMiscia, Takini, Template namespace initialisation script, Terjen, That Guy, From That Show!, Tomotomoko, Tomstoner, Too Old, Trueblood, TuringTestPilot, Tvoz, Ulisesmakana, UnclePaco, Vernonvernon, Vince sarrinen, Virusunknown, Wangqiji, Wavelength, Welsh, Wetman, Wikiklrsc, Wizard1022, WI219, Woohookitty, Wookiepedian, Yamamoto Ichiro, Zachbe, Zigzak, Zoicon5, Гатерас, 372 anonymous edits

Computer programming *Source*: http://en.wikipedia.org/w/index.php?title=Computer_programming *Contributors*: *drew, 1exec1, 206.26.152.xxx, 209.157.137.xxx, 64.24.16.xxx, 84user, 9258fahsflkh917fas, ABF, AKGhetto, AbstractClass, Acalamari, Acdx, Acroterion, AdamCox9, Adrignola, Adw2000, Aeram16, Aeternus, AgentCDE, Ahoerstemeier, Aitias, Akanemoto, Al Lemos, AlanH, Alansohn, Alberto Orlandini, Alex.g, AlistairMcMillan, AllCalledByGod, Alyssa3467, Amiodarone, Amire80, Ancheta Wis, Andonic, Andrejj, Andres, AndrewHowse, Andy Dingley, AnnaFrance, Antonielly, Antonio Lopez, AquaFox, Arnabatcal, ArnoldReinhold, Arvindn, Asijut, AtticusX, Auroranorth, Avoided, Bakabaka, Banaticus, Bangsanegara, Betterworld, Bevo, BiT, Bigk105, Blackworld2005, Bluemoose, Bobo192, Bonadea, Bookofjude, Bootedcat, Boson, Bougainville, Breadbaker444, Brianga, Brichard12, Brighterorange, Brother Dysk, Bubba hotep, Bucephalus, BurntSky, Butterflylunch, C.Fred, C550456, CRGreathouse, Caltas, Can't sleep, clown will eat me, CanadianLinuxUser, Cander0000, Capi, Capi crimm, Capricorn42, Captain Disdain, Centrx, Cflm001, Cgmusselman, CharlesC, CharlotteWebb, Chazcag, Chirp Cricket, Chocolateboy, Chovain, ChrisLoosley, Christopher Agnew, Christopher Fairman, Chriswiki, Chuck369, Ciaccona, Closedmouth, Cmtam922, Cnilep, Cnkids, Colonies Chris, Cometstyles, Conversion script, Crazytales, Cstlarry, Curps, Curvers, Cybercobra, CzarB, DARTH SIDIOUS 2, DMacks, DVD R W, Daekharel, Damian Yerrick, Damieng, DanP, Danakil, Dante Alighieri, Daverose 33, Davey-boy-10042969, DavidCary, DavidLevinson, Davidwil, Dawnseeker2000, Daydreamer302000, Dcljr, Deepakr, Dekisugi, DerHexer, Derek farn, Deryck Chan, Dfmclean, Dialectric, Diberri, Diego Moya, Digitize, Discospinster, Dkasak, Doc9871, Dominic7848, Donald Albury, Donhalcon, DoorsRecruiting.com, Dougofborg, Downtownee, Dravir5, Drphilharmonic, Dureo, Dusto4, Dylan Lake, Dysprosia, EAderhold, ERcheck, Ed Poor, Edderso, Edward, Edward Z. Yang, Eeekster, Eiwot, El C, ElAmericano, Elektrik Shoos, Elendal, Elf, Elkman, Emorr280, Emperorbma, Epbr123, Ephidel, Epolk, Ericbeg, Essexmutant, Extremist, F41t3r, Fakhr245, Falcon Kirtaran, Falcon8765, Fazilati, Femto, Fg, Fratrep, Frecklefoot, FreplySpang, Frosted14, FunPika, Fvw, Galoubet, Gamernotnerd, Gandalf61, Garik, Gary2863, Garzo, GeorgeBills, Geremy659, Ghewgill, Ghyll, Giftlite, Gildos, Gilliam, Glass Tomato, GoodDamon, Goodvac, Gooogler, Gploc, Gracenotes, GraemeL, Graham87, Granpire Viking Man, Gregsometimes, Grison, Grouf, Guaka, Guanaco, Gwernol, Gökhan, Habbo sg, Hadal, Hairy Dude, Hanberke, Handbuddy, Hannes Hirzel, Happyisenough, Harvester, Headbomb, Heltzgersworld, Henry Flower, Hermione1980, Heron, Hipocrite, Hustlestar4, Iamjakejakeisme, Igoldste, Ikanreed, Iliketubesox, Imroy, Intgr, InvertRect, Inzy, Isaac Oyelowo, Ivan Štambuk,

Ixfd64, J. M., J.delanoy, J3ff, JLaTondre, Jackal2323, Jackol, Jacob.jose, Jagged 85, Jason4789, Jason5ayers, Jatos, Jaysweet, Jedediah Smith, Jeff02, Jmundo, Joedaddy09, Joel B. Lewis, Jojhutton, Josh1billion, JoshCarter15, Joshua.thomas.bird, Jpbowen, Jph, Jwestbrook, Jwh335, K.Nevelsteen, KHaskell, KJS77, KMurphyP, Kaare, Keilana, Kenny sh, Kglavin, Kifcaliph, Klutzy, Konstable, Laurusnobilis, Lee J Haywood, Leedeth, Leibniz, LeinadSpoon, Lemlwik, Lerdsuwa, Levineps, Lgrover, Liamlearns, Lightmouse, LilHelpa, LittleOldMe, LittleOldMe old, Loadmaster, Logan, Loren.wilton, Lorenz JJ, Luckdao, Luk, Lumos3, Luna Santin, Lysander89, M4573R5H4K3, M4gnum0n, MER-C, MacMed, Macrakis, Macy, Mahanga, Marek69, Mark Renier, Maroux, Marquez, Martarius, Maryreid, Matthew, Matthew Stannard, Mauler90, Maury Markowitz, Maximaximax, Mdd, Mentifisto, Mesimoney, Metalhead816, Mets501, MiCovran, Michael Drüing, Michael93555, MichaelBillington, Michal Jurosz, MikeDogma, Mindmatrix, Minghong, Minimac, Minna Sora no Shita, Mipadi, Mjchonoles, Mr Stephen, MrFish, MrOllie, Msikma, Mwanner, Mxn, NERIUM, NHRHS2010, Nagy, Nansha, Narayanese, Neilc, Nephtes, Nertzy, Netkinetic, Netsnipe, Neurovelho, NewEnglandYankee, Nigholith, Nikai, Ningauble, Nk, Northamerica1000, Notheruser, Nothingofwater, Nubiatech, Nuno Tavares, Nwbeeson, OSXfan, Obli, Ohnoitsjamie, Optim, Optimist on the run, Orangutan, Orlady, Oxymoron83, P.jansson, Paperfork, Paul D. Buck, Paxse, Pcu123456789, Peberdah, Pedro, Philip Trueman, PhilipO, Phoe6, Piet Delport, Pilotguy, Pimpedshortie99, Pinethicket, Pkalkul, Plugwash, Pm2214, Poco a poco, Pointillist, Poor Yorick, Poweroid, Prashanthellina, Premvvnc, Prgrmr@wrk, PrimeHunter, Promooex, Pt9 9, Qasimb, Qirex, Qrex123, Quadell, RCX, Ragib, Rajnishbhatt, Rama's Arrow, Ranak01, Rasmus Faber, RaveTheTadpole, Rawling, RedWolf, RedWordSmith, RexNL, Ricky15233, Rl, Rmayo, Robert Bond, Robert L, Robert Merkel, Robertinventor, Robin klein, Rodolfo miranda, Ronz, Rrelf, Rror, Rsg, Ruud Koot, Rwwww, S.K., S0ulfire84, SDC, Salv236, Sanbeg, Sardanaphalus, Sasajid, Satansrubberduck, SchfiftyThree, Schrödinger's Neurotoxin, Schwarzbichler, SciAndTech, Scoop Dogy, Scwlong, Sean7341, Senator Palpatine, Seyda, Shahidsidd, Shanak, Shirik, Simeon, SimonEast, SkyWalker, Smalljim, Someone42, SpacemanSpiff, Splang, Starionwolf, SteinbDJ, Stephen Gilbert, Stephenb, Stephenbooth uk, Steven Zhang, Studerby, Suisui, SunCountryGuy01, Suruena, Svemir, Tablizer, TakuyaMurata, Tanalam, Tangent747, TarkusAB, Tedickey, Teo64x, TestPilot, Texture, The Divine Fluffalizer, The Mighty Clod, The Thing That Should Not Be, The Transhumanist, The Transhumanist (AWB), TheRanger, TheTito, Thedjatclubrock, Thedp, Thingg, Thisma, Tide rolls, Tifego, Timhowardriley, Tnxman307, Tobby72, Tobias Bergemann, Tom2we, TomasBat, TonyClarke, Tpbradbury, Trusilver, Turnstep, Tushar.kute, TuukkaH, Tweak232, Twest2665, Tysto, Tyw7, Udayabdurrahman, Ukexpat, Umofomia, Uncle Dick, Unforgettableid, Uniquely Fabricated, Unknown Interval, Userabc, Vanished User 8a9b4725f8376, Versus22, Vipinhari, Viriditas, Vladimer663, WBP Boy, Wadamja, WadeSimMiser, Wangi, Whazzups, Whiskey in the Jar, Wickorama, Wiki alf, Wikiklrsc, Wilku997, Wing (usurped), Witchwooder, Wizard191, Wj32, Worldeng, Wre2wre, Wtf242, Wtmitchell, Wwagner, Xagyg creator programmer, YellowMonkey, Yintan, Yk Yk Yk, Youssefsan, Yummifruitbat, Zeboober, Zkac050, Zoul1380, Zsinj, Zvn, 1071 anonymous edits

Fortran *Source*: http://en.wikipedia.org/w/index.php?title=Fortran *Contributors*: 16@r, 1exec1, Aaron Schulz, Abeliavsky, AdjustShift, Agateller, Agricola44, Aivosto, AmosWolfe, Anarchivist, Andre Engels, Andrejj, Arch dude, ArnoldReinhold, Atlant, Audriusa, AxelBoldt, Bachcell, Badger Drink, Bashen, Bchabala2, Bduke, Beliavsky, BenFrantzDale, Bender235, Benjaminevans82, Betacommand, Between My Ken, Bevo, Bitsmart, Blaxthos, Bobdc, Brad Hughes, Brion VIBBER, Broh., Bryan, Bubba73, Bunnyhop11, CMW275, CRGreathouse, CYD, Captain Fortran, Casey56, Changcho, ChaosCon, Chbarts, ChongDae, Chris, Closeapple, Conversion script, Corti, Corvus cornix, Cromis, Crumley, Csabo, Cybercobra, D. F. Schmidt, DBrane, DMacks, DNewhall, DRady, Damian Yerrick, Dan100, Danakil, Dav4is, David Biddulph, David.Monniaux, Dcoetzee, Dead3y3, Dejvid, Dekart, Dennette, DerHexer, Derek Ross, Derek farn, DesertAngel, Dmsar, DoctorWho42, Dpbsmith, DragonHawk, Drilnoth, Drj, Duja, Dune, Dycedarg, Dysprosia, Eagleal, Elopash, EncMstr, Epbr123, Ericamick, Eschnett, Eubulides, Eustress, Evolauxia, Ewlyahoocom, Falcon8765, Fireuzer, Flex, Flowerheaven, Frecklefoot, Funandtrvl, Furrykef, Fæ, Gaius Cornelius, Gantlord, Gareth Owen, Geoff97, Georg Peter, GeorgeMoney, Ghettoblaster, Gjd001, Glenn, Graham87, Greg L, Greg Lindahl, Gringer, Gscshoyru, Gudeldar, H2g2bob, Hairy Dude, Herbee, Howardjp, Howcheng, I already forgot, I dream of horses, II MusLiM HyBRiD II, Infologue, Intgr, Inwind, Iridescent, IsaacGS, Isis, Iulian.serbanoiu, Ixfd64, JW1805, Jacobolus, Jamesgibbon, Jerryobject, JonEAhlquist, Jossi, Jpfagerback, Jrockley, Julesd, Jvhertum, Jwmwalrus, Jwoodger, Jww19, K-car, Kajasudhakarababu, Karl-Henner, Kbh3rd, Keflavich, Kenyon, Kglavin, KieferSkunk, Kleb, Knebel, KymFarnik, LOL, LOTRrules, LanceBarber, Larsivi, Leandrod, Lerdsuwa, Liao, Ligulem, Little Mountain 5, Ljn917, Lotje, Lousyd, Luminifer, Maghnus, Malaki1874, MarcusMaximus, Mark Foskey, MarkSweep, Mathchem271828, Mathmo, MattGiuca, Matthewdunsdon, Mav, Mboverload, Meisam, Michael Hardy, Misha Stepanov, Mjchonoles, Mortus Est, Mr Wednesday, Mr.Fortran, Muhandis, Muro de Aguas, Nanshu, NapoliRoma, Nbarth, Neuralwiki, Nghtwlkr, Nikai, Nneonneo, Norm mit, Northumbrian, Ojcit, Okedem, Oligomous, Opelio, Ospix, Paul August, Paxsimius, Pgr94, Phil Boswell, Philip Trueman, Plasynins, Pmcjones, Pnm, Pol098, Poor Yorick, Quadrescence, RTC, Rafiko77, Rangek, RaveRaiser, Raysonho, Rchrd, Rcingham, RedAndr, RedWolf, Reedy, Rege, Rich Farmbrough, Rigmahroll, Rjwilmsi, Roadrunner, RobChafer, Robert Merkel, Robo.mind, Rockear, Rogerd, Rowan Moore, Roy Brumback, Rpropper, Rravii, Rudnei.cunha, RupertMillard, Ruud Koot, Rwwww, SMC, Salih, Saxton, Sbassi, Sccosel, Seba5618, Sequentious, Skew-t, Sleigh, Smilitude, Smithck0, SnowRaptor, SpaceFlight89, Spacerat3004, Sprachpfleger, Stevenj, Strait, Stsp0269, Suruena, Svanslyck, T-bonham, TakuyaMurata, Tannin, Tarquin, Taylock, Template namespace initialisation script, The Cute Philosopher, The Recycling Troll, The Thing That Should Not Be, The morgawr, Thestarsatnight, Thom2002, Thumperward, Tiuks, Tokek, Tony Sidaway, Tripodics, Twas Now, UnicornTapestry, Urhixidur, Uriyan, User A1, UtherSRG, Van der Hoorn, Van helsing, Van.snyder, Vicarage, VictorAnyakin, Vina, Waggers, Wavelength, Wcrowe, Wdfarmer, Wernher, Wflong, Who, Widefox, Wiki Wikardo, WikiWookie, Wikiklrsc, Wikip rhyre, Wilkowiki, Williamv1138, Windharp, Woohookitty, Wormholio, Wws, Xamian, Xenfreak, Xlent, YUL89YYZ, Yakushima, Ylai, Yuletide, Yworo, Zap Rowsdower, ZeroOne, Zicraccozian, Zoltar0, 636 anonymous edits

Central Washington University *Source*: http://en.wikipedia.org/w/index.php?title=Central_Washington_University *Contributors*: Absolon, Adhuerta, Almosthonest06, Andy Marchbanks, Angela, Arbustoo, Aricci526, Aspects, BD2412, Billy Hathorn, Bobak, Bobblewik, Bumm13, Can't sleep, clown will eat me, Cascadia, Catapult, Cdc, Centralwashu, Cpastern, Craigy144, Dgabbard, Djharrity, Dynaflow, Eastmain, EdmondsCCPIO, ElKevbo, Emora08, EncyclopediaBrown, EndlessVince, Farwestern, Flowerkiller1692, Freakofnurture, Fuhghettaboutit, Gabe4bs, Gaius Cornelius, George100, Ghewgill, GoneAwayNowAndRetired, Gurch, Hadal, Hammersoft, Ian Pitchford, Izzletodasmizzle, Jllm06, Jmwallin, Johnpacklambert, K3rb, King County, Lightmouse, Logical Cowboy, M.Fanavar, Mabrk, Majorclanger, MarisaDorazio, Marko98506, Martarius, Masonpatriot, Matthewmayer, Maz2004, Momon21, Mrnixon, Neal Finne, Neurolysis, Niteowlneils, Optikos, PMDrive1061, Packerfansam, Pen of bushido, Peter Horn, Pikachelsea, Plastikspork, Pusher, Rich Farmbrough, Robinsos, S, ST47, Scandium, SchaiDog, Skinny McGee, Slyfield, TEB728, Tropicaltree48, Whywhenwhohow, Yath, 225 anonymous edits

General Electric *Source*: http://en.wikipedia.org/w/index.php?title=General_Electric *Contributors*: -Majestic-, 0, 1USCo, 28421u2232nfenfcenc, A Man In Black, AEMoreira042281, AMCKen, AV3000, Aboutmovies, AbsolutDan, Acdx, AdamDeanHall, AdamW, AdnanSa, Adraeus, Aeons, Aerion, Afas1407, Afishler, Aflin, Aizuku, Alan Liefting, Alanlay, Alansohn, Albany NY, Alchemy 142, Alert Investor, Alex.tan, AlexLibman, AlexiusHoratius, Alison9, All Is One, Altenmann, Alvinying, Amcl, Anarchy, Andonic, Andy G, Andy Marchbanks, Angrysockhop, Anhydrobiosis, Anna Lincoln, AnnaFrance, Anniv22, Anschelsc, Antandrus, Antennaman, ApplianceRepair, April kathleen, Aquemini, Arch dude, Aross12345, Art.baron, Arthena, Arunvish, Arx Fortis, AshevillePromise, Aspects, Aster77, Astor14, Astuishin, Athaenara, AtilimGunesBaydin, Attitude2000, Az1568, Azumanga1, B21O303V3941W42371, BRG, Barek, Bastin, Bde1982, Beetstra, Before My Ken, Beinsane, Bender235, Benzocane, BigGuns, Bigmorr, BilCat, Bingoeleven, Bjfg897, Blaxthos, Boarder8925, Bob98133, Boing! said Zebedee, Bongomatic, Bongwarrior, Boothy443, Born2flie, BozMo, Bp102371, Branddobbe, BrekekekexKoaxKoax, BrenDJ, Brouhaha, Bschuko, Btipling, Bubba73, CDA, Caltas, Calwatch, Cannonball 248, Caper13, Capricorn42, CardinalDan, CaribDigita, CaseyPenk, Catapult, Ccrrccrr, Cdogsimmons, Cdonea, Ch Th Jo, Chaitanya.lala, Chendy, Cherkash, Chris the speller, Chris2311, Chrisieboy, Christianceo, Christopher Parham, Chrisv55, Ckatz, Classicstruggle3, CliffC, Cliffb, Codyfinke2008, Comet Tuttle, Computerhistory, Consumer friend, Conversion script, Coolhawks88, Cousteau69, Crocodile Punter, Crysb, Cyrusc, DIEXEL, DMCer, DMG413, DVD R W, DabMachine, Dachshund, DagErlingSmørgrav, Dagrak, Dalenunes, Danallen46, Dancter, DanielPenfield, Dark567, Darkpoet2, Darkwind, Dav115, Davewho2, David Delarge, David Gale, David6.jenkins@ge.com, DavidBlackwell, Davodd, Deli nk, Deltabeignet, Dieselchicken, DigbyDalton, DinosaursLoveExistence, Diomidis Spinellis, Disavian, Dizziealle, Dleonard55, DocWatson42, DocendoDiscimus, Doctor yellow, Docu, Dogru144, Dpbsmith, Dragomiloff, DragonHawk, Drewk, Drmagic, Duffman, Dustingc, Dylan6758, E Pluribus Anthony redux, E. Ripley, Eagleamn, Earlypsychosis, Ebaksa, EdBever, EditorInTheRye, Editthesadparts, Edokter, Edward, Ehn, Eiland, Elaragirl, ElectricEye, Elipongo, Emma Frost 481, Enviroboy, Epbr123, Erikjoncas, Escape Orbit, Eustress, Evannewman830, Evans1982, Eye1ball12, F, Fairlyoddparents1234, Fearfulsymmetry, Ferfish, Filip3311, Financial Zorro, Fingers-of-Pyrex, Finlay McWalter, Flyguy33, Frankie12, Freecyprus, Funandtrvl, G27, GT, Gaius Cornelius, Gallantgriffin2006, Gary King, Gcm, Generalscorch, Gnowxilef, Gogo Dodo, GorillaWarfare, Gr1st, Graham87, Grecko, Greenshed, Greg5030, Gregalton, Grendelkhan, Gridlock Joe, Gsarwa, Guaka, Gurch, Guy Harris, HJ Mitchell, Haham hanuka, Hallii03, Happydemon912, Harro5, Hatcat, Hatster301, Hayfordoleary, Headbomb, Heccy, Helloelan, Heywoodg, Hibernian, Hiphats, Hmmwhatsthisdo, Hoary, Hooverhigh, Horsewack, Hotwire, Htanna, Hu12, Huck57, Hunington-Horstachio, Huntster, Hydrargyrum, Ian3055, Icairns, Icanzhavegoodwiki, Icseaturtles, Idaltu, Ideal gas equation, Ief, Imgaril, Indon, Infrogmation, Inwind, Ipsherman, Ipsingh, Ireyes, Iridescent, Irishguy, Iroll, Ishi Gustaedr, J.P.Lon, J.delanoy, JGXenite, JJay, Jacksonian3623, Jamcib, JamesBWatson, Jamie jca, Jauerback, JavierMC, Jazzamac, Jeet, Jerome Charles Potts, Jerryseinfeld, Jersyko, Jibjibjib, Jkd1242, Jkeene, JoanneB, JoeSmack, Joelfurr, Jogabbeyjr, John Fuzukaka, John K, John Vandenberg, Johnanth, Johnfos, Jonathen Skews, Joseph Solis in Australia, Jprenslo, Jrennie, Jules7484, Jvcdude, K61824, Kamlanjan, Kansan, KansasCity, Karebear 1022, Karimul, Kbdank71, Kelly Martin, Keystoneridin, Kingturtle, Kkm010, Klp363, Knockwood, Kozuch, Kshanks, Ktr101, Kurieeto, Kurse 2799, Kurtbw, Kyle1278, LG4761, LUUSAP, LanceBarber, Langkid1, Larrybob, Leschiffre, LethSquir, Lethe, Leuko, Levineps, Li'l Happy Ending, Ligulem, LilHelpa, Ljenkins13, Lockesdonkey, Logosys, LorenzoB, Lostintherush, Lotje, LtPowers, Lukobe, M-hwang, MK8, MONGO, MacFodder, Madhero88, Mailer diablo, Mairi, Makemi, Manzanita, Marcschulz, Mark83, Markvs88, Martin Wisse, Masque 308, Massfrequency, Materialscientist, Mathieu.petitjean, Maury Markowitz, Mayur, Mbisgaier, Mdavidson98, Meganfoxx, MeltBanana, Mentifisto, Mephistophelian, Messiisking, Mewtwowimmer, Mfourcade, Michael Hardy, Mike Dillon, Millmoss, Mimosalane, Minesweeper, Mirmo!, Mitsukai, Modster, Moo7a, Moocowsrock, Moondancer, Mr. Billion, Mr. Power-Mad!, Mr.bub, MrOllie, Mrceleb2007, Msmusiclaw, Mugunth Kumar, Mulad, Mw938, My76Strat, N328KF, N5iln, NKCTrio, Nakon, Nascar1996, Natalie Erin, NawlinWiki, Ncox, Nczempin, Necromancer, Neelix, NeilN, Nellis, Neonlite, Neutrality, Nichenbach, Nickrg3, NicoNet, Nitin nanda, NoisyJinx, Noroton, Novickas, Noybwiki, Nroberge, Nuno Tavares, Nwbeeson, Ohconfucius, Ohnoitsjamie, Ohpuu, Oihgreugihoer, Oldag07, Oleg Alexandrov, Olivier, Olly150, Onorem, Oo64eva, Orangemonster2k1, OrgasGirl, Ost316, Ottawahitech, Oxygen you can believe in., P1mpy699, PHDrillSergeant, PTSE, PadreNuestro, Patricknewyork, Patricknoddy, PaulHanson, Paulzubrinich, Penale52, Petri Krohn, Phil024, Philip Trueman, Picaroon, Pig de Wig, Plasticup, Politepunk, Porqin, Postdlf, Psiphiorg, Purpleslog, Qc, Qst, QuantumOne, Quidam65, Qxz, REDyellowGreenBLUE, RS101, RTC, Rabhyanker, Radimast, RadioFan, Rberdeen, Rcawsey, RedWolf, Rediahs, Redraiders203, Rehman, Reify-tech, Rencin24, Retro00064, Revo331, Rfc1394, Rgoodermote, Rhobite, Riana, Ribonucleic, Rich Farmbrough, Richard Arthur Norton (1958-), Richard Weil, RideABicycle, Rjwilmsi, Rknasc, Roadrunner3000, Robguru, RoboAction, Rocketman116, Rogerd, Roscoe x, Royalguard11, Rsecker, Rtcpenguin, Ruziklan, Ryan 1269, Ryan Norton, RyanGerbil10, SDC, SamJohnston, Sanjeevmittal, Sardanaphalus, Scalphunter 363, Scififreak95, Sdxvi, Sea.wolf4, Selket, Selmo, Serchdf, Serpent's Choice, Sf5xeplus, Shadowjams, Shawnc, Sheertrror, Sherool, Shizhao, SigKauffman, Sigma 7, Sitethief, Sjsharksrs, Skoosh, SkylineEvolutionIII, Slakr, Slo-mo, Smac2020, Smeaea23, Smmgeek, Solarisworld, Sophie, Soren121, Spalding, Spangineer, SpencerWilson, SriMesh, StaticGull, SteinbDJ, Stella anne victor, Stemonitis, Stephenb, Steven.dai, Steviedpeele, Stifle, Supra guy, Sven4698e, TAnthony, TGCP, TJ Spyke, TWCarlson, Tabletop, Tasteguru, Taxhavensetc, Tcncv, Tedder, Temporaluser, Terafly999, The Flying Spaghetti Monster, The Random Editor, The wub, TheQuandry, Thehelpfulone, Therealcolletepierre, ThinkEnemies, Thomas Larsen, ThomasK, Tide rolls, Tinton5, TitaniumDreads, Tkaizan, Tkessler, Tkgd2007, ToddSweeney, Toonmore, TransporterMan, Tregoweth, Trekphiler, Trevor MacInnis, Trevorwidger, Triplight, TrisDG, Triwbe, Truthsniffer, Truthsort, Tumeric12, TwoOneTwo, Twsx, Tyrider07, UCFirefly, Ufteach, Umpteee, Urbanrenewal, Uris,

Usquam (usurped), Ustye, UtherSRG, Valentinian, Valorian, Vegaswikian, Veghead04, Veritas 0273, Viveksinha in, Vortexrealm, Vroman, WAMC Pirates, WTGDMan1986, Walloon, Warren, Wassermann, Watti Renew, Wavelength, Wcquidditch, Wgungfu, Whosasking, WikiKing1234, Wikieditor06, Wikiuser100, Will Beback Auto, WillMcC, Windwardtrades, Wine Guy, Wknight94, Wongm, Woohookitty, WookieInHeat, World8115, Xavier Canals-Riera, Xienyao, Xnatedawgx, Yurik, ZCaliber, Zachary, Zackaback, Zenosparadox, Ziiv, Zip-Zap 223, Zmiller923, Zntrip, Zr2d2, Zweldon, Zzuuzz, احمد.غامدي.24, , 944 anonymous edits

United States Atomic Energy Commission *Source*: http://en.wikipedia.org/w/index.php?title=United_States_Atomic_Energy_Commission *Contributors*: 2over0, Altenmann, Art LaPella, AutoGeek, Avihu, Cradel, Dale Arnett, DavidLevinson, El C, Emerson7, Epolk, Ewikdjmco, Farras Octara, Fastfission, Figureofnine, Fintor, Giggy, Glenn4pr, Ground Zero, HDRules, Hemlock Martinis, Hugo999, Hydrargyrum, Imaninjapirate, Jetra2, Jmkprime, Johnfos, JonathanDP81, Jrcrin001, Jrtayloriv, Kbdank71, Koavf, Kyle Barbour, Kymacpherson, Lightsabre2001, Mac, Massysett, Midnightcomm, Mikecraig, Mr.98, Orlady, PaulHanson, Pearle, Petri Krohn, Prmacn, Roadrunner, Ryan Postlethwaite, Sherbrooke, Simesa, Sparkit, Trelvis, WVhybrid, Wik, Willoooh, Yardcock, 21 anonymous edits

New York University *Source*: http://en.wikipedia.org/w/index.php?title=New_York_University *Contributors*: 34african34, 3a95a8i9, 72Dino, AEMoreira042281, ANFswims07, AP1787, AUburnTiger, Aboutmovies, AbsoluteFlatness, Abtaylor1992, Acroterion, Addshore, Aeonx, Ajbt dancer, Akrubin, Alai, Alansohn, AlbertGallatin, Alexbouditsky, Amerique, Andrechan, Andrewlp1991, Andrewvdill, Andsoad182, Andy Marchbanks, Anetode, Angela, Angry bee, Arch dude, Archdeceiver, Aricci526, Aristotle1990, Arsene, Art LaPella, ArthurGD, Asa283, Asl352, Asparkle1979, Astuishin, AuCourantStory, Avalon, Avman89, Awadewit, BD2412, BTTNext, Bambollu, Bancham, Barnej, Barticus88, Bender235, Benjamin3939, Benzo, Berkeley69, Beyond My Ken, Bigbluefish, Bill william compton, Billsmith453, Blim8183, Bluefortytwo, Bluetooth954, Bob Burkhardt, Bobak, Bobblewik, Bobo192, Bobstless, Bollywoodbombay, Bongwarrior, BorgQueen, Bprober, BrOnXbOmBr21, BrooklynSteve, Bruxism, Bryantgorman, Bubbachuck, Bubbaprog, Buhbuhbilly, Bullshark44, CLW, CSWarren, Camembert, Can't sleep, clown will eat me, Canderson7, Captainlavender, CarrieBoo22, Casey Abell, Ccacsmss, Cerebella, Cessator, Ceyockey, Charmii, Cheapestcostavoider, Choster, Chris the speller, ChrisRuvolo, Cihan, Clark Street, Clconway, Cmdrjameson, Coasterlover1994, Cohesion, Colloquial, Colonies Chris, Connormah, Cordless Larry, Cornellrockey, Corpx, Corvus cornix, Cosmic Latte, Credmi, Ctrl build, Curlgurlkatharine, Curps, Cyapt81, Cybercobra, D6, DFW HOYA, DMCer, DMacks, Dale Arnett, Dan Guan, DardanAeneas, Darkcore, Darkwind, Darx9url, David Shankbone, David.Monniaux, Deanb, Dguido, DigiBullet, Dina, Dinoid, Directorstratton, Directory7, Discospinster, DocendoDiscimus, Dominus, DooDahm, Dugwiki, EQuacquarelli, EXODUS7, Edudent, Edward, EeepEeep, El C, ElKevbo, Embode, Equalpants, Eric-Wester, Esrever, Ethanolduckie, Everyking, Falard, Fat&Happy, Fenwaysteve, Flamurai, Flatterworld, Flauto Dolce, Flima1990, FloNight, Floydiandroid, Fournax, Foxycat, Franciscoh, Frank12, FreeRadicalX, G0700596, Gaius Cornelius, Galactor213, GallatinMA, Georgeryp, Ghepeu, Giggles321, Gilliam, Gimmetrow, Gkennedy, Gogo Dodo, GoingBatty, Goldsweig, Graham87, GreatWhiteNortherner, Greenshed, Greg kogan, Grey Wanderer, Grsz11, HWV, Ham27, Hammerdrill, Hammersoft, Harel Newman, Hd, Hechung, Helloheyhey, Henry W. Schmitt, Herr Ratselhaft, Higherededitor2, Hogghogg, Hohi, Horsti123, Howcheng, IShadowed, Icetallica, Iss246, Italo, J Milburn, J. Eley, J.delanoy, JDoorjam, JKershenbaum1, JKershenbaum2, JPS1000, JTSchreiber, JaGa, Jainvenus, Jamiew, Jason.alexander4421, Jatkins, Jauhienij, Jbrisport, Jclemens, Jeff G., Jeffrey Boyd, JeremyA, Jersey Devil, JesseRafe, Jevansen, Jiang, Jim.henderson, JimmyGc, Jivecat, Jllm06, Jncraton, JoeKershenbaum, John wesley, JohnGaltJr, Jonathan Williams, Jonathan.s.kt, Joyous!, Jsanstella, Jugander, Jumping cheese, Jweiss11, Jzu200, K-UNIT, Kaku89, Kanonkas, Keilana, Kinari99, Kinu, Kithburd, Kjoonlee, Koavf, Kotjze, Krich, Kurtm, Kushboy, Lagringa, Lambiam, Lamppost51, LarRan, Larry V, LaszloWalrus, Ldpipher, Leszek Jańczuk, Levineps, LiDaobing, LibrarianB, Liface, Liftarn, Lightdarkness, Lightmouse, LtPowers, Ltv100, Lucaseln, Lukepttn, LunarLander, M gray1, M713c041, MER-C, MJO, MONGO, Madcoverboy, Magiclite, Magioladitis, Malepheasant, Mandarax, Marco Guzman, Jr, MarcusLeyva, Marek69, Marluxia.Kyoshu, Martarius, Masonpatriot, Maximus Rex, Maxzook, Meeples, Meersan, MegX, Meganfoxx, Megarian1973, Meghak, MementoVivere, Mentifisto, Merumerume, Mfv2, Mgoren, Mic, Michael Keats, Mike.lifeguard, MikeCapone, Mild Bill Hiccup, Mimihitam, Mirokado, MisfitToys, Mma285, Mneme, Modernist, Modster, Modulatum, Moondyne, Moriogawa, Mrfrankm, N Vale, NYC2TLV, NYULawStud, NYUballer, NYUism, Narrasawa, Nasnema, Natanmda, NawlinWiki, Neilc, Neiman2456, Neshmet12, New.yorker4, NickCT, NicolasJz, Ninababe222, Niteowlneils, Nja234, Nlu, Noeticsage, Noitalever, Nonexistant User, Notsosanepsychogirl15, Npr230, Nricardo, Nuronz, Nv8200p, Nyguy, Ocheta, Ohthelameness, Ommnomnomgulp, Omnis7, Ompandya, Only, Ooodoggies, PMDrive1061, PTSE, PZFUN, Padraic, Part85, Pascal.Tesson, Paul August, Paul Klenk, Paulmcdonald, Pearle, Pegship, Pgk, Pharaoh of the Wizards, Philippe, Piano non troppo, Pilotguy, Pinethicket, Pnkrockr, Postcard Cathy, Fowerpiper, Profmarcp, Prolog, Proon, Punkfoomasta, R'n'B, R. fiend, RA0808, RSpencer7007, Raccoonie, Radiojon, Ran, RandorXeus, RareWolf, Rbs, Red Winged Duck, RedShiftPA, RedWolf, Redf0x, Redguardian, Redthoreau, Regibox, Riana, Rich Farmbrough, Rjwilmsi, Rkevins, Rlitwin, Rms869, Rogerd, RogueNinja, Rothamell, Rtrace, Ryanalford111, Ryulong, Rémih, SDC, Samusb, SandyGeorgia, Saric, Sarregouset, Sayeth, ScottyBerg, Sdrtirs, SeekingOne, Shahpriya, ShakespeareFan00, Shalom Yechiel, Shelat, ShelfSkewed, Sherool, ShinyTool, Shoegal8, Shoreranger, SidneyWindsor, Sinalese, Sionus, Siroxo, Skashkin, SleepyThomas, Slgrandson, Snowmanradio, Some guy, Spellcheck, Squiffybob, Srosenstock, StAnselm, Stay cool, SteinbDJ, Stephen's black friend, StewartMine, Sumahoy, Super Rad!, Supjet, Suruena, Swimdude92, Syed, Sylent, THEMICK, TJBmarv, Tanaats, Tangsyde, Taromsky, Tassedethe, Tbhotch, Tbuckler, Tevi, The Cunctator, The Random Editor, TheMiddleOfTime, Thehornet, Theoldanarchist, Thljcl, Tim Ross, Timwumd, Tinlinkin, TischKid, Tjjd1350, Todfox, TommyP, Tony1, Tothebarricades.tk, Tpbradbury, Trenchcoatjedi, TrevMrgn, Tt 225, Tufflaw, Uconnstud, Ulric1313, VZG, Valentinian, Vegetablesrotting4, Very Input, Veryfutzy, Vgranucci, Vic226, Vicki Rosenzweig, Vuanu, Wahlman10, Waphle, Wasabe3543, Wavetree, Welsh, WhisperToMe, Who, Wideangle, Wikiaway, Wikipimp22, Wikisux, Wikitanvir, Wikiwriter706, Wildhartlivie, WookieInHeat, Wv235, Xiliquiern, Y17k, Y2kcrazyjoker4, YCCHAN, YacozA, Yakuzajoe, Yanks-rule, Yerpo, Yill577, Ylee, ZimZalaBim, Zoe, Zoicon5, Zzyzx11, ^demon, Александър, 1624 anonymous edits

Courant Institute of Mathematical Sciences *Source*: http://en.wikipedia.org/w/index.php?title=Courant_Institute_of_Mathematical_Sciences *Contributors*: Alansohn, Alex Kuper, AuCourantStory, Auntof6, Bender235, Betacommand, Bthomases, Canon.vs.nikon, Charles Matthews, Crowsnest, Danielfong, Deville, ESkog, Edward, Falcon8765, Gaius Cornelius, Giftlite, Giraffedata, Hamiltonious, Hammersoft, Herr Ratselhaft, Hohi, JHunterJ, Japhethwood, Jim.henderson, Johnpacklambert, Jsondow, Lambiam, LarRan, LilHelpa, Liqcrysh, Macallan 12, Markdask, Michael Hardy, Mortense, NapoliRoma, Noeticsage, Nricardo, PMDrive1061, PaulHanson, Pharos, PigFlu Oink, Poco a poco, RSimione, Repliedthemockturtle, Salih, Sam65537, Samuelsen, Scioneso, Sormani, Stammer, Tassedethe, TimonyCrickets, Tomwsulcer, Vegaswikian, Wihenao, Woohookitty, Ylee, 288 anonymous edits

Master of Divinity *Source*: http://en.wikipedia.org/w/index.php?title=Master_of_Divinity *Contributors*: Afterwriting, Ajterril, Aksi great, Amherst5282, An56, Angelbo, Arbustoo, Bigbadbyte, Blauerflummi, Boy in the bands, BrownHairedGirl, Bwilkins, Carolynparrishfan, Carpeyourmom, Cjdowdeswell, Crazynas, Davidkinnen, EdwinHJ, Eequor, Elnwood, Esrever, Gary D, Gmasterman, Grkndeacon, HarvardOxon, Henry plantagenet, Hopquick, Icairns, Jacob grace, JamesMLane, Johnparkw, Leszek Jańczuk, Lisatwo, Maurreen, Mel Etitis, Neutrality, Novaseminary, One Salient Oversight, Pmadrid, Ptsals, Sem2007, SimonP, Stevertigo, Tom harrison, Turnerjazz, Twrist, Uvaphdman, Vandy, Wayward, 63 anonymous edits

Union Theological Seminary in the City of New York *Source*: http://en.wikipedia.org/w/index.php?title=Union_Theological_Seminary_in_the_City_of_New_York *Contributors*: 55Lincoln, Alansohn, AlexanderLondon, Aliceinlampyland, Alienlifeformz, Americus55, Asm76, Billy Hathorn, Black Falcon, Brain Rodeo, BrownHairedGirl, Brunoptsem, Canihaveacookie, Caorongjin, Cjs2111, Colonies Chris, Coolhappysteve, Corcovado, Ctrl build, Cyrius, D-rew, D6, David.M.Carr, December12AC, Dogears, Dreadstar, Ebrownless, Edwardx, EdwinHJ, Emerymat, Emote, Essieblueday, Evan forman, Flex, Fluffernutter, Flyingfarther, Gardar Rurak, Gary D, Gentgeen, GoingBatty, Gryffindor, Gurch, Hede2000, Hroðulf, Iamcuriousblue, Intravenus de Milo, Irn, JASpencer, JHCC, Jayjg, Jessdvd, Jonas Mur, Karlmontague, Kbdank71, Kevindouglashall, Kglavin, Koavf, Ldesilva, Lindsay658, LiniShu, Lnolan, Lol nl, MPS, Makrina, Malindaeb, Masalai, Masonpatriot, Matanariel, Matthewross, Maximus Rex, Michael Hardy, Mkmcconn, Moleskiner, Mtstroud, Nomoskedasticity, Novaseminary, Nyny9480, PSUMark2006, Palnu, Pastorwayne, Petersam, Phil Boswell, Plasma east, Poliocretes, Pragmatistrealist, Prezbo, Psantora, Pubdog, RebelChrysanthemum, Redfox24, Retired username, Rickdomination, SDC, Smallchief, Smjwalsh, Snowolf, SphinxNet, Stephensuleeman, Steve Dufour, Superslum, Sven Manguard, Sweetmoose6, Tedickey, Tesscass, Tim1965, VB101, Vandy, W Nowicki, Weberman7, Wetman, Willthacheerleader18, Ἀλήθεια, 111 anonymous edits

Association for Computing Machinery *Source*: http://en.wikipedia.org/w/index.php?title=Association_for_Computing_Machinery *Contributors*: 100110100, A.A.Graff, Aarkwilde, Aaron charles, Abdull, Abelson, Allen Moore, Altenmann, Alvestrand, Anarchitect, Anders.Warga, Andrei Stroe, Applegrew, Arnstein87, Avraham, Beefyt, Black Falcon, Blainster, Bobblewik, Bratsche, CQ, Cameron Scott, Cek, ChrisLoosley, Cokoli, Conversion script, Coolcaesar, Corsarius, Corti, Curb Chain, Cybercobra, CygnusPius, Danielsmith, David.Monniaux, Dbabbitt, Deodar, Descendall, Dhaluza, Dice789, Dideler, Disavian, Dismas, DixonD, Drewigg, EdBever, Edward Vielmetti, Efficacy, Ehog, Emil Volcheck, Esmito, Eubulides, Fabrictramp, Felixac, Firefly4342, Fmccown, Francislr, Fun.cutt, G3force, Giftlite, Giraffe21, Gmelli, Graham87, Gronky, Hede2000, HenryLi, Hermel, Hooperbloob, Hqb, Iridescent, JLaTondre, JTConroy88, JW1805, Jdmicklos, Jim Horning, Jnc, Joakim Ziegler, Jodi.a.schneider, Johnh, JonHarder, Jpbowen, Jreferee, K.lee, Kalle, Kangguo, Kbdank71, Kelly Martin, Kenyon, Ketiltrout, Krbabu, LanceBarber, Lenzi, Lerdsuwa, Lquilter, Lycurgus, Macrakis, Maduskis, Magicpop, Matteh, Maurice Carbonaro, Metaeducation, Mike Schwartz, Miym, Neel S Patel, Northamerica1000, Parvini, Pcap, Pejman47, Perspective, Petiatil, Pit, Pit-yacker, Porco-esphino, Quadell, Quarl, RMHBeagle, Ras, Rigved, Rnabioullin, Robert K S, Robertvan1, Roscoe x, Ryan Roos, SJK, Salix alba, SchreyP, Siddhant, Siharper, Singleheart, Squideshi, Steelerdon, Stephanefr, Subversive.sound, SupperTina, Suruena, Svick, Synesthetic, Thumperward, Tom Duff, Tom Worthington, Tommstein, Torgree, TreyHarris, Uwe Hermann, Vary, Velle, Vicki Rosenzweig, Wikisouradeeptawiki, Will Clarke, Wo.luren, YPavan, Yaronf, Ynlrc, Δ, 98 anonymous edits

Fellow *Source*: http://en.wikipedia.org/w/index.php?title=Fellow *Contributors*: 13Peewit, ASaidi, Aaslun04, Addedentry, Ajbpearce, Al Lemos, Ale jrb, Andries, Anglius, August11, Bakerccm, Bencherlite, BigAl63, Blisco, Bobo192, Bongwarrior, Boreas74, Bperry7, C628, Casper Gutman, CharlieHuang, Cmcnicoll, Cthulhuslave, Damian Yerrick, David Kernow, Dolphin51, Edtate, Elysianfields, Erianna, Eriksiers, Espanol77ers, Fakist, Finn-Zoltan, Gobonobo, Grkndeacon, Grubber, Hellclanner, Hut 8.5, Hyacinth, Iampreston, Ike9898, InvictaHOG, JForget, JMonroe, JaGa, Jagged 85, Jb0007, Jdlh, Josh Parris, Jpbowen, Kaobear, Ken Gallager, Kwekubo, Legis, LouScheffer, Mangrovian, Masjeff, Mdotley, Michael Hardy, Milesli, Mithent, Mootros, Ncox, Newwhist, Nigel Cross, Ntsimp, OhNoNotSwineFlu, Oliverkeenan, Oxonian2006, Parkwells, Psnae, PurplePlatypus, Quarl, R'n'B, RCEberwein, RJASE1, Rise Above the Vile, Roke, SAKURAI Kazuto, Sbrools, Seeeko, Seglea, SimonArlott, Skomorokh, Sleigh, Squideshi, StAnselm, Stephenb, Subversive.sound, Sukoshisumo, Suruena, Thu, Triona, Tubbs334, Veledan, Wuhwuzdat, דוד55, 111 anonymous edits

Computer Professionals for Social Responsibility *Source*: http://en.wikipedia.org/w/index.php?title=Computer_Professionals_for_Social_Responsibility *Contributors*: AaronSw, AutumnSnow, Carabinieri, Dougschuler, Egil, Horow021, Lquilter, Malcolma, Mephistophelian, Pearle, Pegship, Robertvan1, Ryan2845, SuperDude115, Torla42, Trbdavies, WBardwin, Widefox, Zodon, Zr2d2, 15 anonymous edits

Golden Key International Honour Society *Source*: http://en.wikipedia.org/w/index.php?title=Golden_Key_International_Honour_Society *Contributors*: AdjustShift, Aesopos, Agent 86, Ahouska, Ajdlinux, Amonthemerciful, Aperwich, Arrenlex, AsmCoder8088, Avraham, BD2412, Betacommand, Briaboru, Bueller 007, CKarnstein, Cahk, Cburnett, Clubmeth, CmdrGuard, Crestu, Csk, DevOhm, Dewey Finn, Excirial, Exploding Boy, Falcon8765, Flinders Petrie, Francisx, Fuhghettaboutit, Fulorian, Fæ, Gilliam, Gouveia2, Ground Zero, Gwern, HappyInGeneral, Harrisonharington, Harsimrankaur, Hullaballoo Wolfowitz, Hyad, Icanbeyourfriend, J.delanoy, JRandomF, Jackdanielsaucccccce, Jay-Sebastos, Jayc455, Jbeversluis, Jim Douglas, Julieismywife, Jwulsin, Kaihsu, Kelly Martin, Khatru2, Kotei.Aoki, Koyae, Lacrimosus, Lbbzman, Lee Begg, Lenin1991, Lowercase, M1ss1ontomars2k4, MailOrderYaks, Masonpatriot, MaveenOlam, Moulec, Mystere, NYCRuss, Naraht, Neurophyre, Nthep, PatW326, Pol098, Rhobite, Rjanag, Scottie theNerd, SecretAgent, Seuraza, Shamwatch, Shell Kinney, Snazzyhoppy, Stonemac, Sukitrebek, Tad Lincoln, TheDJ, TheSolomon, TonyFaull, Tonyzhen9, Tracylovitz, Twbellcan, Vgim, Wikipelli, William Ager, Zigzig20s, Zyzzyvas, 208 anonymous edits

Image Sources, Licenses and Contributors

File:Lambda lc.svg *Source*: http://en.wikipedia.org/w/index.php?title=File:Lambda_lc.svg *License*: unknown *Contributors*: Luks, Vlsergey, 1 anonymous edits

File:Sorting quicksort anim frame.png *Source*: http://en.wikipedia.org/w/index.php?title=File:Sorting_quicksort_anim_frame.png *License*: unknown *Contributors*: Howcheng

File:Utah teapot simple 2.png *Source*: http://en.wikipedia.org/w/index.php?title=File:Utah_teapot_simple_2.png *License*: unknown *Contributors*: User:Dhatfield

File:3-Tastenmaus Microsoft.jpg *Source*: http://en.wikipedia.org/w/index.php?title=File:3-Tastenmaus_Microsoft.jpg *License*: unknown *Contributors*: Aka, Darkone, GreyCat, Warden

File:Enigma.jpg *Source*: http://en.wikipedia.org/w/index.php?title=File:Enigma.jpg *License*: unknown *Contributors*: user:Jszigetvari

File:DFAexample.svg *Source*: http://en.wikipedia.org/w/index.php?title=File:DFAexample.svg *License*: unknown *Contributors*: User:Cepheus

File:Wang tiles.png *Source*: http://en.wikipedia.org/w/index.php?title=File:Wang_tiles.png *License*: unknown *Contributors*: Anomie, Blotwell, Ies, Maksim

File:Blochsphere.svg *Source*: http://en.wikipedia.org/w/index.php?title=File:Blochsphere.svg *License*: unknown *Contributors*: Original uploader was MuncherOfSpleens at en.wikipedia

File:Sorting quicksort anim.gif *Source*: http://en.wikipedia.org/w/index.php?title=File:Sorting_quicksort_anim.gif *License*: unknown *Contributors*: Aiyizo, Berrucomons, Cecil, Chamie, Davepape, Diego pmc, Editor at Large, German, Gorgo, Howcheng, Jago84, JuTa, Kozuch, Lokal Profil, MaBoehm, Minisarm, Miya, Mywood, NH, PatríciaR, Qyd, Sayginer, Soroush83, Stefeck, Str4nd, W like wiki, 11 anonymous edits

File:Singly linked list.png *Source*: http://en.wikipedia.org/w/index.php?title=File:Singly_linked_list.png *License*: unknown *Contributors*: User:Dcoetzee

File:SimplexRangeSearching.png *Source*: http://en.wikipedia.org/w/index.php?title=File:SimplexRangeSearching.png *License*: unknown *Contributors*: Original uploader was Gfonsecabr at en.wikipedia. Later version(s) were uploaded by McLoaf at en.wikipedia.

File:Ideal compiler.png *Source*: http://en.wikipedia.org/w/index.php?title=File:Ideal_compiler.png *License*: unknown *Contributors*: LoStrangolatore, Nuno Tavares, Raul654, Surachit, Ysangkok

File:Python add5 syntax.svg *Source*: http://en.wikipedia.org/w/index.php?title=File:Python_add5_syntax.svg *License*: unknown *Contributors*: Lulu of the Lotus-Eaters, Nerzhal, Red Rooster, Xander89, 4 anonymous edits

File:Nicolas P. Rougier's rendering of the human brain.png *Source*: http://en.wikipedia.org/w/index.php?title=File:Nicolas_P._Rougier's_rendering_of_the_human_brain.png *License*: unknown *Contributors*: Nicolas Rougier

File:eye.png *Source*: http://en.wikipedia.org/w/index.php?title=File:Eye.png *License*: unknown *Contributors*: User:Kenny sh

File:Corner.png *Source*: http://en.wikipedia.org/w/index.php?title=File:Corner.png *License*: unknown *Contributors*: McLoaf, Retardo

File:KnnClassification.svg *Source*: http://en.wikipedia.org/w/index.php?title=File:KnnClassification.svg *License*: unknown *Contributors*: User:AnAj

File:User-FastFission-brain.gif *Source*: http://en.wikipedia.org/w/index.php?title=File:User-FastFission-brain.gif *License*: unknown *Contributors*: User:Solipsist

File:data.png *Source*: http://en.wikipedia.org/w/index.php?title=File:Data.png *License*: unknown *Contributors*: User:Adam majewski

File:sky.png *Source*: http://en.wikipedia.org/w/index.php?title=File:Sky.png *License*: unknown *Contributors*: User:Manuel Strehl

File:earth.png *Source*: http://en.wikipedia.org/w/index.php?title=File:Earth.png *License*: unknown *Contributors*: Migdejong, Motopark, Ö

File:neuron.svg *Source*: http://en.wikipedia.org/w/index.php?title=File:Neuron.svg *License*: unknown *Contributors*: User:Dhp1080

File:english.png *Source*: http://en.wikipedia.org/w/index.php?title=File:English.png *License*: unknown *Contributors*: Honza chodec, Mac Wanter

File:HONDA ASIMO.jpg *Source*: http://en.wikipedia.org/w/index.php?title=File:HONDA_ASIMO.jpg *License*: unknown *Contributors*: User:Gnsin

File:NOR ANSI.svg *Source*: http://en.wikipedia.org/w/index.php?title=File:NOR_ANSI.svg *License*: unknown *Contributors*: jjbeard

File:Fivestagespipeline.png *Source*: http://en.wikipedia.org/w/index.php?title=File:Fivestagespipeline.png *License*: unknown *Contributors*: User:Poil

File:SIMD.svg *Source*: http://en.wikipedia.org/w/index.php?title=File:SIMD.svg *License*: unknown *Contributors*: User:Cburnett

File:Operating system placement.svg *Source*: http://en.wikipedia.org/w/index.php?title=File:Operating_system_placement.svg *License*: unknown *Contributors*: Photos:GolfthemanGolftheman

File:NETWORK-Library-LAN.png *Source*: http://en.wikipedia.org/w/index.php?title=File:NETWORK-Library-LAN.png *License*: unknown *Contributors*: User:Hcberkowitz

File:Emp Tables (Database).PNG *Source*: http://en.wikipedia.org/w/index.php?title=File:Emp_Tables_(Database).PNG *License*: unknown *Contributors*: User:Jamesssss

File:Padlock.svg *Source*: http://en.wikipedia.org/w/index.php?title=File:Padlock.svg *License*: unknown *Contributors*: Anomie, Ixfd64, Rich Farmbrough, Stephen Bain

File:Roomba original.jpg *Source*: http://en.wikipedia.org/w/index.php?title=File:Roomba_original.jpg *License*: unknown *Contributors*: Larry D. Moore (Nv8200p on en.wikipedia)

File:flowchart.png *Source*: http://en.wikipedia.org/w/index.php?title=File:Flowchart.png *License*: unknown *Contributors*: Cwbm (commons), Mintz l, Patil mahesh, Superborsuk, Ysangkok

File:Lorenz attractor yb.svg *Source*: http://en.wikipedia.org/w/index.php?title=File:Lorenz_attractor_yb.svg *License*: unknown *Contributors*: User:Dschwen, User:Wikimol

File:Quark wiki.jpg *Source*: http://en.wikipedia.org/w/index.php?title=File:Quark_wiki.jpg *License*: unknown *Contributors*: User:Brianzero

File:Naphthalene-3D-balls.png *Source*: http://en.wikipedia.org/w/index.php?title=File:Naphthalene-3D-balls.png *License*: unknown *Contributors*: Benjah-bmm27

File:1u04-argonaute.png *Source*: http://en.wikipedia.org/w/index.php?title=File:1u04-argonaute.png *License*: unknown *Contributors*: Opabinia regalis

File:neuron.png *Source*: http://en.wikipedia.org/w/index.php?title=File:Neuron.png *License*: unknown *Contributors*: User:Caiguanhao

File:Wacom graphics tablet and pen.png *Source*: http://en.wikipedia.org/w/index.php?title=File:Wacom_graphics_tablet_and_pen.png *License*: unknown *Contributors*: User:Metoc, User:Wookie

Image:Ccnymedal.jpg *Source*: http://en.wikipedia.org/w/index.php?title=File:Ccnymedal.jpg *License*: unknown *Contributors*: Artyoung

File:Shepard Hall.JPG *Source*: http://en.wikipedia.org/w/index.php?title=File:Shepard_Hall.JPG *License*: unknown *Contributors*: Su & Soe

File:CityCollegeofNewYork.JPG *Source*: http://en.wikipedia.org/w/index.php?title=File:CityCollegeofNewYork.JPG *License*: unknown *Contributors*: User:Гатерас

Image:Shepard1.jpg *Source*: http://en.wikipedia.org/w/index.php?title=File:Shepard1.jpg *License*: unknown *Contributors*: CCNY

File:CityCollegeNewYorkGeneralWebbHarlem.JPG *Source*: http://en.wikipedia.org/w/index.php?title=File:CityCollegeNewYorkGeneralWebbHarlem.JPG *License*: unknown *Contributors*: User:Гатерас

Image:CCNY Grove school jeh.JPG *Source*: http://en.wikipedia.org/w/index.php?title=File:CCNY_Grove_school_jeh.JPG *License*: unknown *Contributors*: User:Jim.henderson

Image:Freeacad.jpg *Source*: http://en.wikipedia.org/w/index.php?title=File:Freeacad.jpg *License*: unknown *Contributors*: Original uploader was Wikiklrsc at en.wikipedia

Image:CUNY-main.jpg *Source*: http://en.wikipedia.org/w/index.php?title=File:CUNY-main.jpg *License*: unknown *Contributors*: Unknown

Image:CCNY tower W139 jeh.jpg *Source*: http://en.wikipedia.org/w/index.php?title=File:CCNY_tower_W139_jeh.jpg *License*: unknown *Contributors*: Llamabr

Image:Ccnyg1.jpg *Source*: http://en.wikipedia.org/w/index.php?title=File:Ccnyg1.jpg *License*: unknown *Contributors*: Original uploader was Wikiklrsc at en.wikipedia

Image:Adolph Lewisohn Stadium.jpg *Source*: http://en.wikipedia.org/w/index.php?title=File:Adolph_Lewisohn_Stadium.jpg *License*: unknown *Contributors*: Original uploader was PTosh at en.wikipedia

File:North Academic Center jeh.jpg *Source*: http://en.wikipedia.org/w/index.php?title=File:North_Academic_Center_jeh.jpg *License*: unknown *Contributors*: User:Jim.henderson

Image:Ccnysc1.jpg *Source*: http://en.wikipedia.org/w/index.php?title=File:Ccnysc1.jpg *License*: unknown *Contributors*: Not credited

Image:Ccnysc3.jpg *Source*: http://en.wikipedia.org/w/index.php?title=File:Ccnysc3.jpg *License*: unknown *Contributors*: Jim.henderson, Wikiklrsc

Image:IBM402plugboard.Shrigley.wireside.jpg *Source*: http://en.wikipedia.org/w/index.php?title=File:IBM402plugboard.Shrigley.wireside.jpg *License*: unknown *Contributors*: User:ArnoldReinhold

Image:PunchCardDecks.agr.jpg *Source*: http://en.wikipedia.org/w/index.php?title=File:PunchCardDecks.agr.jpg *License*: unknown *Contributors*: mehul panchal

Image:H96566k.jpg *Source*: http://en.wikipedia.org/w/index.php?title=File:H96566k.jpg *License*: unknown *Contributors*: Courtesy of the Naval Surface Warfare Center, Dahlgren, VA., 1988.

File:Fortran acs cover.jpeg *Source*: http://en.wikipedia.org/w/index.php?title=File:Fortran_acs_cover.jpeg *License*: unknown *Contributors*: Uncredited

File:Ibm704.gif *Source*: http://en.wikipedia.org/w/index.php?title=File:Ibm704.gif *License*: unknown *Contributors*: Lawrence Livermore National Laboratory

File:FortranCardPROJ039.agr.jpg *Source*: http://en.wikipedia.org/w/index.php?title=File:FortranCardPROJ039.agr.jpg *License*: unknown *Contributors*: Arnold Reinhold

File:FortranCodingForm.png *Source*: http://en.wikipedia.org/w/index.php?title=File:FortranCodingForm.png *License*: unknown *Contributors*: Original uploader was Agateller at en.wikipedia

File:CentralWashingtonUniversitySeal.png *Source*: http://en.wikipedia.org/w/index.php?title=File:CentralWashingtonUniversitySeal.png *License*: unknown *Contributors*: Original uploader was Chocobot18 at en.wikipedia Later versions were uploaded by Arwcheek at en.wikipedia.

File:Wordmark-of-Central-Washington-University.png *Source*: http://en.wikipedia.org/w/index.php?title=File:Wordmark-of-Central-Washington-University.png *License*: unknown *Contributors*: Aricci526, Nyttend, Skier Dude

Image:2008-1019-02-CentralWashingtonUniversity.jpg *Source*: http://en.wikipedia.org/w/index.php?title=File:2008-1019-02-CentralWashingtonUniversity.jpg *License*: unknown *Contributors*: Bobak Ha'Eri

Image:Central Washington University.jpg *Source*: http://en.wikipedia.org/w/index.php?title=File:Central_Washington_University.jpg *License*: unknown *Contributors*: User:Farwestern

File:Magnify-clip.png *Source*: http://en.wikipedia.org/w/index.php?title=File:Magnify-clip.png *License*: unknown *Contributors*: User:Erasoft24

File:General Electric logo.svg *Source*: http://en.wikipedia.org/w/index.php?title=File:General_Electric_logo.svg *License*: unknown *Contributors*: Jeff G., Kakurady, Presidentman, Quibik, Tkgd2007, Wtshymanski

File:Decrease2.svg *Source*: http://en.wikipedia.org/w/index.php?title=File:Decrease2.svg *License*: unknown *Contributors*: User:Sarang

File:Increase2.svg *Source*: http://en.wikipedia.org/w/index.php?title=File:Increase2.svg *License*: unknown *Contributors*: Sarang

File:GE Fairfield Entrance.jpg *Source*: http://en.wikipedia.org/w/index.php?title=File:GE_Fairfield_Entrance.jpg *License*: unknown *Contributors*: User:Markvs88

File:Early General Electric logo 1899.png *Source*: http://en.wikipedia.org/w/index.php?title=File:Early_General_Electric_logo_1899.png *License*: unknown *Contributors*: The General Electric Company (logo); The United States Patent and Trademark Office (1990 renewal registration certificate, which this logo was obtained from)

File:GE Building by David Shankbone.JPG *Source*: http://en.wikipedia.org/w/index.php?title=File:GE_Building_by_David_Shankbone.JPG *License*: unknown *Contributors*: David Shankbone

Image:23TonGELocomotiveSRM.jpg *Source*: http://en.wikipedia.org/w/index.php?title=File:23TonGELocomotiveSRM.jpg *License*: unknown *Contributors*: User:SriMesh

Image:GeneralElectricSign.jpg *Source*: http://en.wikipedia.org/w/index.php?title=File:GeneralElectricSign.jpg *License*: unknown *Contributors*: Bubba73 (talk), Jud McCranie. Original uploader was Bubba73 at en.wikipedia

Image:LocomotiveGaugesSRM.jpg *Source*: http://en.wikipedia.org/w/index.php?title=File:LocomotiveGaugesSRM.jpg *License*: unknown *Contributors*: User:SriMesh

Image:US Atomic Energy Commission logo.jpg *Source*: http://en.wikipedia.org/w/index.php?title=File:US_Atomic_Energy_Commission_logo.jpg *License*: unknown *Contributors*: Awg1010, Fastfission, Tetris L, 3 anonymous edits

File:New York University Seal.svg *Source*: http://en.wikipedia.org/w/index.php?title=File:New_York_University_Seal.svg *License*: unknown *Contributors*: Connormah

File:NYU logo.svg *Source*: http://en.wikipedia.org/w/index.php?title=File:NYU_logo.svg *License*: unknown *Contributors*: Connormah

Image:Albert Gallatin 3.JPG *Source*: http://en.wikipedia.org/w/index.php?title=File:Albert_Gallatin_3.JPG *License*: unknown *Contributors*: Original uploader was Jsanstella at en.wikipedia

Image:Nyuuniheights.jpg *Source*: http://en.wikipedia.org/w/index.php?title=File:Nyuuniheights.jpg *License*: unknown *Contributors*: Original uploader was Noeticsage at en,wikipedia

Image:Main buildingNYU.JPG *Source*: http://en.wikipedia.org/w/index.php?title=File:Main_buildingNYU.JPG *License*: unknown *Contributors*: Croml, Nishkid64

Image:NYU's Bobst library-2.jpg *Source*: http://en.wikipedia.org/w/index.php?title=File:NYU's_Bobst_library-2.jpg *License*: unknown *Contributors*: Marilyn Cole from Atlanta, GA, USA

File:First Free Congregational Poly jeh.jpg *Source*: http://en.wikipedia.org/w/index.php?title=File:First_Free_Congregational_Poly_jeh.jpg *License*: unknown *Contributors*: User:Jim.henderson

File:DibnerLibrary.JPG *Source*: http://en.wikipedia.org/w/index.php?title=File:DibnerLibrary.JPG *License*: unknown *Contributors*: Polytechnic Institute of NYU

File:11 W42 calendar jeh.JPG *Source*: http://en.wikipedia.org/w/index.php?title=File:11_W42_calendar_jeh.JPG *License*: unknown *Contributors*: User:Jim.henderson

Image:NYU Maison francaise.gif *Source*: http://en.wikipedia.org/w/index.php?title=File:NYU_Maison_francaise.gif *License*: unknown *Contributors*: Original uploader was Gkennedy at en.wikipedia

Image:Washington Square Village.jpg *Source*: http://en.wikipedia.org/w/index.php?title=File:Washington_Square_Village.jpg *License*: unknown *Contributors*: Beyond My Ken, Jim.henderson, Nishkid64, Padraic, Skeezix1000, Xnatedawgx

Image:NYU-Gallatin School.jpg *Source*: http://en.wikipedia.org/w/index.php?title=File:NYU-Gallatin_School.jpg *License*: unknown *Contributors*: User:Padraic

Image:NYU Program Board Logo.png *Source*: http://en.wikipedia.org/w/index.php?title=File:NYU_Program_Board_Logo.png *License*: unknown *Contributors*: User:AEMoreira042281, User:Cydebot, User:Esrever, User:Noeticsage, User:Part85, User:Polbot

Image:NYU Thomas SLF235 30620 on Shuttle Route A.jpg *Source*: http://en.wikipedia.org/w/index.php?title=File:NYU_Thomas_SLF235_30620_on_Shuttle_Route_A.jpg *License*: unknown *Contributors*: User:AEMoreira042281

Image:NYUAthleticsLogo.jpg *Source*: http://en.wikipedia.org/w/index.php?title=File:NYUAthleticsLogo.jpg *License*: unknown *Contributors*: Rms869

Image:NYU Hockey.jpg *Source*: http://en.wikipedia.org/w/index.php?title=File:NYU_Hockey.jpg *License*: unknown *Contributors*: Michael Schamis

Image:NYU volleyball.jpg *Source*: http://en.wikipedia.org/w/index.php?title=File:NYU_volleyball.jpg *License*: unknown *Contributors*: Michael Schamis from New York, NY, USA

Image:NyuTorch.png *Source*: http://en.wikipedia.org/w/index.php?title=File:NyuTorch.png *License*: unknown *Contributors*: User:ChrisRuvolo, User:Isamuel

Image:CourantInstitute.jpg *Source*: http://en.wikipedia.org/w/index.php?title=File:CourantInstitute.jpg *License*: unknown *Contributors*: Courant Institute of Mathematical Sciences

Image:CourantInstituteView.jpg *Source*: http://en.wikipedia.org/w/index.php?title=File:CourantInstituteView.jpg *License*: unknown *Contributors*: NYU Student

File:CIMS Lecture Hall.jpg *Source*: http://en.wikipedia.org/w/index.php?title=File:CIMS_Lecture_Hall.jpg *License*: unknown *Contributors*: User:AuCourantStory

File:CIMS Classroom.jpg *Source*: http://en.wikipedia.org/w/index.php?title=File:CIMS_Classroom.jpg *License*: unknown *Contributors*: User:AuCourantStory

Image:Games for Learning Institute.jpg *Source*: http://en.wikipedia.org/w/index.php?title=File:Games_for_Learning_Institute.jpg *License*: unknown *Contributors*: User:AuCourantStory

Image:Applied Mathematics Lab.jpg *Source*: http://en.wikipedia.org/w/index.php?title=File:Applied_Mathematics_Lab.jpg *License*: unknown *Contributors*: NYU Student

Image:CenterAtmosphereSciences.jpg *Source*: http://en.wikipedia.org/w/index.php?title=File:CenterAtmosphereSciences.jpg *License*: unknown *Contributors*: Center for Atmosphere-Ocean Science

Image:CSplashTeacher.jpg *Source*: http://en.wikipedia.org/w/index.php?title=File:CSplashTeacher.jpg *License*: unknown *Contributors*: NYU cSplash

File:Union Theological Seminary NYC 001 002 combined.jpg *Source*: http://en.wikipedia.org/w/index.php?title=File:Union_Theological_Seminary_NYC_001_002_combined.jpg *License*: unknown *Contributors*: User:Fpo, User:Gryffindor

Image:Union Theological Seminary LC-USZ62-74646.jpg *Source*: http://en.wikipedia.org/w/index.php?title=File:Union_Theological_Seminary_LC-USZ62-74646.jpg *License*: unknown *Contributors*: Dogears, Gryffindor, Lupo

File:UnionTheological.jpg *Source*: http://en.wikipedia.org/w/index.php?title=File:UnionTheological.jpg *License*: unknown *Contributors*: Foad Torshizi

Image:Association for Computing Machinery logo.png *Source*: http://en.wikipedia.org/w/index.php?title=File:Association_for_Computing_Machinery_logo.png *License*: unknown *Contributors*: Ctjf83, David.Monniaux, Skier Dude, Tom Morris, Tyrol5

Image:Twopennplaza.jpg *Source*: http://en.wikipedia.org/w/index.php?title=File:Twopennplaza.jpg *License*: unknown *Contributors*: Wikipedia user name: w::en:User:CoolcaesarlCoolcaesarl -

Image:Golden Key.jpg *Source*: http://en.wikipedia.org/w/index.php?title=File:Golden_Key.jpg *License*: unknown *Contributors*: Cahk, The Pink Oboe

File:Golden Key Honor Society Key.JPG *Source*: http://en.wikipedia.org/w/index.php?title=File:Golden_Key_Honor_Society_Key.JPG *License*: unknown *Contributors*: User:Avraham

MIX
Papier aus verantwortungsvollen Quellen
Paper from responsible sources
FSC® C105338

Printed by Books on Demand GmbH, Norderstedt / Germany